Fundamentals of Buddhism and Ethics

Fundamentals of Buddhism and Ethics

I.N. Singh

PRASHANT PUBLISHING HOUSE
DELHI-110094

Published by :
Prashant Publishing House
C-34, 28 Foota Road, Gali-3,
West Karwal Nagar, Delhi-110094
Phone : 011-22963970, Mob. : 9810396373
e-mail.: prashantpublishinghouse@gmail.com

Fundamentals of Buddhism and Ethics

First Published 2019

ISBN 978-93-88526-14-2

PRINTED IN INDIA

Published by Mr. R.K. Jha M/s Prashant Publishing House and Published at H.S. Offset House Press, Delhi.

Contents

Preface

The Buddhist tradition acknowledges that life is complex and throws up many difficulties, and it does not suggest that there is a single course of action that will be right in all circumstances. Indeed, rather than speaking of actions being right or wrong, Buddhism speaks of the being skilful (kusala) or unskilful (akusala). In Triratna, our faith in the Three Jewels of Buddha, Dharma and Sangha finds everyday practical expression in our aspiration to live by ethical precepts, to the best of our ability.

Moral conduct for Buddhists differs according to whether it applies to the laity or to the Sangha or clergy. A lay Buddhist should cultivate good conduct by training in what are known as the "Five Precepts". These are not like, say, the ten commandments, which, if broken, entail punishment by God. The five precepts are training rules, which, if one were to break any of them, one should be aware of the breech and examine how such a breech may be avoided in the future. The resultant of an action (often referred to as Karma) depends on the intention more than the action itself. It entails less feelings of guilt than its Judeo-Christian counterpart. Buddhism places a great emphasis on 'mind' and it is mental anguish such as remorse, anxiety, guilt etc. which is to be avoided in order to cultivate a calm and peaceful mind.

The emphasis on actions, however, should not obscure the intensive interest Buddhist thinkers have taken in the virtues and dispositions that produce them. Since Buddhists locate moral culpability in intention and volition rather than solely in the action itself, the operations of moral choice are central to ethical reflection. Buddhism offers a close analysis of mind, investigating the emotions, dispositions, and tendencies that drive our action and shape the world. Early Buddhism produced a very sophisticated moral psychology called abhidharma, which articulated an analysis of the constituents of the mind and their relationships that are crucial for the development of virtuous dispositions. This moral psychology, as well as other discourses on the mind, assert that the key to developing moral character is to replace negative and harmful mental states and emotions with positive and other-regarding mental states.

Thus in spite of superficial similarities, Buddhist ethics differs from other ethical systems when analysed in detail. In the Noble Eightfold Path the elements corresponding to morality and ethics are Right Speech, Right Action and Right Livelihood. These three together constitute siila. The cultivation of siila normally proceeds alongside progress in the other two great constituents of the Path, namely mental training (bhavana) and wisdom-insight (panna). Because of the mutually supportive nature of the three components of morality, mental development and wisdom, it is difficult to argue about the relative importance of these three components. Nonetheless it has long been the generally accepted view that panna is both the threshold as well as the culmination of Buddhist practice, with the other two components of sla and bhavana being the chief means to the realization of this great objective.

This is a reference book. All the matter is just compiled and edited in nature, taken from the various sources which are in public domain.

This book contains the fundamental and basic information of subject and the selection of contents makes it an appropriate textbook for the students.

—Editor

1

Introduction to Buddhism

THE ORIGIN AND CHARACTERISTICS OF BUDDHISM

Religion is a social phenomenon and studying it with a view to understanding its historical development has special significance today. We can see similar trends in other countries where the rapid developments of science and technology do not in any significant way lessen the people's sense of, nor interests in, religion. Even the people of China, for some reason or other, show similar interests in the development of religion. This phenomenon is enough to raise several theoretical questions concerning the need for a better understanding of religion: what is the nature of religion? Does the human psyche require a religious faith? Is religion synonymous with religious belief? Is religious belief beneficial to social life? Is science complementary to, or inconsistent with, religious belief? Can religion be a modernizing agent? and so forth. This paper does not pretend to deal specifically with these questions, But, why do we study the history of religions? Should an ideal history of religions be time-conscious? Can such an history help people think seriously about the problems of religion that exist in the world today? All historians of religions need to address themselves to these kinds of problems.

The religions which had been popular in Chinese history include Buddhism, Buddhism, Islam, Christianity and animism. However, of all these religious traditions, only Buddhism is indigenous to China. To be sure, Buddhism is a Chinese religion; it has characteristics peculiar to the Chinese. Besides, it has exercised considerable influence on the development of Chinese culture and psychology, customs and habits, science and technology, philosophy and thought, medicine and hygiene, and even political life. Can our investigation into one of the more influential religions--the origin of Buddhism, its development and characteristics--help us deepen our understanding of Chinese culture, personality and way of thinking? Can it indirectly help us understand, more intimately, the theoretical and practical problems of religion in the world today? I think it can and toward this end the present discussion is an attempt to analyze and discuss the following issues.

General Background

The development of Buddhism was an attempt to orientate the Han Chinese to their social, political, economic, moral and psychological lives at the end of the Eastern Han.

Why did Buddhism develop only at the end of the Eastern Han period? Historically, such Daoist ideas, as `immortality' and `sanctification of the bodies' had already existed during the time of the Warring States (Zhanguo). They became even more popular during the Qin and Han dynasties--why? We know that not just any kind of superstition can be called religion, although religion often embodies a good deal of superstitious elements. Neither can we say that any theistic discourse can become a religion, even if it is capable of extending its influence over a sizeable cross-section of the population. Its growth and development were directly related to the social life of the people, their history, and other objective facts. The development of Buddhism during the Eastern Han may be attributed to the following factors.

First, the reality of social life at the end of the Eastern Han had laid fertile grounds for the growth of Buddhism. The social and political conditions, since Shundi of the Eastern Han, had begun to deteriorate. There was outside interference in the day-to-day administration and the administrative machinery was in the hands of a bureaucracy. Debauchery, unruly behaviour and social strife, both from within and without, were the order of the day. Finally there were crop failures due to severe drought, and large numbers of people died in ditches (Chong Zhangdong, Changyuan). Undue economic exploitations and political pressure at that time had made it impossible for the populace to lead a decent life; bankruptcy and emigration were common. The conflict between the ruling class and the ruled was intense and acute. According to historical records, from Shundi's time, peasant uprisings were rampant. At that time, apart from the common class-interest that united them in social movements, their leaders resorted to magic and superstitions as organizing agents. That is why, in history books, the rebels after Shundi's time were often called yaozei, or `the goblin thieves'.

Two conclusions may be drawn from the above discussion. First, a period of economic and political unrest, as well as spiritual and moral decay, provided an objective vantage for the development of religion. Second, as the leaders of the peasantry had used magic and superstitions to rally support in their movements, they knew that these could be used as tools for mobilizing the people, thus paving the way for the widespread development of religion. As is always the case, social turbulence often caused great hardship and suffering to the lower class. Thus, when people became desperate they tended to hinge their hopes upon some kind of spiritual power, or shenling. This was one of the most common avenues through which people, in antiquity, reconciled themselves with their social reality. This also explains why a majority of the early Daoist believers were members of the lower social strata.

Second, the social conditions at the end of the Eastern Han had provided useful material for the founding of Buddhism. Since the time of Han Wudi, when Dong Zhongshu pointed out that "of the hundred schools, only Confucianism is the most revered," Confucian thought had adapted itself to the needs of building a unified feudal society and serving as an ideology for the ruling class. From then on the development of Confucianism depended primarily on the teaching of a reciprocal relationship between heaven and man, followed by an increased interest in the development of theology and metaphysics. Though ideally a religion is theistic, not any form of theism is adequate or sufficiently meaningful to become a religion. This is because such a religion (namely, the religion of the masses) must include not only the worship of spiritual beings, but also possess a body of canon together with an endurable form of church organization, doctrines and dogmas, and an historical medium for the dissemination of religious knowledge. Generally, religion must see the world in two forms: the real and the supernatural. Based on this premise, human beings feel that they can only disengage themselves from the problems of social life in a supernatural world--believing that an ideal life can manifest itself only in the yonder shore of the supernatural world.

Despite the fact that Confucianism acknowledged the existence of Shen or God, especially during the Han dynasty, it had never thought it necessary that its ideals be fulfilled outside the world, but required rather that the ideals of "governing the state and pacifying the world" (zhi guo ping tianxia) be actualized in the real world, even though this were merely an illusion. Although religion had played a very important role in feudal China, it had never become a force to reckon with. Instead it had, many a time, occupied a secondary position, which state of affairs clearly bespoke as well the dominance of Confucian ideology.

From the developmental point of view, after the Eastern Han Confucianism could very well have become a religion, because its metaphysics together with the conception of the sacred could be easily converted into religion. However, Confucianism did not become a religion during the Han dynasty for the simple reason that it attempted to materialize the ideals of "governing the state and pacifying the world" in the real world. Thus, following the decay of the Han dynasty, Confucian ideology not only fell short of becoming a religion but its position as an ideology of the ruling class continued to decline. Because of this decline, Confucian thought had given way to the growth of Buddhism. History shows that, whenever the dominant ideology of the ruling class lost its power, it often signalled the growth and dominance of a countervailing religion.

Even though Confucianism had declined at the end of the Eastern Han, certain facets of its ideology could still be absorbed and put to good use by an ongoing religion. The fact that Confucian ideas are found in Buddhism is clear proof that such assimilation did take place. For example, the idea of "the ultimate peace in the unity of the three (heaven, earth and man) in one" (tian-di-ren san heyi zhi taiping) shows that the Confucianists were concerned about political reality and the notion of sancai (three endowments) mentioned in Yi Zhuan. The idea that the sky and the universe were formed by breath (qi) could have derived from the knowledge of world creation as well as the yin-yang principles and the five elements mentioned in the apocryphal texts. All these ideas were closely connected to Han Confucian thought. That most of the scholars who studied the development of Buddhism focused their attention on its relationship with Daoist sources and overlooked the nexus between Daoist and Confucianist ideas is a bias.

Buddhism could have another source in its gradual mingling with the tradition of the saints. Although there was a connection between the Daoists and the saints of the early Qin, both seem to belong to quite different schools of thought. Until the beginning of the Western Han, the popular Huang-Lao learning was essentially Daoist. It frequently emphasized the exemplary qualities of the sage and was thus deemed capable of exercising its power over the state and the cosmos. That is why Sima Qian, in his preface, commented that the importance of the Huang-Lao learning lies in the doctrine of "self-actualization through non-action, and self-correction through expiation" (wuwei zihua, qingjing zizheng).

The Huang-Lao Daoist learning underwent a change during the Eastern Han: part of its adherents sought the help of the gods installed in shrines, thus becoming unified with the saints. Huandi, for example, made sacrifices to Laozi (Lao Tzu) at the latter's shrine with the aim to "preserve shen for the uplift of character and the ultimate ascent to heaven," thus signalling the initial transformation of Huang-Lao's Daoist teaching. Also, as early as the end of the Western Han, there was already in existence what was known as "Huang-lao's Dao" (the Way of Huang-Lao) and, later on, the "Fangxian's Dao" (the Way of the Saints), all of which actually belonged to the immortalist sects. Further, the saints' underlying objective was to attain `eternal life' (changsheng busi) and to cause the bodies to be sanctified (routi chengxian).

Thus, once it merged with the Daoist ideas of "attaining peace through inaction, and remaining in peace through abstinence" (qingjing wuwei, tiandan guayu), it increasingly began to attract the masses and became a powerful social force. Lastly, the basic tenets of Buddhism, such as "immortality" and "the sanctification of the bodies," although derived from the Way of the Saints, became part of the Daoist system. Hence, its transformation also represents an important factor contributing to the growth of Buddhism.

From the above viewpoints, Buddhism as a religion may be said to have deviated from the Confucianists' and Daoist' schools of thought. However, its source of ideas was inseparable from both. Hence, from the beginning, it had distinguished itself as a religious system in which Confucian and Daoist ideas supplemented each other. This system represents some of the characteristics typical of Chinese culture, psychology and way of thinking.

Third, the introduction of Buddhism into China had greatly stimulated the development of Chinese religion. From the time Buddhism spread to China during the Western Han till after the middle of the Eastern Han, it maintained a steady level of propagation. Buddhism, acting like a catalyst, escalated the development of Buddhism. Actually, the school of the saints was already popular during the Western Han, and disciples frequently had given tributes to Huang-Lao. This was evidenced in the existing learnings of "Huang-Lao's Dao" and "Fangxian's Dao." The former sanctified Huangdi and worshipped him in shrines dedicated to him; the latter talked about "non-death and everlasting life" (zhongshen busi). Shiji records that the teacher of the river elder, Le Jigong, learned about Huangdi.

The book of Fengchan records that Huangdi became an immortal because of Fengchan. Yujie (more appropriately, Ganjie), who compiled the Daoist scripture Taiping Jing, suggested that the book was originally by Laozi (Lao Tzu). During Han Mingdi, Chu Wangying had already worshipped Huangdi and Foutu. Chu Wangying recited Huang-Lao's words and honored Foutu's shrine. Huandi erected Huang-Lao's and Foutu's shrines in his palace. The fact that Huang-Lao and Foutu were worshiped manifestly shows that Huangdi was at that time regarded as a deity or a Buddha. Sainthood was in fact a form of sagehood. Living the life of an immortal is but a human discipline. There was no formal, nor endurable form of organization to be used as a base for the interaction of the religious community. But after the spread of Buddhism to China, it became an organized form of religion, possessing not only a set of teaching which differed from that of traditional China, but also an organized church, with a religious canon and a spiritual community, all of which served as a blueprint for the founding of Buddhism.

It is true that Buddhism had served as a model for the establishment of Buddhism. Of even greater importance is that Buddhism was alien to Chinese culture, and its propagation in China was greeted with protests by the bearers of Xia's cultural tradition. This defensive attitude acted as a stimulus spurring the Chinese to strive even harder towards establishing an indigenous religion. When an ethnic culture encountered an alien culture it often gave rise to mutual absorption or rejection.

This situation was particularly marked in the case of the Chinese response to Indian Buddhism. We can provide evidence to show how it was actually reflected in the earliest Daoist scripture, Taiping Jing. In this scripture, we see how some Buddhist ideas, like benqi (the primal beginning) and sanjie (the three worlds), had their origins in the Buddhist canon. On the other hand, there were criticisms about Buddhism, for example, the talks that "the conduct of the four destructions collectively denigrates the spiritual way of heaven" (Shihui zhi xing, gong wuru huangtian zhi shendao). Moreover, upon the establishment of Buddhism, its adherents circulated the story about Laozi (Lao Tzu)'s role in bringing about a renaissance among the northern Chinese (Laozi [Lao Tzu] huahu). This was designed not only as a blow to Buddhism but also as an attempt to boost the image of Buddhism. All this suggests a kind of antagonistic reaction against the entry of the alien culture.

Therefore, it is not at all surprising that the end of the Eastern Han period saw the need for the development of an indigenous religion. The founding of this religion could be traced to the existing tradition of the saints. The fact that it adopted Confucian and Daoist ideas as a basis for the development of Buddhism is even less surprising. Once it emerged, it immediately became charged with an intense ethnic fervor and came into direct conflict with the alien Buddhist religion. The outcome is, precisely, a manifestation of an indigenously endowed Chinese culture.

THE MEANING OF BUDDHISM

The teaching founded by the Buddha is known, in English, as Buddhism. It may be asked, who is the Buddha? A Buddha is one who has attained Bodhi; and by Bodhi is meant wisdom, an ideal state of intellectual and ethical perfection which can be achieved by man through purely human means. The term Buddha literally means enlightened one, a knower. Buddhists believe that a Buddha is born in each aeon of time, and our Buddha-the sage Gotama who attained enlightenment under the bo tree at Buddh Gaya in India-was the seventh in the succession.

Gotama was born the son of an Indian king on the border of modern Nepal 623 years before Christ. The wise men of the kingdom foresaw that he would become either an emperor or a Buddha, and his father, wanting him to be an emperor, kept him utterly secluded from all unpleasant things, so that he might not become wise by seeing life. But the gods knew that Gotama must become the Buddha, and so they visited earth in various forms to let him see them. On three successive days, while on his way to the royal park, Gotama saw an old man, a sick man, and a corpse, and thus he learned that men-all men-must suffer and die. On the fourth day he saw a monk; from this he understood that to learn the way of overcoming man's universal sorrow lie must give up worldly pleasures. Accordingly, in his twenty-ninth year, he renounced his kingdom and became an ascetic.

Gotama wandered about the countryside, a seeker after truth and peace. He approached many a distinguished teacher of his day, but none could give him what he sought. He strenuously practiced all the severe austerities of monkish life, hoping to attain Nirvana. Eventually his delicate body was reduced almost to a skeleton. But the more he tormented his body the further away he was from his goal. Realizing the futility of self-mortification, he finally decided to follow a different course, avoiding the extremes of pain and indulgence.

The new path which he discovered was the Middle Way, the Eightfold Path, which subsequently became part of his teaching. By following this path his wisdom grew into its fullest power, and he became the Buddha.

As a man Prince Gotama, by his own will, love, and wisdom, attained Buddhahood-the highest possible state of perfection-and he taught his followers to believe that they might do the same. Any man, within himself, possesses the power to make himself good, wise, and happy.

All the teachings of the Buddha can be summed up in one word: Dhamma. It means truth, that which really is. It also means law, the law which exists in a man's own heart and mind. It is the principle of righteousness. Therefore the Buddha appeals to man to be noble, pure, and charitable not in order to please any Supreme Deity, but in order to be true to the highest in himself.

Dhamma, this law of righteousness, exists not only in a man's heart and mind, it exists in the universe also. All the universe is an embodiment and revelation of Dhamma. When the moon rises and sets, the rains come, the crops grow, the seasons change, it, is because of Dhamma, for Dhamma is the law of the universe which makes matter act in the ways revealed by our studies of natural science.

If a man will live by Dhamma, he will escape misery and come to Nirvana, the final release from all suffering. It is not by any kind of prayer, nor by any ceremonies, nor by any appeal to a God, that a man will discover the Dhamma which will lead him to his goal. He will discover it in only one way-by developing his own character. This development comes only through control of the mind and purification of the emotions. Until a man stills the storm in his heart, until he extends his loving-kindness to all beings, he will not be able to take even the first step toward his goal.

Thus Buddhism is not a religion at all, in the sense in which the word is commonly understood. It is not a system of faith or worship. In Buddhism, there is no such thing as belief in a body of dogma which must be taken on faith, such as belief in a Supreme Being, a creator of the universe, the reality of an immortal soul, a personal savior, or archangels who are supposed to carry out the will of the Supreme Deity. Buddhism begins as a search for truth. The Buddha taught that we should believe only that which is true in the light of our own experience, that which conforms to reason and is conducive to the highest good and welfare of all beings. Men must rely on themselves. Even though he may "take refuge in Buddha," the expression used when a man pledges himself to live a righteous life, he must not fall victim to a blind faith that the Buddha can save him. The Buddha can point out the path, but he cannot walk it for us.

The truth which the Buddhist sees when he looks around him is the truth of cause and effect. Every action, no matter how insignificant, produces an effect; every effect in its turn becomes a, cause and produces still further effects. It is meaningless to inquire for a First Cause. A First Cause is inconceivable; rather, cause and effect are cyclical, and this universe when it dies and falls apart will give rise to another universe, just as this one was formed from the dispersed matter of a previous universe. The origin of the universe, like that of every individual person or thing in it, is dependent on the chain of previous causes, which goes on and on in an endless cycle of birth, death, and rebirth. This is the principle of dependent origination.

What of the soul? The Buddha taught that there is no soul or self, and he used the metaphor of the cart. If you take away the wheels and axles, the floorboards and sides, the shafts, and all the other parts of the cart, what remains? Nothing but the conception of a cart, which will be the same when a new cart is built. So the uninterrupted process of psychophysical phenomena moves from life to life. Each life passes instantaneously in death to a new life, and the new life is the effect of the causes in the old life. A candle flame at this instant is different from the flame that burned an instant ago, yet the flame is continuous.

Thus in the chain of interdependent causation all phenomenal existence is constantly changing. The elements combine and recombine with no underlying substance, or soul, to give them permanence. This is the Wheel of Life. The main cause of the restlessness, the suffering, which is the lot of beings turning on the Wheel of Life, is craving or selfish desire for existence, and it is this desire which sets the life force in motion. Desire is manifested in action. This action is in reality volition or will power, which is responsible for the creation of being. It is called karma in Sanskrit, but in the Pali language, which the Buddha spoke and in which all the Buddhist scriptures were written, it is softened to kamma.

In this universe in which nothing is permanent all change is governed by kamma or the kammic force. Kamma means action. In its general sense, kamma means all good and bad actions. Kamma refers to all kinds of intentional actions whether mental, verbal, or physical, that is, all thoughts, words, and deeds. In its ultimate sense kamma means all moral and immoral volition.

Kamma, though it activates the chain of cause and effect, is not determinism, nor is it an excuse for fatalism. The past influences the present, but does not dominate it. The past is the background against which life goes on from moment to moment; the past and the present influence the future. Only the present moment exists, and the responsibility for using the present moment for good or ill lies with each individual.

Every action produces an effect; it is cause first and effect afterward. We therefore speak of kamma as "the law of cause and effect." If you throw a stone into a pond, the ripples spread out to the shore, but that is not all, for the ripples return inward until they touch the stone again. The effects of our actions come back to us, and as long as our actions are done with evil intent, the waves of effect will come back to us as evil. But if we are kind and keep ourselves peaceful, the returning waves of trouble will grow weaker until they die down and our good kamma will come back to us in blessing.

In the world around us there are many inequalities in the lot of man-some are rich, others are poor, some live full lives, others die young, etc. According to Buddhism, the inequalities which exist are due, to some extent, to environment-which is itself shaped by cause and effect-and to a greater extent to causes, that is kamma, which are in the present, the immediate past, and the remote past. Man himself is responsible for his own happiness and misery. Thus kamma is not fate nor destiny nor blind determinism. Man has a certain amount of free will; he can modify his actions and affect his future. Each act, whether mental or physical, tends to produce its like. If a man does a good deed or thinks a good thought, the effect upon him is to increase the tendencies to goodness in him.

The understanding of kamma gives us power. The more we make the doctrine of kamma a part of our lives, the more power we gain, not only to direct our future, but also to help our fellow beings more effectively. The practice of good kamma, when fully developed, will enable us to overcome evil and even to overcome kamma itself, thus bringing us to our goal, Nirvana.

The principle of dependent origination and the law of kamma provide the background for understanding the nature of rebirth. According to Buddhism, death is "the temporary end of a temporary phenomenon." It is not the complete annihilation of the being, for although the organic life has ceased, the kammic force which hitherto actuated it is not destroyed. Our physical forms are only the outward manifestations of the invisible kammic force. When the present form perishes, another form takes its place according to a good or bad volitional impulse-the kamma that was the most powerful-at the moment before death.

At death the kammic force remains entirely undisturbed by the disintegration of the physical body, and the passing away of the present consciousness creates the conditions for the coming into being of a fresh body in another birth. The stream of consciousness flows on like a river which is built up by its tributaries and dispenses its water to the countryside through which it passes. The continuity of flux at death is unbroken in point of time; there is no breach in the stream of consciousness, and therefore there is no room whatever for an intermediate stage between this life and the next. Rebirth takes place immediately.

The present being, present existence, is conditioned by the way one faced circumstances in the last and in all past existences. One's present character and circumstances are the result of all that one has been up to the present, but what one will be in the future depends on what one does now in the present. The true Buddhist regards death as a momentary incident between one life and its successor and views its approach with calmness. His only concern is that his future should be such that the condition of that life may provide him with better opportunities for perfecting himself.

Buddhism teaches that with the practice of meditation and concentration the memory can be trained. By meditation and mind culture one can acquire the power to see one's rebirth as a link, or a succession of links, in a chain of births; one can also acquire the power of looking back into one's previous lives. Not only this, but Buddhism also teaches that with the attainment of Nirvana in this life itself, through enlightenment and true wisdom, one can reach the end of this chain of rebirths.

Nirvana, the state to which all Buddhists aspire, is the cessation of desire and hence the end of suffering. Nirvana in Sanskrit means "the blowing out." It is understood as the extinguishment of the flame of personal desire, the quenching of the fire of life. Among Westerners Nirvana is often thought of as a negative state, a kind of "nothingness." But in the Buddhist scriptures it is always described in positive terms; the highest refuge, safety, emancipation, peace, and the like. Nirvana is freedom, but not freedom from circumstance; it is freedom from the bonds with which we have bound ourselves to circumstance. That man is free who is strong enough to say, "Whatever comes I accept as best."

Nirvana is the dying of the kammic force. The Buddhist ascends to Nirvana through many stages of the Middle Way, the path of wisdom, morality, and control. There is not space enough here even to mention these phases or the various aspects of the regimen recommended by the Buddha in his vast scriptures; but it may be taken for granted that the life of the conscientious Buddhist is full and rich. Through the cycle of rebirths he ascends, he perfects himself, he conquers his cravings through wisdom and love. Slowly the kammic force ebbs away, the flame dies down.

At the root of man's trouble is his primal state of ignorance. From ignorance comes desire, which sets the kammic force in motion. Hence the way to Nirvana lies through knowledge, and we come again full circle to Dhamma, the Buddha's teachings. For in Dhamma, as truth, lies release from ignorance and desire and perpetual change, and the Buddha has shown us the way to truth.

What, then, is the meaning of Buddhism? Ultimately Buddhism, although not strictly speaking a religion, is a systematic exercise in spirituality, certainly one of the greatest ever conceived. It offers the individual a means by which he may fulfill himself through understanding, reaching eventually the plane of the supraperson on which both the self and self-knowledge are no longer useful. Meister Eckhart, the great Christian mystic, said: "The kingdom of God is for none but the thoroughly dead." The Buddhist would agree, though he would probably prefer a less grim way of saying it. Nirvana in life, the peace which "passeth all understanding," is the conquest of life, the discovery of the permanent in its flux of psychophysical accidents and circumstances. The Buddhist believes that through meditation and good hard thought he can follow the Buddha through the successive stages of enlightenment and achieve at last the perfect wisdom which surmounts all need.

But by no means all Buddhists are monks or adepts. What does Buddhism mean for the ordinary person going about his work in the world? All through the Buddha's teaching, repeated stress is laid on self-reliance and resolution. Buddhism makes man stand on his own feet, it arouses his self-confidence and energy. The Buddha again and again reminded his followers that there is no one, either in heaven or on earth, who can help them or free them from the results of their past evil deeds. The Buddhist knows that the powers of his own mind and spirit are enough to guide him in the present and shape his future and bring him eventually to the truth. He knows that he possesses a strength which is ultimately unsurpassable. Moreover, Buddhism points unequivocally to the moral aspect of everyday life. Though Nirvana is amoral, in the sense that final peace transcends the conflict of good and evil, the path to wisdom is definitely a moral path. This follows logically from the doctrine of kamma. Every action must produce an effect, and one's own actions produce an effect in one's own life. Thus the kammic force which carries us inevitably onward can only be a force for good, that is, for our ultimate wisdom, if each action is a good action.

This doctrine finds its highest expression in metta, the Buddhist goal of universal and all-embracing love. Metta means much more than brotherly feeling or kindheartedness, though these are part of it. It is active benevolence, a love which is expressed and fulfilled in active ministry for the uplifting of fellow beings. Metta goes hand in hand with helpfulness and a willingness to forego self-interest in order to promote the welfare and happiness of mankind. It is metta which in

Buddhism is the basis for social progress. Metta is, finally, the broadest and intensest conceivable degree of sympathy, expressed in the throes of suffering and change. The true Buddhist does his best to exercise metta toward every living being and identifies himself with all, making no distinctions whatsoever with regard to caste, color, class, or sex.

In addition, of course, the teachings of the Buddha are a prime cultural force in Oriental life, just as the Bible is the ultimate source of much Western art and thought. The Buddhist scriptures are larger and more detailed than the Christian Bible, however, and in translation would fill a dozen volumes. In Pali, the language of the scriptures, the Buddha's teachings are called Tripitaka, which means "The Three Baskets."

Vinaya Pitaka, "The Basket of Discipline," consists of five books which expound the rules of monastic life. Sutta Pitaka, "The Basket of Discourses," is a collection of discussions, stories, poems, and proverbs, written in simple language, imparting all the precepts of practical Buddhism. The third basket, Abhidhamma Pitaka, or "Basket of Ultimate Things," deals with epistemological, metaphysical, and psychological matters and is of interest mainly to trained philosophers.

Thus the Tripitaka offers cohesive guidance at every level of intellectual, ethical, and spiritual activity. The Buddha's word is light, a lamp for Burma-and for everyone.

THE DEVELOPMENT OF BUDDHISM

The Process through which Buddhism developed into an organized religion also a clear manifestation of how a religious community came into being. What is the nature of religion? It can be defined in a great number of ways. Even in Marx's writings, religion is conceived differently under different circumstances. He said, "religion is the opiate of the people," which is interpreted in terms of the use of religion as a way of hypnotising the masses. This statement came not from Marx but Feuerbach. It means that the purveyors of religion who claimed that it could bring comfort to humankind were not being honest. Lenin conceived of "religion as the workers' groaning sound," which is interpreted as relating to the agony of the proletariat. Brezhnev said, "Religion has a countless number of definitions. . . . It may be interpreted as a form of relationship that helps to realize the existence of the mystical superhuman power, for humans believe that they can depend on this power." Brezhnev's definition seems to be more relevant and practical, but is there such a mystical power? How do we adjust to the existence of such a power? Why do people find it necessary to believe in such a power? Is belief in a mystical superhuman power superstitious? This raises some philosophical problems, viz., the problems of religion vis-a-vis superstition and belief.

Is religion a superstition? This question can be debated for a long time and no one knows when it will end, but devout believers most certainly will reject the pronouncement that "religion is superstition." Why? It is because believers frequently rely upon certain ideal principles to interpret what often is called the "mystical superhuman power" in the form of ultimate "truth, goodness, and beauty" (zhen, shan, mei), or else they often look upon the ideals of "truth, goodness, and beauty" as a form of "mystical superhuman power." They sincerely believe it to be true and try very hard to apply these ideals in their social life. Probably the belief in, and dependence upon, this ultimate "truth, goodness and beauty" in the guise of a "mystical superhuman power" is a matter of the human psyche's response to specific social conditions. But believers of the "mystical superhuman power" assume superstition and religion to be two different things. To them, `superstition' can only be a trick played upon those who lack scientific knowledge, i.e. a manifestation of spiritual poverty due to a lack of ideals. Devotees who believe that the "mystical superhuman power" is a manifestation of "truth, goodness, and beauty" may perhaps accept the idea that "religion is synonymous with belief" but certainly will not accept that "religion is superstition." According to them people should have faith: even the agnostics believe in agnosticism.

Religion and belief are undoubtedly related. Religion is based on belief, but whether belief is based on religion, in the classical sense, is a different matter. As a matter of illustration we can say that "we believe in the scientific explanation of atheism" or even accept that "we believe in Confucian philosophy." Nonetheless, there is no doubt that atheism is not a religion, but a scientific doctrine. Even Confucianism may be said to have embodied certain religious elements, although it is not a religion. Therefore, we should distinguish not only between `religion' and `belief,' but also between `religion' and `religious thought.' Otherwise, almost any kind of philosophical discourse could be regarded as a religion, and if that be the case, it would be as good as abnegating the existence of religion.

Based on our understanding of the human psyche, we may postulate that human beings really need a certain kind of belief. The question is whether there is the need for a religious belief. If we could divide religion into two categories--one a scientific belief--and another a non-scientific belief - religion may be said, generally, to belong to the latter category. What follows immediately will be questions like whether human spiritual life requires a certain kind of self-satisfaction obtained from a non-scientific discipline, or whether social life looks upon religious belief itself as a psychological need. This is too gigantic a problem to be discussed here. We can only postulate that for a non-scientific belief to become an organized religion, it must offer some kind of theoretical bases or support. Also, these arguments must be able to reflect the spirit of the time. If there were no religious teachings to be used as a theoretical system, non-scientific beliefs could become an established religion. Besides, as an established religion, especially one that had coloured the history of the social masses, there must be a perduring church organization, a religious canon, a community of devotees, and a history of religion. In Chinese history, there were thousands of the so-called "religious sects," but not all of them could be regarded strictly as "religious organizations." In fact, a number of them could only be looked upon as "superstitious cults." If that be the case, what then may be thought to be an organized religion? We shall analyze the growth of Buddhism first before illuminating the really meaningful form of religious organization.

An organized religion must have a canon with a philosophical base of its own. The religious teachings should not be nonsensical, but must contain a well-organized system of ideas for the advancement of humankind. The reason why Indian Buddhism has become an influential world religion is that it provides an impressive system of thought which is capable of enlightening the human mind. If Buddhism merely confined itself to a haphazard way of thinking, as is represented in the Taiping Jing, it would have been difficult to become an established religion in China.

Thus, from the end of the Han dynasty, through the Three Kingdoms, till after the Western and Eastern Jin, there emerged Daoists like Ge Hong, Lu Xiujing, Kou Qianzhi, Tao Hongjing and others who, in an attempt to fulfill the requirement of the time, not only integrated some of the Daoist and Confucian ideas but also absorbed some of the Buddhist elements to enrich Buddhism.

A really meaningful and influential religious community must have a formal or more serious form of church organization. Even though the ideas of `immortality' and `the sanctification of the bodies' were subsequently incorporated into the Daoist religion, the saints relied heavily on personal devotion without developing a distinctive church, and so they failed to develop a religion. It was not until the end of the Han dynasty that Buddhism became an established religion with a permanent membership of disciples, together with a body of clergy and church leaders. However, the regimes of the Three Kingdoms and the Western Jin banned this organization, subjecting it to dissolution until the Eastern Jin when Du Zhigong and others revived it and once again set it on course.

An organized religion must also have a more permanent set of religious teaching and canon. Although Buddhism had its own precepts and canon when it was first instituted at the end of the Eastern Han, they were rather simple and impermanent in nature. From the Eastern Han onward, Buddhism gradually became more firmly established under the impact of Buddhism and with the tireless efforts of Lu Xiujing, Kou Qianzhi and others.

An organized religion must have its own canon and scriptures for the guidance of its believers. Although there were a number of Daoist books, like the Laozi (Lao Tzu) and the Zhuangzi, before the Wei and the Jin dynasties, these books came to be accepted as scriptures only after being popularized by the devotees. All these books were written by Daoist philosophers of the early Qin, and they had hardly any connection with Daoist religion. It was due to the believers' attempt to look for historical evidences that they decided to upgrade them as scriptures.

Taiping Jing, for example, was written before the inception of the Daoist religion. Hence, it served only as a groundwork for the development of Buddhism. However, by the time of the Eastern Jin and the Northern and Southern dynasties, when Buddhism was firmly rooted and a church was organized, a large quantity of scriptures expounding the Daoist canon began to appear (Ge Hong's Pao Pozi, This period saw the appearance of three distinctive categories of scriptures: Sanhuangjing (the Three Emperors Scripture), Shangqingjing (the High Pure Scripture), and Lingbaojing, (the Spirit Protected Scripture).

All these scriptures subsequently combined to form the `three caves' (sandong) of the Dizhangjing, namely: the cave of the real (dongzhen), the cave of the gods (dongshen), and the cave of the occult (dongxuan).

An established religion must have a spirit being, or shenling, as a specific object of worship and a history of its own. When Buddhism was first instituted it had inherited part of the saints' tradition. The Daoist disciples claimed that it was imparted to them by the immortals, mostly with Laozi (Lao Tzu)'s assistance. Until the Northern and the Southern dynasties, Daoist disciples created the "rank of the real being" based on the conception of the social hierarchy prevailing at the time.

Tao Hongjing's Zhenlin Yueweitu (Real Spirit's Occupational Status Chart) divided the immortals into seven classes, the highest of which was occupied by the first three: the Primal Lord of Heaven (Yuanshi Tianzun), the Daoist Lord on High (Gaoshang Daojun), and the First Divine Daoist Lord (Yuanhuang Daojun). From then on, these three deities became the most honored in the objects of worship in the Daoist temples (daoguan). Since a religion always finds it necessary to undermine the existence of other competing religions, it has to create a history of its own in order to raise its own status. Thus, being an indigenous Chinese religion, Buddhism had to tackle the entry of alien Buddhism. Besides emphasizing the differences between `Chinese' and `non-Chinese' (huayi zhi bian) to undermine Buddhism, Daoists also spread the story of "Laozi (Lao Tzu) huahu" and elevated Laozi (Lao Tzu)'s position to that of Buddha Sakyamuni's teacher. Consequently, both Buddhism and Buddhism remained in conflict for a long time.

However, it was not until the Eastern Jin and the Northern and Southern dynasties that Buddhism finally became an established religion. The various stages of its development may be summarized as follows. First, from the Eastern Jin onward, the Daoists began to revive their religion by reorganizing the Daoist community which had become scattered and unstable. At the same time, in order to overcome the inadequacy of Daoist teaching and theoretical formulations, Ge Hong and others had provided a body of Daoist canon and precepts.

Thereafter, as an attempt to consolidate the founding of the Daoist church, a set of religious teaching was formulated; and in order to propagate Daoist teaching the required scriptures were made available.

Lastly, so as to set the religion on a proper footing, a compendium of fairy tales and legendary stories was kept alive. The various phases involved in the development of Buddhism may thus be said to be characteristic of the circumstances under which a religious body came into existence. One of our aims of studying the history of religion is to use it as a source for illuminating the various phases of its development so as to enable us to assess, more accurately, the role it played in society.

DHARMA

Dharma or Dhamma in Buddhism has two primary meanings:

- the teachings of the Buddha which lead to enlightenment
- the constituent factors of the experienced world

In East Asia, the character for Dharma is pronounced fa in Mandarin and ho in Japanese. The Tibetan translation of this term is chos (cho).

Buddha's Teachings

What is called Buddhism in the west has been referred to in India (the teachings' place of origin) and the east generally for many centuries as buddha-dharma. This term has no sectarian connotations but simply means "Path of Awakening" and thus conforms to a universal understanding of dharma.

The status of dharma is regarded variably by different traditions. Some regard it as an ultimate and transcendent truth which is utterly beyond worldly things, somewhat like the Christian logos. Others, who regard the Buddha as simply an enlightened human being, see dharma as the 84,000 different teachings that the Buddha gave to various types of people based on their needs.

The teachings are expedient means of raising doubt in the hearer's own cherished beliefs and view of life; when doubt has opened the door to the truth, the teaching can be put aside.

"Dharma" usually refers inclusively not just to the sayings of the Buddha but to the later traditions of interpretation and addition that the various schools of Buddhism have developed to help explain and expand upon the Buddha's teachings. For others still, they see the dharma as referring to the "truth" or ultimate reality or "the way things are".

The dharma is one of the Three Jewels of Buddhism of which practitioners of Buddhism seek refuge in (what one relies on for his/her lasting happiness).

The three jewels of Buddhism are the Buddha (mind's perfection of enlightenment), the dharma (teachings and methods) and the Sangha (awakened beings who provide guidance and support).

Buddha's Dharma Body

The qualities of the Dharma (Law, truth) is the same as the qualities of the Buddha and forms his "truth body" or "Dhamma Kaya": In the Samyutta Nikaya, Vakkali Sutta, Buddha said to his disciple Vakkali that,

"Yo kho Vakkali dhammam passati so mam passati"

Vakkali, whoever sees Dhamma, sees me [the Buddha]

Another reference from the Agganna Sutta of the Digha Nikaya, says to his disciple Vasettha:

"Tathagatassa h'etam Vasettha adivacanam Dhamma-kayo iti pi...":

O Vasettha! The Word of Dhammakaya is indeed the name of the Tathagata

Qualities of Buddha Dharma

The Teaching of the Buddha also has six supreme qualities:

1. *Svakkhato:* The Dhamma is not a speculative philosophy, but is the Universal Law found through enlightenment and is preached precisely. Therefore it is excellent in the beginning (sila-Sanskrit sila-moral principles), excellent in the middle (samadhi-concentration) and excellent in the end (panna-Sanskrit prajna... Wisdom),
2. *Sanditthiko*: The Dhamma can be tested by practice and therefore he who follows it will see the result by himself through his own experience.

3. *Akaliko:* The Dhamma is able to bestow timeless and immediate results here and now, for which there is no need to wait until the future or next existence.
4. *Ehipassiko*: The Dhamma welcomes all beings to put it to the test and come see for themselves.
5. *Opanayiko*: The Dhamma is capable of being entered upon and therefore it is worthy to be followed as a part of one's life.
6. *Paccattam Veditabbo Vinnuhi*: The Dhamma can be perfectly realized only by the noble disciples (Ariyas) who have matured and enlightened enough in supreme wisdom.

Knowing these attributes, Buddhists believe that they will attain the greatest peace and happiness through the practice of the Dhamma. Each person is therefore fully responsible for himself to put it in the real practice. Here the Buddha is compared to an experienced and skilful doctor and the Dhamma to proper medicine. However efficient the doctor or wonderful the medicine may be, the patients cannot be cured unless they take the medicine properly. So the practice of the Dhamma is the only way to attain the final deliverance of Nibbana.

These teachings ranged from understanding karma (Pali: kamma) (cause and effect) and developing good impressions in one's mind, to reach full enlightenment by recognizing the nature of mind.

Dharmas in Buddhist Phenomenology

Other uses include dharma, normally spelled with a small "d" (to differentiate), which refers to a phenomenon or constituent factor of human experience.

This was gradually expanded into a classification of constituents of the entire material and mental world. Rejecting the substantial existence of permanent entities which are qualified by possibly changing qualities, Buddhist Abhidharma philosophy, which enumerated seventy-five dharmas, came to propound that these "constituent factors" are the only type of entity that truly exists.

This notion is of particular importance for the analysis of human experience: Rather than assuming that mental states inhere in a cognizing subject, or a soul-substance, Buddhist philosophers largely propose that mental states alone exist as "momentary elements of consciousness" and that a subjective perceiver is assumed. One of the central tenets of Buddhism, is the denial of a separate permanent "I" and is outlined in the three marks of existence. The three signs: 1. Dukkha (Pali: Dukkha)-Suffering, 2. Anitya (Pali: Anicca)-Change/ Impermanence, 3. Anatman (Pali: Anatta)-Non-self. At the heart of Buddhism, is the denial of a "self" or "I" (and hence the delusion) as a separate self-existing entity.

Later, Buddhist philosophers like Nagarjuna would question whether the dharmas (momentary elements of consciousness) truly have a separate existence of their own. (*i.e.* Do they exist apart from anything else?) Rejecting any inherent reality to the dharmas, he asked (rhetorically):

> *When all dharmas are empty, what is endless? What has an end?*
>
> *What is endless and with an end? What is not endless and not with an end?*
>
> *What is it? What is other? What is permanent? What is impermanent?*
>
> *What is impermanent and permanent? What is neither?*
>
> *Auspicious is the pacification of phenomenal metastasis, the pacification of all apprehending;*
>
> *There is no dharma whatsoever taught by the Buddha to whomever, whenever, wherever.--Mulamadhyama-kakarika, nirvanaparikna, 25:22-24*

Dharma as Righteousness

According to S. N. Goenka, teacher of Vipassana Meditation, the original meaning of dhamma is "dhareti ti dhamma', or "that which is contained". Dharma in the Buddhist scriptures has a variety of meanings, including "phenomenon" and "nature" or "characteristic". Dharma also means 'mental contents' and is paired with citta, which means heart/mind. The pairing is paralleled with the pairing of kaya (body) and vedana (feelings or sensations, that which arise within the body but experienced through the mind), in major sutras such as the Mahasatipatthana sutra.

Dharma is also used to refer to the teachings of the Buddha, not in the context of the words of one man, even an enlightened man, but as a reflection of natural law which was re-discovered by this man and shared with the world. A person who lives their life with an understanding of this natural law, is a "dhammic" person, which is often translated as "righteous".

2

Buddhist Councils

1ST BUDDHIST COUNCIL (5TH CENTURY BCE)

The first Buddhist council was held soon after the nirvana of the Buddha under the patronage of king Ajatashatru, and presided by the monk Mahakasyapa, at Rajagaha (today's Rajgir). Its objective was to record the Buddha's sayings (sutta) and the monastic discipline or rules (Vinaya). The Suttas were recited by Ananda, and the Vinaya was recited by Upali. Also the Sangha made the unanimous decision to keep all the rules of the Vinaya, even the lesser and minor rules.

2nd Buddhist Council (383 BCE)

The historical records for the so-called 'Second Buddhist Council' derive primarily from the canonical Vinayas of various schools (Theravada, Sarvastivada, Mulasarvastivada, Mahasanghika, Dharmaguptaka, and Mahiuasaka). In most cases, these accounts are found at the end of the 'Skandhaka' portion of the Vinaya. While inevitably disagreeing on points of details, they nevertheless agree on roughly the following.

100 (or 110) years after the Buddha's Nibbana, a monk called Yasa, when visiting Vesali, noticed a number of lax practices among the local monks. A list of 'ten points' is given; the first and most important was that the Vesali monks, known as Vajjiputtakas, consented to accepting money. Considerable controversy erupted when Yasa refused to follow this practice. He was prosecuted by the Vajjiputtakas, and defended himself

by quoting in public a number of canonical passages condemming the use of money by monastics. Wishing to settle the matter, he gathered support from monks of other regions, mainly to the west and south. A group consented to go to Vesali to settle the matter. After considerable maneuvering, a meeting was held, attended by 700 monks. A council of eight was appointed to consider the matter. This consisted of four locals and four 'westerners'; but some of the locals had already been secretly won over to the westerners' case. Each of the ten points was referred to various canonical precedents. The committee found against the Vajjiputtaka monks. They presented this finding to the assembly, who consented unanimously. The canonical accounts end there.

3rd Buddhist Council (c. 250 BCE)

In striking contrast to the uniform accounts of the Second Council, there are records of several possible 'Third Councils'. These different versions function to authorize the founding of one particular school or other.

According to the Theravada commentaries and chronicles, the Third Buddhist Council was convened by the Mauryan king Ashoka (260–218 BC) at Pataliputra (today's Patna), under the leadership of the monk Moggaliputta Tissa. Its objective was to purify the Buddhist movement, particularly from opportunistic factions which had been attracted by the royal patronage. The king asked the suspect monks what the Buddha taught, and they claimed he taught views such as eternalism, etc., which are condemned in the canonical Brahmajala Sutta. He asked the virtuous monks, and they replied that the Buddha was a 'Teacher of Analysis' (Vibhajjavadin), an answer that was confirmed by Moggaliputta Tissa. The Council proceeded to recite the scriptures once more, adding to the canon Moggaliputta Tissa's own book, the Kathavatthu, a discussion of various dissentient Buddhist views now contained in the Theravada Abhidhamma Pitaka.

Also, emissaries were sent to various countries in order to spread Buddhism, as far as the Greek kingdoms in the West (in particular the neighbouring Greco-Bactrian Kingdom, and possibly even farther according to the inscriptions left on stone pillars by Ashoka). According to Frauwallner (Frauwallner, 1956), several of these missionaries were responsible for founding schools in various parts of India: Majjhantika was the father of the Kasmiri Sarvastivadins; Yonaka Dhammarakkhita may have been the founder of the Dharmaguptaka school; Mahadeva, sent to the Mahisa country may have been the founder of the Mahisasakas; and several teachers travelled to the Himalayas where they founded the Haimavata school, including a certain Kassapagotta, who may be connected with the Kasyapiyas. Relics of some of these monks have been excavated at Vedisa. (Willis, 2001) The most famous of the missionaries, and the main focus of interest for these Theravada histories, is Mahinda, who travelled to Sri Lanka where he founded the school we now know as Theravada.

The Theravada's own Dipavamsa records a quite different Council called the 'Greal Recital' (Mahasangiti), which it claims was held by the reformed Vajjiputtakas following their defeat at the Second council. The Dipavamsa criticizs the Mahasangitikas (who are the same as the Mahasanghikas) for rejecting various texts as non-canonical: the [Vinaya] Parivara; the 6 books of the Abhidhamma; the Patisambhida; the Niddesa; part of the Jatakas; and some verses. (Dipavamsa 76, 82)

The Mahasanghika, for their part, remember things differently: they allege, in the Sariputraparipriccha available in Chinese translation, that there was an attempt to unduly expand the old Vinaya. Although this account is set much later than the Dipavamsa's account, both accounts agree that the dispute was over the extent of what works could be considered canonical.

An entirely different account of Mahasanghika origins is found in the works of the Sarvastivada group of schools. Vasumitra tells of a dispute in Pataliputra at the time of Ashoka over five heretical points: that an arahant can have nocturnal emission; that he can have doubts; that he can be taught by another; that he can lack knowledge; and that the path can be aroused by crying 'What suffering!' These same points are discussed and condemned in Moggaliputta Tissa's Kathavatthu, but there is no mention of this Council in Theravadin sources. The later Mahavibhasa develops this story into a lurid smear campaign against the Mahasanghika founder, who it identifies as 'Mahadeva'. This version of events emphasizes the purity of the Kasmiri Sarvastivadins, who are portrayed as descended from the arahants who fled persecution due to 'Mahadeva'.

The Two Fourth Buddhist Councils (c. 30 BCE and 100 CE)

The Fourth Buddhist Council of the Mahayana was convened by the Kushan emperor Kanishka, around 100 CE at Jalandhar or in Kashmir, and is usually associated with the formal rise of Mahayana Buddhism. Theravada Buddhism does not recognize the authenticity of this council, and it is sometimes called the "council of heretical monks".

It is said that Kanishka gathered 500 Bhikkhus in Kashmir, headed by Vasumitra, to edit the Tripitaka and make references and remarks. It is said that during the council, there were all together three hundred thousand verses and over nine million statements compiled, and that it took twelve years to complete.

The Mahayana Fourth Buddhist Council did not rely on the original pali canon (the Tipitaka). Instead, a set of new scriptures were approved, as well as fundamental principles of Mahayana doctrine. The new scriptures, usually in the Gandhari vernacular and the Kharosthi script, were rewritten in the classical language of Sanskrit, to many scholars a turning point in the propagation of Buddhist thought.

The new Mahayana form of Buddhism was characterized by an almost God-like treatment of the Buddha, by the idea that all beings have a Buddha-nature and should aspire to Buddhahood, and by a syncretism due to the various cultural influences within northwestern India and the Kushan Empire, especially from Zoroastrianism and Greco-Buddhism.

From that point on, and in the space of a few centuries, Mahayana was to flourish and spread into Central Asia, China, Korea and Japan (introduction of Buddhism in 538 CE).

The First General Conference of the World Fellowship of Buddhists

The first time in the history of Buddhism since the third council, monks and laitiy representatives from nearly every school and organisation of Buddhism in the Mahayana, Theravada and Vajrayana from 27 countries in Asia, Europe and North America gathered to found The World Fellowship of Buddhists (WFB). The Aims and Objectives of the World Fellowship of Buddhists are:

1. To promote among the members strict observance and practice of the teachings of the Buddha
2. To secure unity, solidarity, and brotherhood amongst Buddhists
3. To propagate the sublime doctrine of the Buddha
4. To organize and carry on activities in the field of social, educational, cultural and other humanitarian services
5. To work for happiness, harmony and peace on earth and to collaborate with other organizations working for the same ends.

Theravada Buddhist Council in 1871 (5th Buddhist Council)

Another Buddhist Council, this time presided by Theravada monks took place in Mandalay Burma now known as Myanmar in 1871 in the reign of King Mindon. The chief objective of this meeting was to recite all the teachings of the Buddha and examine them in minute detail to see if any of them had been altered, distorted or dropped. It was presided over by three Elders, the Venerable Mahathera Jagarabhivamsa, the Venerable Narindabhidhaja, and the Venerable Mahathera Sumangalasami in the company of some two thousand four hundred monks (2,400). Their joint Dhamma recitation lasted for five months. It was also the work of this council to cause the entire Tripitaka to be inscribed for posterity on seven hundred and twenty-nine marble slabs in the Myanmar script after its recitation had been completed and unanimously approved. This monumental task was done by some two thousand four hundred (2,400) erudite monks and many skilled craftsmen who upon completion of each slab had them housed in beautiful miniature 'pitaka' pagodas on a special site in the grounds of King Mindon's Kuthodaw Pagoda at the foot of Mandalay Hill where it and the so called 'largest book in the world', stands to this day.

Theravada Buddhist Council in 1954 (Sixth Buddhist Council)

The Sixth Council was called at Kaba Aye in Yangon, formerly Rangoon in 1954, eighty-three years after the fifth one was held in Mandalay. It was sponsored by the Burmese Government led by the then Prime Minister, the Honourable U Nu. He authorized the construction of the Maha Passana Guha, 'the great cave', an artificial cave very like India's Sattapanni Cave where the first Buddhist Council had been held. Upon its completion The Council met on the 17th of May, 1954.

As in the case of the preceding councils, its first objective was to affirm and preserve the genuine Dhamma and Vinaya. However it was unique in so far as the monks who took part in it came from eight countries. These two thousand five hundred learned Theravada monks came from Myanmar, Cambodia, India, Laos, Nepal, Sri Lanka, Thailand. The late Venerable Mahasi Sayadaw was appointed the noble task of asking the required questions about the Dhamma of the Venerable Bhadanta Vicittasarabhivamsa who answered all of them learnedly and satisfactorily. By the time this council met all the participating countries had the Pali Tipitaka rendered into their native scripts, with the exception of India.

The traditional recitation of the Buddhist Scriptures took two years and the Tripitaka and its allied literature in all the scripts were painstakingly examined and their differences noted down and the necessary corrections made and all the versions were then collated. It was found that there was not much difference in the content of any of the texts. Finally, after the Council had officially approved them, all of the books of the Tipitaka and their Commentaries were prepared for printing on modern presses and published in the Myanmar (Burmese) script. This notable achievement was made possible through the dedicated efforts of the two thousand five hundred monks and numerous lay people. Their work came to an end in May, 1956, two and a half millennia after the Lord Buddha's Parinibbana.

Doubts on the 6th Buddhist Council's Tipitaka

Since the year 2000, the authenticity of the currently published version of Tipitaka of the Sixth Buddhist Council has been in some doubt, as some findings from the Dhamma Society Fund in Thailand have become more well known. The Dhamma Society Fund claims it has proof that after the first printing of the Tipitaka of Sixth Buddhist Council in 1958, it had been secretly replaced with the previous Burmese Fifth Buddhist Council Tipitaka. The Dhamma Society Fund is currently printing the 'real' Sixth Buddhist Council Tiptaka with sponsorship from the Thai King and other Thai royalty, for distribution amongst the most prestigious libraries and institutes around the world. After this, they plan to publish the Sixth Buddhist Counil Tipitaka for free, via the internet.

- Sanskrit (or Buddhist Hybrid Sanskrit): primarily Mahayana Buddhism
- Tibetan (Tib): Tibetan Buddhism
- Thai: Theravada Buddhism
- Burmese (Bur): Theravada Buddhism
- CJKV languages
    - o Chinese (Cn): Chinese Buddhism
    - o Japanese (Jp): Japanese Buddhism
    - o Korean (Ko): Korean Buddhism
    - o Vietnamese (Vi): Vietnamese Buddhism.

FOUR NOBLE TRUTHS

The Four Noble Truths are one of the most fundamental Buddhist teachings, they appear many times throughout the most ancient Buddhist texts, the Pali Canon. They are among the truths the Buddha realised during his enlightenment experience. Why the Buddha taught in this way is illuminated by the social context of the time in which he lived. The Buddha was a Sramana, a wandering ascetic whose "aim was to discover the truth and attain happiness". The Buddha claimed to have achieved this aim while under a bodhi tree near the Ganges River; the Four Noble Truths are a formulation of his understanding of "suffering", the fundamental cause of all suffering, the escape from suffering, and what effort a person can go to so that they themselves can *"attain happiness."*

These truths are not expressed as a theory or tentative idea, rather the Buddha says:

"These Four Noble Truths, monks, are actual, unerring, not otherwise. Therefore, they are called noble truths."

The Buddha said that he taught them...

"...because it is beneficial, it belongs to the fundamentals of the holy life, it leads to disenchantment, to dispassion, to cessation, to peace, to direct knowledge, to enlightenment, to Nirvana. That is why I have declared it."

This teaching was the basis of the Buddha's first discourse after his enlightenment.

Mahayana Buddhism contains within itself an alternative version of the Four Noble Truths, in which the immortality of the Buddha occupies a central position.

Four Noble Truths

Suffering (Dukkha): Now this, monks, is the noble truth of suffering: Birth is suffering, aging is suffering, sickness is suffering, death is suffering; union with what is displeasing is suffering; separation from what is pleasing is suffering; not to get what one wants is suffering; in brief, the five aggregates subject to clinging are suffering.

Source of Suffering (Samudaya): Now this, monks, is the noble truth of the origin of suffering: It is this craving which leads to renewed existence, accompanied by delight and lust, seeking delight here and there; that is, craving for sensual pleasures, craving for existence, craving for extermination.

The Cessation of Suffering (Nirodha): Now this, monks, is the noble truth of the cessation of suffering: It is the remainder less fading away and cessation of that same craving, the giving up and relinquishing of it, freedom from it, and non-reliance on it.

The Way Leading to the Cessation of Suffering (Magga): Now this, monks, is the noble truth of the way leading to the cessation of suffering: It is this Noble Eightfold Path; that is, right view, right intention, right speech, right action, right livelihood, right effort, right mindfulness, right concentration."

Variant Four Noble Truths in Mahayana Buddhism

Certain major Mahayana sutras, including the Mahaparinirvana Sutra and the Angulimaliya Sutra, present variant versions of the Four Noble Truths in line with their own metaphysics and soteriology. In the Mahaparinirvana Sutra, the Buddha declares that:

The Truth of Suffering relates to the failure to recognise the eternity of the Buddha; The Truth of the Cause of Suffering concerns the perversion and distortion of the True Dharma; The Truth of the Cessation of Suffering relates to the correct meditative cultivation of the tathagatagarbha (indwelling Buddha Essence in all beings) and not erroneously viewing it as non-Self and empty; cessation of suffering also arises with the elimination of inner defilements, when one can then enter into the Buddhic Essence within oneself: "When the afflictions have been eradicated, then one will perceive entry into the tathagata-garbha"; the Truth of the Path to the Cessation of Suffering entails envisioning the Buddha, Dharma and Sangha as eternal, immovable and indestructible.

The Angulimaliya Sutra similarly emphasises the seeing and knowing of the Buddha's eternality, immutability and peace as the key factors in liberation from suffering; failure to see this eternal nature of ultimate reality is said to constitute the primary cause of beings' continued entrapment in the sufferings of samsara.

STAGES IN THE HISTORY OF BUDDHISM

The history of Buddhism in India, which lasted about 1500 years, can be divided into 500 year periods, during which distinctive forms of Buddhism emerged. This is an idealized and schematic picture, but it is convenient, and it can be matched up with where Buddhism spread during these periods and what forms of Buddhism became dominant there. Buddhist doctrine and practice in the earliest period were agreed upon in a series of Councils, sometimes reckoned to be three, or four.

1. The First Council was held shortly after the Buddha's death, at Rajagriha (capital of the Kingdom of Magadha). Issues about the conduct of the *Sangha*, the monastic community, in the absence of the Buddha appear to have been settled.
2. The Second Council was held about a century after the Buddha's death, at Vaisali (under Magadhan control). Sometimes this is considered the First Council, or is confused with the previous one. It began to agree on the content of the Buddhist Canon and on the monastic discipline, the *vinaya*.
3. The Third Council was called by the Emperor Ashoka and held at Pataliputra. The content of the Pali *Tripitaka*, "Three Baskets," is supposed to have been settled at this Council, or thereabouts in this period, consisting of the *Sutra-pitaka* [*Sutta* in Pali], the sermons of the Buddha, the *Vinaya-pitaka*, the monastic discipline, and the *Abhidharma-pitaka* [*dharma* is *dhamma* in Pali], the philosophical development of Buddhist doctrine. Buddhism was introduced into Sri

Lanka (Ceylon) as the result of Ashoka's own efforts, and the Canon in Pali was preserved there.

4. The Fourth Council was called under the Emperor Kanishka I and held at Jalandhara (or Purushpura, Peshawar, Kanishka's capital). This is not attested in Pali sources, and so one often hears that there were only three Councils. The Council is supposed to have supervised the translation of the *Tripitaka* into Sanskrit. The Canon apparently had not only existed in Pali, but in other Prakrits, which were all consulted for a standard Sanskrit version. It appears to be the Sanskrit texts that were subsequently spread to China. The sutras of the Mahayana may have existed only in Sanskrit from the beginning.

Theravada ("Teaching of the Elders") Buddhism (called "Hinayana," the "Lesser Vehicle," by the Mahayana): In India, 5th century BC to 1st century AD.

- Distinctive doctrines:
  1. The Buddha (Siddhartha Gautama, Shakyamuni) is gone, and individual practitioners must work out their salvation on their own.
  2. The Buddha was unique, and individual practitioners cannot become Buddhas, only *arhats* ("saints"). There will be a future Buddha, Maitreya, but not for thousands of years.
  3. *Nirvana* (liberation) and *samsara* (the place of death and rebirth) are definitely different. *Samsara* is a place of suffering to be left behind. *Nirvana* is a liberation that is free of death and rebirth but is beyond description and rational understanding.

Mahayana ("Great Vehicle") Buddhism: In India, 1st century AD to 6th century.

- Distinctive doctrines:
  1. The Gautama Buddha is *not* gone, and individual practitioners are *not* on their own. Instead, the Buddha taught the dharma out of compassion, and

his compassion would prevent him from being unavailable to practitioners now. Indeed, to emulate the compassion of the Buddha, practitioners become *bodhisattvas*, who vow to carry all beings with them into salvation. Bodhisattvas are also available, like the Buddhas, to help people work out their salvation. Maitreya is presently a bodhisattva, but the most important bodhisattva is probably Avalokiteshvara, who developed into the Chinese goddess of Mercy, *Guanyin* (*Kwan-in* in Wade-Giles, *Kannon* in Japan).

2. The Buddha was *not* unique, and individual practitioners who have become bodhisattvas *can* become Buddhas. There are already multiple Buddhas besides Shakyamuni. Most important are Mahavairocana and Amitabha. Amitabha is famous for his Western Paradise, or Pure Land, where he has Vowed to cause anyone who calls on him for help to be born, so they will be free of the world of suffering to work out their ultimate liberation. In Japan Amitabha is known as *Amida* and Mahavairocana as *Dainichi*. Most of the famous Buddha statues in Japan are *not* Shakyamuni: the great outdoor bronze Buddha at Kamakura is Amida, and the Buddha enshrined in the *Todaiji* ("Great Eastern") Temple in Nara (the largest wooden building in the world), is another Buddha named Locana.
3. *Nirvana* and *samsara* are *no longer* definitely different. The "Fourfold Negation" is applied to the relationship between the two. *Samsara* and *Nirvana* are thus neither the same, nor different, nor both the same and different, nor neither the same nor different. This allows some room for maneuver, which may have made Buddhism more palatable in China, where Confucianism never did approve either of the world-denying metaphysics or the monasticism of Buddhism. Distinctively Chinese schools of

Buddhism developed, like T'ien-t'ai (*Tendai* in Japan) and Ch'an (*Seon* [*Son*] in Korea, *Thien* in Vietnam, *Zen* in Japan), for whom samsara and Nirvana were virtually identical, so that enlightenment and Nirvana *transformed* the world rather than eliminated it. The paradoxical metaphysics of Buddhism could be assimilated to the similar paradoxical doctrines of the native Chinese philosophical school of Taoism.

- Places where Mahayana spread: Mahayana Buddhism is presently practiced in China, Korea, Vietnam, and Japan. Buddhism was propagated in China by missionaries from India, like Kumarajiva (344-413), who arrived in China in 401, and Buddhabhadra (359-429), who arrived in 408, and by Chinese pilgrims who travelled to India, like Fa-Hsien (Faxian[3]), who travelled to India between 399 and 414, and Hsuan-tsang (Xuanzang[3], 600-664), who went to India between 629 and 645. Most of these figures concern a China of the Northern and Southern Empires (266-589), when the country was fragmented, and when barbarians, perhaps more susceptible to a foreign doctrine, ruled the North. These journeys were difficult, either by sea around Malaya, where many ships were attacked by pirates or sunk by storms, or by land through Central Asia, on the "Silk Road" caravan route, through deserts and over some of the highest mountains in the world. The highest peaks of the Pamirs and related mountain chains, called *Bam-e Donya* in Persian, "the Roof of the World," are all over 24,000 feet [note]. One story of a Buddhist missionary crossing the Pamirs, Kumarayana, father of Kumarajiva, is that he carried a Buddha image during the day — and the Buddha image carried him during the night! Kumarajiva, Fa-Hsien, and Hsuan-tsang all brought Buddhist texts from India to China and translated them. The Buddhist canon as it arrived in China was in Sanskrit, and it included many special

Mahayana Sutras that are not in the Pali Canon (though many are now suspected of being Chinese forgeries). The stories of Fa-Hsien and Hsuan-tsang's travels are important parts of Chinese literature, and Fa-Hsien's account of India during the reign of Chandra Gupta II (375-415) is an important document for the history of India.

Vajrayana ("Thunderbolt Vehicle") Buddhism: In India, 6th to 11th century.

- Distinctive doctrines: Vajrayana Buddhism is *Tantric* Buddhism, often called "esoteric" Buddhism. Although it is sometimes also translated as "diamond" (i.e. "hard"), the *vajra* (*kongo* in Japanese) was originally the thunderbolt of Indra; and in Vajrayana it symbolizes the magical power of Tantrism. Tantric magic could be worked through *man.d.alas*, sacred diagrams, *mantras*, sacred formulas for recitation (the most famous one being, "Om, mane padme hum"— "The jewel is in the lotus"), and *mudras*, sacred gestures. This Tantric magic could be merely thaumaturgical ("wonder working") or could be regarded as means of achieving liberation in addition to or apart from meditative or meritorious practices. Just as Hindu Tantrism expresses its magical power through goddesses like Kali, Vajrayana emphasizes female figures. Vajrayana comes to balance male Bodhisattvas with female Bodhisattvas as attendants of the various Buddhas. And while Buddhas tend to be regarded as male in all branches of Buddhism, Tibetan Buddhism supplies female figures corresponding to each Buddha, like the "savioresses" Green Tara, White Tara, and Mamaki, who actually vow to always be reborn as women in the process of leading all beings to salvation. Vajrayana symbolism always balances male and female: the Vajra Mandala (or the "jewel" above) corresponds to the Womb (or Matrix) Mandala (the "lotus"). The extent to which Vajrayana *practiced* real sexual union, been the physical male "vajra" and the physical female womb, as part of its Tantrism is unclear and disputed. Often "right-handed" Tantrism is distinguished from "left-handed" Tantrism, in which the former practiced the union of male and female, in symbolic, iconographic form, while the latter practiced it literally. While the "right-handed" forms are mainly what remain in Tibet and in Japanese Shingon today, there is little doubt that real "left-handed" practices existed in the past and survive to an extent in the present, and Tibetan art sometimes still portrays the more violent and disturbing aspects of Tantric practice — rape, bestiality, etc.

- Places where Vajrayana spread: Vajrayana Buddhism most importantly spread to Tibet and then Mongolia. In Tibet it assumed distinctive forms that are usually called *Lamaism*, since the monks are called Lamas. The present Dalai Lama, who was the priestly ruler of Tibet until he fled the Communist Chinese in 1959, is from a line that is reputed to be successive incarnations of the Bodhisattva Avalokiteshvara. Vajrayana Buddhism also entered China, Japan, etc., as special "esoteric" schools, like the Japanese *Shingon* school. The great temple at Borobudur, outside Jakarta on the island of Java, dates from this period (c.800), and embodies Vajrayana Mandala forms; but in Indonesia Buddhism soon thereafter gave way to Islam.

The end of Buddhism in India. Buddhism may have died out in India in the 11th century because: 1) It had become almost indistinguishable from the Tantric forms of Hinduism. Sophisticated Buddhist doctrine did not appeal to most people, and the actual practices and iconography of Vajrayana could easily be assimilated into Hinduism. And, 2) Islam arrived in earnest in India with the Afghan prince Mahmud of Ghazna, who defeated a coalition of Hindu princes in 1008 and soon annexed the Punjab. As Buddhism was persecuted, conversions to Islam increased, and Buddhism declined. By the time the British arrived, about 25% of India was Moslem. That ultimately led to the partition of the country into India and Pakistan. The

Gautama Buddha himself has ended up being regarded as the 9th Incarnation (*Avatar*) of the great Hindu God Vishnu, although the unflattering take on it is that he deliberately taught a false doctrine (i.e. Buddhism) in order to deceive and destroy demons.

The Final Dharma Age

Another way of dividing the history of Buddhism emerged in the Buddhist tradition as a way of dealing with the prediction of the Buddha himself that the *Dharma* would only last 500 years. This became a matter of concern in China, where Buddhism did not even become established until nearly 1000 years after the time of the Buddha. Indeed, there was uncertainty about when the time of the Buddha had been, but soon enough it was obvious that far more than 500 years had passed. The doctrine that was formulated in response to this we find in K'uei-chi (Tz'u-en, 632-682), founder of the Fa-hsien school early in the T'ang Dynasty, in his *I-lin-chang*, "The Grove of Meanings." There we find a division into three periods based on the existence of Buddhist teaching, Buddhist practice, and Buddhist "proof," i.e. results — supernatural powers and Nirvana:

- The Age of the True Dharma (Sanskrit *Saddharma*, Japanese *shobo*). In the first 500 years of Buddhism (sometimes put at 1000 years, however), the teaching, the practice, and the proof of Buddhism are all evident and effective. This becomes the Buddhist equivalent of the "age of the Apostles" in Christianity or of the "companions of the Prophet" in Islam — when the best exemplars of the religion lived, people whose achievements are now largely beyond the reach of believers (as most Protestants do not believe that any modern Christians can perform miracles on the scale of the Apostles). It becomes, naturally, particularly associated with Buddhism in India, the first step in the *Sangoku*, or "three nations," ideology that later developed in Japan.

- The Age of the Counterfeit Dharma (Sanskrit *Saddharma-pratirupaka*, Japanese *zoho*). In the 1000 years following the True Dharma, the teaching and the practice of Buddhism are evident but the proof fails. While uncertainty about the length of the True Dharma Age could postpone a reckoning, Buddhism in China — which now becomes particularly associated with the second Age — eventually had to face the fact that the full force of the Dharma, as defined by the Buddha himself, was spent. This would seem to remove the point of Buddhist belief and practice altogether, but it was also something whose full implications most Buddhists were unwilling to accept. One result was the popularity of devotionalistic forms of Buddhism, which substitute intermediate goals before final *Nirvana*. In Pure Land practice, the Vow of the Buddha Amitabha enables devotees to be reborn in a Pure Land, where they will be free of suffering, let alone the Hells, and can work out their salvation without distractions (like hunger or sex). Pure Land Buddhism, indeed, became the most popular form of Buddhism in China and Japan. Another approach, which we see in the T'ien-tai (Japanese *Tendai*) and Ch'an (*Zen*) Schools, was to redefine the "proof," so that avoiding rebirth was no longer the goal of Buddhist practice. Instead, life in the world of *samsara* can become the equivalent of *Nirvana*. This gives to Buddhism itself a very different character, unlike the world-denying tendencies of India and more conformable to the sensibilities of both Confucianism and Taoism. This goes along with discussions about whether it was really necessary to keep Buddhist Precepts. Nevertheless, we do have a continuation of traditional monasticism, and of course not everyone agrees with the new tendencies in thinking.
- The Age of the Final Dharma (Sanskrit *Saddharma-vipralopa*, Japanese *mappo*). If the Counterfeit Dharma posed a disturbing challenge for Buddhism, the Final

Dharma was even worse. At that point the real practice and proof of Buddhism are both supposed to no longer be possible. Only the teaching remains. While K'uei-chi didn't yet quite have to worry about that, by the time we get to the Kamakura Period (1186-1336) in Japanese history, it becomes widely accepted that the Final Dharma, *Mappo*, is upon them. This is expected to last no less than 10,000 years. After that, Buddhism will simply be forgotten, and ages will pass, perhaps a million years, before the arrival of the Future Buddha, Maitreya. By this time, of course, Buddhism was already vanishing in India itself. Some Japanese expected this, or were aware of it, others didn't believe it. But it was the kind of thing to reinforce the sense of the fading of the Dharma. The response was a period of religious creativity, in which a number of Chinese schools were adopted and reworked (Tendai, Zen, Jodo), and some original Japanese schools (Jodo Shin, Nichiren) emerged. Japanese monks ceased taking full monastic vows, clerical marriage became tolerated, sometimes sanctioned (in Jodo Shin), later even expected, and Japanese monks could easily gain reputations as formidable drinkers, despite the Precept against intoxicants. To Buddhists elsewhere, this kind of thing often makes it seem that Japanese monks are no longer proper Buddhists.

While many Buddhists now no longer worry about the problem of the fading Dharma, there is no denying the statement of the Buddha, or the role that dealing with this has played in the history of Buddhism.

NOBLE EIGHTFOLD PATH

The Noble Eightfold Path is, in the Buddhist tradition as taught by the Buddha Uakyamuni, considered to be the way that leads to the end of suffering. It forms the fourth part of the Four Noble Truths, which are the most fundamental Buddhist teachings.

The Noble Eightfold Path is essentially a practical guide of ethics, mental rehabilitation and mind deconditioning, and is believed, by Buddhists, to result in an end to *dukkha*, or suffering, which is a goal that has informed and driven the entire Buddhist tradition since its inception 2500 years ago. As the name indicates, there are eight elements in the Noble Eightfold Path, and these are further subdivided into three basic categories as follows:

- Wisdom (Sanskrit: *prajna*, Pali: *panna*)
  1. Right understanding
  2. Right intention
- Ethical conduct
  1. Right speech
  2. Right action
  3. Right livelihood
- Mental discipline
  1. Right effort
  2. Right mindfulness
  3. Right concentration.

In all of the elements of the Noble Eightfold Path, the word "right" is a translation of the word *samyanc* (Sanskrit) or *samma* (Pali), which denotes completion, togetherness, and coherence, and which can also carry the sense of "perfect" or "ideal".

Though the path is numbered one through eight, it is generally not considered to be a series of linear steps through which one must progress; rather, as the Buddhist monk and scholar Walpola Rahula points out, the eight elements of the Noble Eightfold Path "are to be developed more or less simultaneously, as far as possible according to the capacity of each individual.

They are all linked together and each helps the cultivation of the others".

In Buddhist symbology, the Noble Eightfold Path is often represented by means of the Dharma wheel, whose eight spokes represent the eight elements of the path.

Wisdom (*Prajna* · *Panna*)

The "wisdom" subdivision of the Noble Eightfold Path is constituted by those elements that refer primarily to the mental or cognitive aspect of a Buddhist practitioner's practice.

Right Understanding

Right understanding can also be translated as "right view" or "right perspective". This element of the Noble Eightfold Path refers explicitly to the Four Noble Truths of Buddhism, stating that these must be fully understood by the Buddhist practitioner. In the *Mahasatipammhana Sutta*, one of the Buddha Uakyamuni's discourses, right understanding is explained directly in terms of the Four Noble Truths:

And what, O bhikkhus, is right understanding? To understand suffering, to understand the origination of suffering, to understand extinction of suffering, to understand the path leading to the extinction of suffering; this is called right understanding.

Additionally, right understanding is sometimes considered to encompass an understanding of the Buddhist idea of the non-permanence, or even non-existence, of the self, an idea known as *anatman* in Sanskrit and *anatta* in Pali.

There are two stages for every stage of the eightfold path, a preliminary stage and the higher stages gradually obtained through the journey towards enlightenment. The preliminary stage of Right Views or right understanding is the knowledge of the Four Noble Truths. The higher stage require more than the comprehension of the Four Noble Truths, it also includes the knowledge and understanding of the not-self doctorine, imperminence, dependent origination, the five aggregates, *kamma* and rebirth, and so on.

Right Thought

Right thought can also be translated as "right intention", "right resolve", or "right aspiration". This element of the Noble Eightfold Path deals, fundamentally, with the Buddhist practitioner's reasons for practising Buddhism, and with his or her outlook towards the world. It enjoins renunciation of worldly things and an accordant greater commitment to spiritual matters; good will; and a commitment to non-violence, or *ahimsa*, towards other living beings. In the *Magga-vibhanga Sutta*, it is simply explained as follows:

And what is right thought? Being resolved on renunciation, on freedom from ill will, on harmlessness: This is called right thought.

Ethical Conduct (*Uila*)

The "ethical conduct" (Uila) subdivision of the Noble Eightfold Path is constituted by those elements that are driven by and ultimately conducive to the Buddhist idea of *karuna*, which is generally translated as *compassion* and somewhat akin to the Christian notion of *agapç*, or "unconditional love". This aspect of the Noble Eightfold Path is the most outward-oriented aspect of the Noble Eightfold Path insofar as it deals directly with a Buddhist practitioner's relationship with other members of his or her society.

Right Speech

Right speech, as the name implies, deals with the way in which a Buddhist practitioner would best make use of his or her words. In the *Magga-vibhanga Sutta*, this aspect of the Noble Eightfold Path is explained as follows: And what is right speech? Abstaining from lying, abstaining from divisive speech, abstaining from abusive speech, abstaining from idle chatter: This, monks, is called right speech.

Walpola Rahula glosses this by stating that not engaging in such "forms of wrong and harmful speech" ultimately means that "one naturally has to speak the truth, has to use words that are friendly and benevolent, pleasant and gentle, meaningful and useful".

Right Action

Right action can also be translated as "right conduct" and, as the name implies, deals with the proper way in which a

Buddhist practitioner would act in his or her daily life. In the *Magga-vibhanga Sutta*, this aspect of the Noble Eightfold Path is explained as follows:

And what, monks, is right action? Abstaining from taking life, abstaining from stealing, abstaining from unchastity: This, monks, is called right action.

Together with the idea of *ahimsa* and right speech, right action constitutes the Five Precepts, which form the fundamental ethical code undertaken by lay followers of Buddhism, and which are as follows:

1. To refrain from destroying living beings.
2. To refrain from stealing.
3. To refrain from sexual misconduct (adultery, rape, etc.).
4. To refrain from false speech (lying).
5. To refrain from intoxicants which lead to heedlessness.

Right Livelihood

Right livelihood is based around the concept of *ahimsa*, or harmlessness, and essentially states that Buddhist practitioners ought not to engage in trades or occupations which, either directly or indirectly, result in harm to other living beings. Such occupations include "trading in arms and lethal weapons, intoxicating drinks, poisons, killing animals, [and] cheating", among others. "[B]usiness in human beings"—such as slave trading and prostitution—is also forbidden, as are several other dishonest means of gaining wealth, such as "[s]cheming, persuading, hinting, belittling, [and] pursuing gain with gain".

Mental Development (*Samadhi*)

The "mental development" subdivision of the Noble Eightfold Path is constituted by those elements that deal with how a Buddhist practitioner can best go about shaping his or her outlook towards the world.

Right Effort

Right effort can also be translated as "right endeavour", and involves the Buddhist practitioner's continuous effort to, essentially, keep his or her mind free of thoughts that might impair his or her ability to realize or put into practice the other elements of the Noble Eightfold Path; for example, wishing ill towards another living being would contradict the injunction—contained in the "Right thought" element—to have good will towards others, and the "Right effort" element refers to the process of attempting to root out such an ill wish and replace it with a good wish.

The Buddhist monk Ajahn Chah, of the Thai forest tradition of Theravada Buddhism, described right effort as follows:

Proper effort is not the effort to make something particular happen. It is the effort to be aware and awake in each moment, the effort to overcome laziness and defilement, the effort to make each activity of our day meditation.

By making right effort, a Buddhist practitioner is considered to be engaging in an effort that is wholesome in terms of *karma*; that is, in terms of that effort's ultimate consequences to the practitioner.

Right Mindfulness

Right mindfulness, also translated as "right memory", together with right concentration, is concerned broadly with the practice of Buddhist meditation. Roughly speaking, "mindfulness" refers to the practice of keeping the mind alert to phenomena as they are affecting the body and mind. In the *Magga-vibhanga Sutta*, this aspect of the Noble Eightfold Path is explained as follows:

And what, monks, is right mindfulness?

(i) There is the case where a monk remains focused on (his/her) *body* in and of itself... ardent, aware, and mindful... having already put aside worldly desire and aversion.

(ii) (He/she) remains focused on *feelings* in and of themselves... ardent, aware, and mindful... having already put aside worldly desire and aversion.

(iii) (He/she) remains focused on *the mind* in and of itself... ardent, aware, and mindful... having already put aside worldly desire and aversion.

(iv) (He/she) remains focused on *mental qualities* in and of themselves... ardent, aware, and mindful... having already put aside worldly desire and aversion.

This, monks, is called right mindfulness.

Bhikkhu Bodhi, a monk of the Theravadin tradition, further glosses the concept of mindfulness as follows:

The mind is deliberately kept at the level of *bare attention*, a detached observation of what is happening within us and around us in the present moment. In the practice of right mindfulness the mind is trained to remain in the present, open, quiet, and alert, contemplating the present event. All judgments and interpretations have to be suspended, or if they occur, just registered and dropped.

Right Concentration

Right concentration (*samyak-samadhi* · *samma-samadhi*), together with right mindfulness, is concerned broadly with the practice of Buddhist meditation.

And what, monks, is right concentration?

(i) Quite withdrawn from sensuality, withdrawn from unwholesome states, a monk enters in the first jhana: rapture and pleasure born from detachment, accompanied by movement of the mind onto the object and retention of the mind on the object.

(ii) With the stilling of directed thought and evaluation, (he/she) enters and remains in the second jhana: rapture and pleasure born of concentration; fixed single-pointed awareness free from movement of the mind onto the object and retention of the mind on the object; assurance.

(iii) With the fading of rapture, (he/she) remains in equanimity, mindful and fully aware, and physically sensitive of pleasure. (He/She) enters and remains in the third jhana which the Noble Ones declare to be "Equanimous and mindful, (he/she) has a pleasurable abiding."

(iv) With the abandoning of pleasure and pain...as with the

> earlier disappearance of elation and distress...(he/she) enters and remains in the fourth jhana: purity of equanimity and mindfulness, neither in pleasure nor in pain.

The Ninth and Tenth Elements

In the *Great Forty Sutra* (Mahacattarisaka Sutta), which appears in the Pali Canon, the Buddha explains that cultivation of the Eightfold Path leads to the development of two further stages once enlightenment has been reached. These also fall under the category of panna and are *Right Knowledge* (sammanana) and *Right Liberation* (or *Right Release*; sammavimutti). Some consider *Right Association* as an implicit ninth aspect of the Path.

The Noble Eightfold Path and Cognitive Psychology

From the standpoint of modern cognitive psychology, the Noble Eightfold Path can be seen as rooted in what is called cognitive dissonance, which is the perception of incompatibility between two cognitions. In the essay "Buddhism Meets Western Science", Gay Watson explains this dissonance as it relates to Buddhist teaching:

Buddhism has always been concerned with feelings, emotions, sensations, and cognition. The Buddha points both to cognitive and emotional causes of suffering. The emotional cause is desire and its negative opposite, aversion. The cognitive cause is ignorance of the way things truly occur, or of three marks of existence: that all things are unsatisfactory, impermanent, and without essential self.

The Noble Eightfold Path is, from this psychological viewpoint, an attempt to resolve this dissonance by changing patterns of thought and behaviour. It is for this reason that the first element of the path is right understanding (*samma-dimmhi*), which is how one's mind views the world. Under the wisdom (*panna*) subdivision of the Noble Eightfold Path, this worldview is intimately connected with the second element, right thought (*samma-samkappa*), which concerns the patterns of thought and intention that controls one's actions. These elements can be seen at work, for example, in the opening verses of the *Dhammapada*:

Preceded by perception are mental states,
For them is perception supreme,
From perception have they sprung.
If, with perception polluted, one speaks or acts,
Thence suffering follows
As a wheel the draught ox's foot.
Preceded by perception are mental states,
For them is perception supreme,
From perception have they sprung.
If, with tranquil perception, one speaks or acts,
Thence ease follows
As a shadow that never departs.

Thus, by wilfully altering one's distorted worldview—as well as the behaviours stemming from that worldview—and bringing out "tranquil perception" in the place of "perception polluted", one is enabled to potentially escape from suffering and develop one's mind. Watson points this out from a psychological standpoint:

THE FIVE PRECEPTS

The five precepts constitute the basic Buddhist code of ethics, undertaken by lay followers of the Buddha Gautama in the Theravadin tradition.

The laity undertake to follow these training rules at the same time as they become Buddhists, taking refuge in the *Triple Gem*: In the Buddha (teacher), in the Dharma (teaching) and thirdly in the Sangha (community of monks and nuns). A lay practitioner who has undertaken the precepts is called an Upasaka.

The Buddha is said to have taught the five precepts out of compassion, not out of any desire to control his followers, and so they are to be undertaken voluntarily rather than as commandments from a god. They are to be seen as guidelines to how one who is awakened lives, not as mere moral injunctions imposed from outside and to be obeyed literally at all times.

The Buddha said that undertaking the precepts is a gift to oneself and others. He also described the rewards of following the precepts and the bad consequences of breaking the precepts.

The following are the five precepts rendered in English and then Pali.

1. I undertake the precept to refrain from taking the life (killing) of living beings.

   Panatipata veramani sikkhapadam samadiyami

2. I undertake the precept to refrain from stealing.

   Adinnadana veramani sikkhapadam samadiyami

3. I undertake the precept to refrain from sexual misconduct (adultery, rape, etc.).

   Kamesu micchacara veramani sikkhapadam samadiyami

4. I undertake the precept to refrain from false speech (lying).

   Musavada veramani sikkhapadam samadiyami

5. I undertake the precept to refrain from intoxicants which lead to heedlessness.

   Sura meraya majja pamadatthana veramani sikkhapadam samadiyami

Chinese Version of Five Precepts

The Chinese version as found in the *Supplement to the Canon* hardly differs:

1. As the Buddha refrained from killing until the end of his life, so I too will refrain from killing until the end of my life.
2. As the Buddha refrained from stealing until the end of his life, so I too will refrain from stealing until the end of my life.

As the Buddha refrained from sexual misconduct until the end of his life, so I too will refrain from sexual misconduct until the end of my life.

As the Buddha refrained from false speech until the end of his life, so I too will refrain from false speech until the end of my life.

3. As the Buddha refrained from alcohol until the end of his life, so I too will refrain from alcohol until the end of my life.

3

Buddhist Ethics and Wisdom

PAI LU-TIEN, a famous Chinese poet, author, and statesman who lived in the thirteenth century of the Christian era, once went to see an eminent Buddhist monk whose saintly life was known far and near, and asked him if he would instruct him in the essentials of Buddhist doctrine. The monk assented and recited the following gatha:

"Commit no wrong, but good deeds do,
And let thy heart be pure,
All Buddhas teach this truth,
Which will for aye endure."

The statesman-poet was not at all satisfied with this simple moral teaching, for he expected to have something abstruse, recondite, and highly philosophical from the mouth of such a prominent and virtuous personality. Said the poet, "Every child is familiar with this Buddhist injunction. What I wish to learn from you is the highest and most fundamental teaching of your faith." But the monk retorted, "Every child may know of this gatha, but even a silvery-haired man fails to put it into practice." Thereupon, it is said, the poet reverentially bowed and went home meditatively.

If we are requested today to state what is the most fundamental in Buddhist ethics, we have to make the same assertion. There may be and in fact are many schools and denominations in Buddhism, each claiming to have transmitted the true spirit of Buddha; but they will be unanimous in declaring that the gatha aforementioned is one of the common grounds on which they all stand. "Sabba papassa akaranam" is heard in all Southern monasteries, and the lines "Chu wo mo tso, etc.," are seen everywhere in the Eastern lands of Buddhism. If Buddhism were called a sort of ethical culture society on account of this simple code of morality, its followers would make no objection to it, for the recognition of a personal God, or the conception of original sin, or belief in a risen Christ is not thought indispensable to Buddhist salvation. Let a man do what is good and avoid what is bad and have his heart as pure as he can of all egotistic impulses and desires, and he will be delivered from the clutches of ignorance and misery. What ever his dogmatic views on religion, he is one of the enlightened who are above bigotry, intolerance, vanity, conceit, pedantry, and prejudice. He must truly be said to be one whose spiritual insight has penetrated into the depths of existence.

Now, the question is: What is good? What is evil? And how is the heart to be cleansed? I am not going to discuss here these great ethical and religious problems from a mere theoretical point of view. Buddhism has nothing to do with utilitarianism or intuitionalism or hedonism or what not. Buddhism is most practical in its announcement of what constitutes goodness. It dogmatically and concretely points out good deeds one by one. First, negatively, it enumerates ten deeds of goodness (kusalam) as most fundamental in Buddhist ethics; while, positively, it considers the six paramitas (virtues of perfection) or eightfold path as the route leading to a virtuous life.

The ten deeds of goodness are: (1) Not to kill any living being; (2) Not to take anything that does not belong to oneself; (3) Not to look at the other sex with an unclean heart; (4) Not to speak falsehood; (5) Not to calumniate; (6) Not to use vile language; (7) Not to make sensational utterances; (8) Not to be greedy; (9) Not to be out of temper; and lastly, (10) Not to be confused by false doctrines. Later Buddhists, however, make ten affirmative propositions out of those just mentioned, thus: It is good (1) to save any living being, (2) to practise charity,

(3) to be clean-minded, (4) to speak truth, (5) to promote friendship, (6) to talk softly and gently, (7) to be straightforward in speech, (8) to be content with one's own possessions, (9) to be meek and humble, and (10) to think clearly and rightly.

The six paramitas or virtues of perfection are: (1) Charity, which includes the giving away of worldly possessions as well as the proclamation of the Good Law, (2) The observation of the moral precepts as formulated by Buddha, (3) Meekness, (4) Strenuosity, (5) Contemplation, (6) Spiritual enlightenment.

The eightfold path is: (1) Right view, (2) Right reflection, (3) Right speech, (4) Right deed, (5) Right livelihood, (6) Right striving, (7) Right understanding, (8) Right contemplation. In these various enumerations of Buddhist virtues, what is most unique are perhaps the virtues of strenuosity and those of contemplation and enlightenment. To be good Buddhists, we must never be indolent, whiling away our time to no purpose. Mere piety will not do, so long as there is some work to be accomplished for the sake of humanity and civilization. Love, again, must be accompanied with enlightenment, for the affection is very frequently wasted on account of its blindness. God-fearing is recommendable, but without contemplation we fail to recognize the purport of our own position in the system of the universe. Mere passion leads to fervour and violence if not properly guided by contemplation which brings enlightenment, revealing the reason of existence and purifying the heart of ignorance.

Ignorance, according to Buddhism, is the root of all evil, and therefore it advises us in strong terms to have ignorance completely destroyed. And it is only then that the all-illuminating light of enlightenment guides us gloriously to the destination of all beings, where we gain purity of heart, and whatever flows from this eternal fountain of purity is good.

It is evident, then, that by purity of heart is meant absence of ignorance and self-will. But it is not a negative condition, for the most essential postulate of Buddhism is that in each of us there abide the indwelling reason of the universe, which, when released from the temporal bondage of ignorance and self-will, becomes the master of itself by reducing everything to subjection and restoring it to its right place. In a pure heart, therefore, the universal reason manifests itself in its full glory and works its own destiny unmolested. What one with such a heart wills is what makes the bird sing and the flower smile, what has raised the mountain and makes the water flow. He is hungry and the universe wishes to eat; he is asleep and all the world hybernates. This sounds extraordinary, but the enlightened understand it perfectly well. We cannot make the blind see what we ourselves see. The blind may protest that we are deceiving them; but could we do otherwise, inasmuch as they are deprived of the sense we have, or they have not yet learned how to make use of it? It is declared by Buddhists, therefore, that to realize fully the sanctity of religious life one must have Buddha-wisdom awakened from its unconscious slumber in which it is indulging from time out of mind.

Analytically, purity of heart consists of sympathy and intelligence, and on this groundwork the structure of practical Buddhism is founded. Sympathy is the tremulation of the spiritual cord which unites the hearts of all sentient beings; and it is intelligence that discovers the presence of the sacred cord in every one of us and keeps it from being entangled. The cord freely responds to cries of suffering. The heart contrives to effect all the possible means to relieve sentient beings from misery and ignorance. The ten deeds of goodness, the eightfold path, the six virtues of perfection, and many other good things all flow from this one source of pure-heartedness.

It is, then, of unqualified importance in the ethics of Buddhism to have one's heart perfectly cleansed and free from the dust of egotism which has been accumulating through the want of enlightenment. In this sense "blessed are the pure in heart"; they may not see God as he is superficially and superstitiously understood, but they will surely come into personal touch with the ultimate authority of conduct and also perceive that the author is not residing outside of their being but within themselves. We read in the Dharmapada:

"Manopubbangama dhamma, manosettha, manomaya;
Manasa, ce padutthana bhasati va karoti va,
Tato nam dukkham anveti, cakkara va vahato padam.
"Manopubbangama dhamma, manosettha, manomaya;
Manasa ce pasannena bhasati va karoti va,
Tato nam sukhara anveti, chaya va anapayinî."

In this respect Buddhism can be said to have a decidedly idealistic tendency, since it fully recognizes the paramountcy of ideas in the moral realm. But we must not lose sight of the fact that Buddhism is not a system of metaphysics, but a religion which is practical more than anything else. What it teaches is the profound spiritual experience of every enlightened man, while the philosopher and theorist will speculate on the facts and offer whatever interpretation they may please or feel compelled to give to account adequately for them.

Buddhism is often charged with passiveness and quietism, lacking the "push" of some other religions; and the backwardness of Asiatic nations in the general march of humanity is sometimes ascribed to the influence of Buddhism. Though I am not here entering upon any lengthy polemics, a few words may not be altogether inopportune to refute such an erroneous opinion as this.

If there is anything passive in Eastern culture, which is often no more than tolerance or indifference or self-restraint, it is not due to Buddhism but to the racial idiosyncrasy of Asiatic peoples. Buddhism teaches contemplation and tranquillity and at the same time strenuosity, indefatigable energy in following truth and in destroying ignorance. We see many admirable examples among its believers who have fully illustrated these virtues in their person. The history of Buddhism, while perfectly free from bloodshed and inhumanity, evidences how far its moral teachings have been carried out. Buddhist ethics is not certainly passive or negative, unless the absence of arrogance, aggressiveness, intolerance, bigotry, and fanaticism could be called so.

Religion in its social aspect is not omnipotent, nor is it absolute, as is imagined by some. It is, like many other things created by man, a human institution; it has been discovered, shaped, developed according to the inner necessity of mankind; and as long as he is imperfect and steering his course through innumerable obstacles, religion also must share his imperfection and adapt itself to ever-changing surroundings.

Instead of imposing its ideals upon man tyrannically and absolutely, religion reconciles itself to his needs, going through all the necessary modifications. Therefore, one religion is diversely interpreted by different peoples among whom it may thrive.

To suppose that religion could do anything it desires without regard to individual, national, racial peculiarities is far from the fact. The difference between Oriental and Occidental civilization is by no means due to the difference between Christianity and Buddhism.

On the other hand, the difference between the two religions is due to the difference between the two great types of Civilization. Truth, be it religious or philosophical or scientific, is universal, and as such does not allow any modification or distortion. But it suffers modification in its practical application, for it is like a mathematical formula or figure. When conceived a priori, it is formal and not subject to any concrete individualization, which latter in fact is the condition of its particular forms.

In conclusion let me say most emphatically that the ethics of Buddhism is summed up in the purification of the heart, in keeping oneself unspotted even though living in the world; and from this eternal root must sprout such things of God as love, a heart of compassion, the virtue of strenuosity, humbleness of mind, longsuffering, forbearing one another, forgiving one another, and freedom from all evils. It is said that there were eighty-four thousand virtues of perfection practised by all Bodhisattvas, but they are no more than so many leaves and branches growing from the one stem of pure-heartedness.

"NON-THEISTIC ETHICS" AND "BUDDHISM AND PHENOMENOLGY"

Non-Theistic Ethics

Presenters:

- Edward Ted Slingerland (University of Colorado, Boulder): "Confucius as Virtue Ethicist.
- Presenters Sallie B. King (James Madison University): "From Is to Ought: Natural Law in Theravada"

In her paper, Professor King explores the role of the natural law (Pali: dhamma) in Theravada Buddhist ethics and argues that such an ethics, especially in the interpretation of Phra Prayudh Payutto, supports democratic systems of government and individual rights.

King commences her argument by citing Stephen Buckle's definition of natural law as "an unchanging normative order that is part of the natural world." Thus defined, natural law grounds ethics in the order of the cosmos as the natural rather than supernatural source of normative behavior.

Similarly, King argues, Theravada Buddhism grounds ethical reasoning in the dhamma, which Buddhadasa Bhikkhu paraphrases as "nature itself," "the laws of nature," and "a person's duty to act in accordance with the laws of nature." Payutto further distinguishes between "saccadhamma" as "the conditions... of dhamma" and "cariyadhamma" as the "knowledge pertaining to the application of saccadhamma."

That which harmonizes human behavior with the conditions of reality Buddhadasa calls "sila." Thus defined morality constitues normalcy, that is, harmony with the nature of things, individually and socially. In this sense, Theravada Buddhism replaces the moral extremes of "bad" and "good" with "unskillful" and skillful."

The natural law, specified as the law of conditioned origination (paticca-samuppada) and the law of karma is merely desciptive rather than normative. King argues that Theravada Buddhist ethics differs from the Confucian natural law theory in that the latter is normative in character while the former is predominantly descriptive. The moral imperative as implied in the law of karma explicates this descriptive nature of Theravada ethics. King explains: "if one violates the moral law, or in other words, behaves in an anti-dhammic fashion, it is inevitable that unpleasant consequences will follow, since that is how the universe is constructed."

Morality, then, becomes a matter of conforming to and harmonizing with "the way things are." Metta, love, karuna, compassion, upekkha, equanimity, and samaggi, unity, constitute the appropriate response to the world and its order. Buddhism comprises the observation that humans tend to be in disharmony with nature and experience suffering (dukkha) and provides a "cure" for this problem, as formulated in the four noble truths.

In the second half of her paper, King asks how such an ethics based on the observation of the natural law and an "emphatic, caring, compassionate response" to the human predicament, can support the value of the individual and respond to unjust governments?

She argues that the notions of causal interdependence and harmony with "the way things are" does not justify tyranny as one aspect of the interdependence between government and its people but rather implies "non-egocentricism" and harmony with the natural law (not that of "a particular social system"). To the contrary, a government that does not harmonize with the dhamma violates the natural order itself and "could be easily challenged on that ground, simply for the sake of putting an end to suffering." Even Buddhadasa argues that a violation of the dasarajadhamma (the ten virtues of a ruler) justifies rebellion.

However, while Buddhadasa and Payutto agree that independent critical thinking is necessary, they disagree in their interpretation of the relationship between individuals and society. Buddhadasa, who proposes a "dhammic socialism," argues that liberalism and individualism underestimate the power of human defilements (kleseas) and, therefore, interprets non-egocentricism to privilege society over the individual.

Payutto, on the contrary, argues that the freedom of the individual is interrelated to the freedom of other individuals and thus is important to society. Based on his interpretation of interdependence, Payutto formulates the idea of a "dhammic democracy" which "balances the interests of individual and society."

Thus Buddhadasa seems to emphasize the importance of human defilements, on the one hand, while Payutto stresses human potential, on the other. King argues that Payuttto's view is both "more philosophically adequate" and "truer to the values of Shakyamuni Buddha."

Professor Twiss commences his response by outlining the three different kind of complexities involved in a comparative study.

Comparative studies face methodological complexities insofar as they apply, critique, or dialogue categories across cultures and traditions; they face social complexities insofar as they cross cultural and religious boundaries; and they face the problem of having to negotiate complexities with individual traditions. Since both, Slingerland and King refrain from a cross-cultural critique of ethical categories, Twiss concludes they are "implicitly rather than self-consciously comparative."

Finally, he acknowledges his bias in favour of an interpretation of Buddhist ethics as virtue ethics and thus against King's reading of Theravada Buddhist ethics as a natural law theory.

Nevertheless, he acknowledges that King's interpretation is "plausible" and decides to focus on King's definition of natural law. By the same token, he suggests that while he contends that King's interpretation of Confucianism as natural law ethics is "not utterly off-the-wall," he definitely leans towards an interpretation of Confucian ethics as value ethics.

In general, Twiss argues that Kings definition of the natural law neglects "an emphasis on the role of reason" and " the sociomoral functions of natural law ethics." Central to a natural law theory are general and specific principles which enable a moral life, a social order, and a critique thereof.

These principles are found in "the natural cosmic order," in what it means to be human, by "general consensus," or in divine revelation. Based on this expanded notion of natural law, Twiss argues, that a consideration of the "epistemic warrants" of the Theravada position could highlight "the uniqueness of the Buddhist view" and would engage in a "fruitful dialogue with natural law positions in other traditions." At the heart of this issue, however, lies the question, whether a natural law or a law of karma, for this matter, can serve as the basis for a moral theory if it is purely descriptive and devoid of any normative character. It is the answer to this question which will determine the value of the Buddhist natural law theory for the reconstruction of a Buddhist social ethics.

MEDICAL ETHICS

Despite Buddhism's long association with the healing arts, little attention has been paid to the ethical issues which arise from the practice of medicine. A small number of monographs provide introductions to the issues and dilemmas which arise in medical practice. These are Ratanakul (1986), Nakasone (1990) and Keown (1995), and these volumes should be consulted in conjunction with the sources listed under the specific subject-headings below. Also relevant is the unpublished Masters thesis by Shoyu Taniguchi (1987a). For general discussions in the periodical literature see Taniguchi (1987b), Mettanando (1991), and Ratanakul (1988; 1990). A useful discussion of Buddhism in terms of the "four principles" approach to medical ethics developed by Beauchamp and Childress (1989) is provided by Robert Florida (1994).

The Encyclopedia of Bioethics contains articles on medical ethics in India (Jaqqi, 1987), Asia (Unschuld, 1987), and Japan in the nineteenth century (Kitagawa, 1987). Also on Japan see Umezawa (1988). On medical ethics in imperial China see

Unschuld (1979) and on Thailand Violette Lindbeck (1984) and Ratanakul (1988; 1990).

The principal issues to be addressed in contemporary medical ethics may be summarised as moral personhood (the question of who is and who is not entitled to moral respect), abortion, embryo experimentation, genetic engineering, consent to treatment, resource allocation, defining death, organ transplantation, living wills, the persistent vegetative state, and euthanasia. Little systematic attention has yet been directed to these subjects by Buddhist practitioners or scholars, and some subjects have not been discussed at all from a Buddhist perspective. The arrangement of the topics below is neither comprehensive nor final. It is inevitable there will be overlap between the sections, and items which appear under one category may contain discussion of issues or principles which have broader relevance.

At this time, however, it seems useful to identify three groups of issues and related literature. These concern: moral personhood, issues surrounding life at its beginning, and issues surrounding life at its end. There is insufficient literature on resource-allocation, socio-economic issues, or other questions about general medical practice to justify a category on those topics in this review. There are signs, however, that a Buddhist perspective on certain aspects of medical treatment is beginning to appear, for example Epstein (1993) and Kabat-Zinn's (1990, 1994) integration of Buddhist meditation into medical practice, and the growing literature on Buddhism and social justice, such as Jones (1989) and Sizemore and Swearer (1993).

MORAL PERSONHOOD

Personhood is both a central problem for Buddhist ethics and Western medical ethics, and consequently a very promising area for a dialogue between the two. The problem for Buddhist ethics has always been why should people act ethically if there is no act, no actor and no consequences of action (Collins, 1982). If there is no self or other, how can there be karmic consequences, responsibility, loyalty, or even compassion? Theravadin scholars continue to be divided over whether Buddhism suggests different ethics for those who persist in the illusion of self (kammic ethics) and for those who would transcend the illusion of self (nibbanic ethics). The paradoxical unity of compassionate ethics and nihilistic insight into selflessness has been the central koan of Mahayana Buddhism. Tantra and Zen suggest that the person who sees that there is no "I" is beyond good and evil.

For bioethics, struggles over abortion, animal rights and brain death have brought personhood to the forefront (Nelkin, 1983). Opponents of abortion and euthanasia, and advocates for the disabled and animals, on the other hand, assert that mere humanness or merely being alive should bestow a "right to life."

But most bioethicists believe that human beings and animals take on ethical significance to the extent that they are "persons." Some, such as Tooley (1984), would set a standard which would exclude almost all animals, newborns, and the severely retarded or demented. When they specify which elements of sentience and neurological integrity create the illusion of personhood, Western bioethicists begin to sound remarkably Buddhistic: "the awareness of the difference between self and other; the ability to be conscious of oneself over time; the ability to engage in purposive actions" (see, for instance, Fletcher, 1979).

At the same time, Western bioethicists have become increasingly troubled by questions about the autonomy, continuity and authenticity of the self. Do anti-depressants create an inauthentic self, or is the self more authentic when its cheerful? Is one respecting a patient's autonomy by respecting the treatment preferences they expressed when healthy, or those they express in the throes of illness? Is it ever possible for a patient to give truly free and informed consent to treatment?

The most radical challenge to Western ethics of self-determination came in 1984 with the publication of British philosopher Derek Parfit's Reasons and Persons. In this meticulously argued tome, Parfit rejects the existence of continuous selves and concludes that an individual is as discontinuous from itself at some later time as it is from other individuals. Consequently, working for the future welfare of all beings is the same as working for one's own future welfare, since there will be no "I" to benefit in the future.

Bioethicists are only now incorporating Parfit's argument. For instance, researchers find that is impossible to accurately anticipate one's state of mind when one is sick or dying, much less when one is unconscious, undercutting the assumption of continuous personhood undergirding "living wills."

From a Buddhist/Parfitian perspective, the search for "real" preferences, central to the identity of the person, is a pointless one. With this acknowledgement, it is less troubling to place our trust in our family and friends to make decisions for our future selves (Kuczewski, 1994). More to the point, a Buddhist/ Parfitian would encourage citizens to look beyond their personal preferences in dying, which may be to "die with dignity" but may also be to use as many resources as possible to stave off death, and instead participate in creating a health care system that served the needs of everyone in society.

Another area of potential dialogue is in the efforts to go beyond Cartesian (and Hindu etc.) mind-body dualism in defining life and death. Over the last twenty years the West has slowly accepted that a "person" is dead if their brain is destroyed, even if the body continues to function. Yet it still troubles many Westerners and Buddhists to declare the permanently unconscious "dead," believing that this is an example of inappropriate mind-body dualism. Other Westerners and Buddhists believe that only a "neocortical" definition of death recognizes the centrality of consciousness and personhood in ethics (Gervais, 1986). More challenging, some Western ethicists have begun to discuss the status of personhood as future technologies make possible the continuity of personality from one body to another (More, 1994). When medical technology offers reincarnation, Buddhist bioethics will certainly flourish.

ABORTION

Buddhism, like all religious and secular philosophies, focuses on two central questions concerning abortion: (a) when does the embryo or fetus acquire the property which makes termination of pregnancy "killing"?; and (b) is termination of a pregnancy, before or after this point, ever justifiable?

While there was a minority tradition in classical Hindu embryology that held that incarnation does not occur till as late as the seventh month (Lipner, 1989), most Buddhist commentators have adopted classical Hindu teachings that the transmigration of consciousness occurs at conception, and therefore that all abortion incurs the karmic burden of killing. Before modern embryology, however, in both Buddhist countries and the West, ideas about conception were scientifically inaccurate, and often associated the beginning of life with events in the third or fourth month of pregnancy (for a discussion of traditional Tibetan embryology, see Dhonden, 1980 and Lecso,1987).

Another problem in early Buddhists' embryology is their assumption that the transmigration of consciousness is sudden rather than gradual. Based on the findings of modern neuro-embryology Buddhists today might maintain that the fetus does not fully embody all five skandhas and the illusion of personhood until after birth; this is the argument developed by most Western ethicists to defend abortion (Tooley, 1984; Flower, 1985; Bennett, 1989).

If the fetus is not yet a fully embodied person, then the karmic consequences of abortion would be even less than the killing of animals, which Buddhism teaches do have moral status. This neurological interpretation of the skandhas may be more consistent with Western Buddhism, which often sees the doctrine of rebirth as peripheral or interprets rebirth metaphorically rather than literally (Batchelor, 1992; King, 1994).

The second question is whether abortion always generates bad karma, or in Western terms, is it ever "justified." This relates to the debate about whether Buddhist ethics are absolutist, utilitarian or "virtuist," i.e. seeing the good in the development of personal qualities. The absolutist would hold that bad karma is incurred from any act of murder, whatever the justifications. The utilitarian would argue that murder can be a compassionate act with positive karmic consequences, taking into account factors such as the health of the fetus or mother, the population crisis, and the readiness of the parents to raise a child.

A virtue-oriented Buddhist would argue that the attitude and motivations of the pregnant woman and her collaborators would determine the ethics of an abortion. Along this line, Tworkov (1992) argues that the karmic skilfulness of an abortion is related to whether the person became pregnant and made her decision to abort without serious mindfulness. From this perspective, aborting a fetus conceived without an effort at contraception would be more karmically significant than an abortion necessitated in spite of contraception.

The much discussed Japanese tolerance for, and ritualization of, abortion appears to combine both utilitarian and virtue approaches. The Japanese believe that abortion is a "sorrowful necessity," and Buddhist temples sell rituals and statues intended to represent parents' apologies to the aborted, and wishes for a more propitious rebirth. The Japanese have reached these accommodations consensually, with little debate, and without discussion of the rights of women or the unborn (LaFleur, 1990, 1992).

The Theravadin commentator Buddhaghosa appears to have combined all three views. He held that killing produces karma jointly through the mental effort and intensity of the desire to kill, and the virtue of the victim (Florida, 1991). Since killing big animals required more effort, and was therefore worse than killing small animals, the karma of feticide would be less than murder of adults, and less in earlier stages of pregnancy. On the other hand, for Buddhaghosa, the karma of feticide would be greater than that of killing villains in self-defence.

Buddhists have thus far given little thought to the third important question, the connection between morality and law, specifically how, and on what grounds, the state should regulate abortion. Some Buddhists have adopted the stance of many moderates in the West: abortion is murder of a person, but women should have that choice (for instance, Imamura, 1984 and Lecso, 1987). Since most Buddhists have no problem with laws to discourage and punish murder in general, implicit in this position is that murder is either justifiable when it conflicts with bodily autonomy or, since few Buddhists would imprison butchers, that fetuses are closer in status to animals. Clearly there is much room for clarification of the relationship between religious ethics and law in pluralistic societies.

Some scholars (such as Ling, 1969, and LaFleur, 1992) have looked beyond the strictly ethical concerns with abortion to examine the cultural aspects of the question. From this perspective it is sometimes pointed out that Buddhism is not "pro-natalist," i.e. does not hold that reproduction is a religious duty-quite the reverse in fact-and does not advocate "family values," at least in the sense that Confucianism did. Buddhist skepticism about family and reproduction was a central cause of Confucian and Shinto persecution. The Sinhalese embrace of contraception and abortion was so enthusiastic in the 1960s, compared to Sri Lanka's Muslims, Catholics and Hindus, that racialist monks began to argue that Buddhists had an obligation to "race-religion-nation" to reproduce.

DEATH, DYING AND EUTHANASIA

The themes of impermanence, decay and death are omnipresent in Buddhist literature. In many Asian cultures Buddhism is identified as the authority par excellence on matters pertaining to death, and is closely linked to the rites and ceremonies associated with the transition from this life to the next. Buddhist literature emphasises the importance of meeting death mindfully since the last moment of one life can be particularly influential in determining the quality of the next rebirth.

General reflections on death will be found in Philip Kapleau's 1972 anthology The Wheel of Death and his 1989 The Wheel of Life and Death. Stephen Levine is the author of several books dealing with the subject of death from a Zen perspective while a contemporary Tibetan perspective is provided by Sogyal Rinpoche's popular Tibetan Book of Living and Dying, Glenn H. Mullin (1986) and John Powers (1995, Ch.10). James Whitehill (1974) discussed what can be learned from the death of the Buddhist masters, and the development of a corpus of "Great Death" stories of various Buddhist masters is examined by LaFleur (1974). Other writings on death in Buddhism include Smart (1968), Amore (1974), and Bowker (1991).

In a 1993 monograph on the subject of death in Buddhism, Becker asserts that the Buddhist tradition, especially in Japan, is very tolerant of suicide and euthanasia. Evidence of this is the Buddha's tolerance of suicide by monks (Wiltshire, 1983) and Japanese stories praising suicide by monks, samurai and laypeople. Becker suggests that Buddhism values self-determination and praises those who decide when and how they will die when they do so in order to have a dignified conscious death. Becker also concludes that the key point is not whether there is still warmth or reflexes (as suggested by some readings of the Visuddhimagga) but whether the patient's skandhas have permanently left, i.e. the patient is permanently unconscious. In other words, Buddhism would endorse a brain death definition of death. On the understanding of death in Japanese religion see also Picken (1977).

A number of issues in medical ethics turn upon the problem of defining death, but few writers have addressed the question of a Buddhist definition of death directly. Only van Loon (1978), Keown (1995), and Mettanando (1991) have argued for a specific definition: van Loon equates death with neocortical death whereas Keown and Mettanando support the "whole brain" criterion.

There has been considerable resistance to the adoption of the brain death standard in Japan, both from the public and within the medical profession, due in no small measure to its association with organ transplantation. The brain death criterion allows organs to be harvested with the minimum delay, thereby enhancing the prospects for a successful transplant.

Japanese tradition, however, requires the performance of rituals over a lengthy period before an individual is regarded as having passed on, and is also reluctant to countenance plundering the bodily organs of future ancestors. Some commentators suggest that public acceptance of brain death is growing as professional groups and universities develop criteria, and as pressure from potential beneficiaries grows. Also, countries such as the Philippines have raised objections to Japanese patients going abroad for transplants rather than building an organ retrieval system of their own.

The best analysis available (in English) of the Japanese situation is Hardacre (1994), but relevant material may also be found in Lock and Honde (1990), Feldman (1988), Becker (1990), and Nudeshima (1991). For discussions of the issue outside of Japan see Ratanakul (1988, 1990), Sugunasiri (1990), and Nakasone (1994). A more positive attitude towards transplantation is revealed in Tsomo (1993). The author surveyed teachers from many different traditions about their attitudes to donation. All were very positive, and emphasized that the corpse is merely an empty vessel, and that to give of oneself is a great thing, and an act of compassion.

EUTHANASIA

There are no monographs devoted specifically to euthanasia in Buddhism. There are a few periodical articles and the subject is dealt within one or two books. Relevant issues are the distinction between various forms of euthanasia (e.g. "active" and "passive") and the use of narcotics in palliative care which may cloud the mind and interfere with the process of dying (Keown, 1995; Kapleau, 1989; Lecso, 1986; Ratanakul, 1988, 1990).

Kapleau's volume The Wheel of Life and Death (1989) contains a short discussion of euthanasia in conjunction with suicide and it is suggested that Buddhism would reject the practice of either. Ratanakul concurs, reporting "a growing consensus among the Thai public that euthanasia (passive or active) is morally unjustifiable" (1990:27). Keown and Keown (1995) explore Buddhist and Christian attitudes to euthanasia and suggest both oppose it for similar reasons. Nakasone, however, is of the opinion that "Evidence indicates that Buddhists would favour the 'right-to-die' position" (1990:76). Jennifer Green's short article "Death with Dignity: Buddhism" (1989:40-41) discusses only the practicalities of funeral arrangements and does not mention euthanasia. Neuberger (1987) is likewise concerned with practical as opposed to moral issues.

Euthanasia has been a special feature in two Buddhist magazines, Raft, and Tricycle. London-based Raft, the Journal of the Buddhist Hospice Trust, devoted its No. 2 Winter 1989/90 issue to Euthanasia. Sixteen pages in length it contains short pieces by authors such as Elisabeth Kubler-Ross, Ajahn Sumedho, Dame Cicely Saunders and David Stott, exploring the cases for, against, and in terms of a middle way. A similar range of opinions will be found in the Winter 1992 edition of Tricycle, which contains short articles by Patricia Anderson, Jeffrey Hopkins, Philip Kapleau, Chogyam Trungpa, and an interview with author Stephen Levine.

TRIPITAKA

The Tipitaka (Pali ti, "three," + pitaka, "baskets"), or Pali canon, is the collection of primary Pali language texts which form the doctrinal foundation of Theravada Buddhism. The Tipitaka and the paracanonical Pali texts (commentaries, chronicles, etc.) together constitute the complete body of classical Theravada texts.

The Pali canon is a vast body of literature: in English translation the texts add up to thousands of printed pages. Most (but not all) of the Canon has already been published in English over the years. Although only a small fraction of these texts are available on this website, this collection can be a good place to start. The three divisions of the Tipitaka are:

VINAYA PITAKA

The collection of texts concerning the rules of conduct governing the daily affairs within the Sangha-the community of bhikkhus (ordained monks) and bhikkhunis (ordained nuns). Far more than merely a list of rules, the Vinaya Pitaka also includes the stories behind the origin of each rule, providing a detailed account of the Buddha's solution to the question of how to maintain communal harmony within a large and diverse spiritual community.

THE WAY OF WISDOM

The Five Spiritual Faculties

Spiritual progress depends on the emergence of five cardinal virtues - faith, vigor, mindfulness, concentration and wisdom. The conduct of the ordinary worldling is governed by his sense-based instincts and impulses. As we progress, new spiritual forces gradually take over, until in the end the five cardinal virtues dominate and shape everything we do feel and think. These virtues are called, in Sanskrit and Pali, indriya, variously translated by faculties, controlling faculties, or spiritual faculties. The same five virtues are called powers (bala) if emphasis is on the fact that they are "unshakable by their opposites."

Faith

Faith is called "the seed," and without it the plant of spiritual life cannot start at all. Without faith one can, as a matter of fact, do nothing worthwhile at all. This is true not only of Buddhism, but of all religions, and even the pseudo-religions of modern times, such as Communism. And this faith is much more than the mere acceptance of beliefs. It requires the combination of four factors - intellectual, volitional, emotional and social.

Intellectually, faith is an assent to doctrines which are not substantiated by immediately available direct factual evidence. To be a matter of faith, a belief must go beyond the available evidence and the believer must be willing and ready to fill up the gaps in the evidence with an attitude of patient and trusting acceptance. Faith, taken in this sense, has two opposites, i.e., a dull unawareness of the things which are worth believing in, and doubt or perplexity. In any kind of religion some assumptions are taken on trust and accepted on the authority of scriptures or teachers.

Generally speaking, faith is, however, regarded as only a preliminary step, as a merely provisional state. In due course direct spiritual awareness will know that which faith took on trust, and longed to know: "Now we see through a glass darkly, but then face to face." Much time must usually elapse before the virtue of wisdom has become strong enough to support a vigorous insight into the true nature of reality. Until then quite a number of doctrinal points must be taken on faith.

What then in Buddhism are the objects of faith? They are essentially four: (1) the belief in karma and rebirth; (2) the acceptance of the basic teachings about the nature of reality, such as conditioned co-production, emptiness, etc.; (3) confidence in the "Three Refuges," the Buddha, the Dharma and the Order; and (4) a belief in the efficacy of the prescribed practices, and in Nirvana as the final way out of our difficulties. I shall say more about them when I have dealt with the other aspects of faith.

In this skeptical age we, anyway, dwell far too much on the intellectual side of faith. shraddha (Pali: saddha) the word we render as "faith," is etymologically akin to Latin cor, "the heart," and faith is far more a matter of the heart than of the intellect. It is, as Prof. Radhakrishnan incisively puts it, the "striving after self-realization by concentrating the powers of the mind on a given idea." Volitionally, faith implies a resolute and courageous act of will. It combines the steadfast resolution that one will do a thing with the self-confidence that one can do it. Suppose that people living on the one side of a river are doomed to perish from many enemies, diseases and famine. Safety lies on the other shore. The man of faith is then likened to the person who swims across the river, braving its dangers, saving himself and inspiring others by his example. Those without faith will go on dithering along the hither bank. The opposites to this aspect of faith are timidity, cowardice, fear, wavering, and a shabby, mean and calculating mentality.

Emotionally, faith is an attitude of serenity and lucidity. Its opposite here is worry, the state of being troubled by many things. It is said that someone who has faith loses the "five terrors," i.e., he ceases to worry about the necessities of life, about loss of reputation, death, unhappy rebirth and the impression he may make on an audience. It is fairly obvious that the burden of life must be greatly lightened by belief in karma, emptiness, or not-self. Even an unpleasant fate can be accepted more easily when it is understood as a dispensation of justice, when vexations are explained as an inevitable retribution, when law seems to rule instead of blind chance, when even apparent loss is bound to turn into true gain. And if there is no self, what and whom do we worry about? If there is only one vast emptiness, what is there to disturb our radiance?

Socially, and that is more difficult to understand, faith involves trust and confidence in the Buddha and the Sangha. Its opposite here is the state of being submerged in cares about one's sensory social environment, cares which spring from either social pressure or social isolation. The break with the normal social environment is, of course, complete only in the case of the monk who, as the formula goes, "in faith forsakes his home." To a lesser extent it must be carried out by every practitioner of the Dharma, who must "live apart" from his society, in spirit if not in fact.

The company of others and the help we expect from them are usually a mainstay of our sense of security. By going for refuge to the Buddha and the Sangha one turns from the visible and tangible to the invisible and elusive. By placing one's reliance on spiritual forces one gains the strength to disregard public opinion and social discouragement. Some measure of defiant contempt for the world and its ways is inseparable from a spiritual life. The spiritual man does not "belong" to his visible environment, in which he is bound to feel rather a stranger. He belongs to the community of the saints, to the family of the Buddha. Buddhism substitutes a spiritual for the natural environment, with the Buddha for the father, the Prajnaparamita for the mother, the fellow-seekers for brothers and sisters, relatives and friends. It is with these more invisible forces that one must learn to establish satisfactory social relations. In carrying out this task, faith requires a considerable capacity for renunciation.

This concludes our survey of the four factors which go into the making of faith. Like other spiritual qualities, faith is somewhat paradoxical in that in one sense it is a gift which one cannot obtain by merely wanting to, and in another sense it is a virtue that can be cultivated. The capacity for faith varies with the constitution of the individual and his social circumstances. It is usual to classify types of personality according to whether they are dominated by greed, hatred or confusion. Those who walk in greed are said to be more susceptible to faith than the other two, because of the kinship which exists between faith and greed. To quote Buddhaghosa (Visuddhimagga III,75): "As on the unwholesome plane greed clings and takes no offense, so faith on the wholesome plane. As greed searches for objects of sense-desire, so faith for the qualities of morality, etc. As greed does not let go that which is harmful, so faith does not let go that which is beneficial."

As regards social conditions, there are ages of faith and ages of unbelief. The present age rather fosters unbelief. It puts a premium on intellectual smartness, so that faith is easily held to indicate nothing but a weak head or a lack of intellectual integrity. It multiplies the distractions from the sensory world to such an extent that the calm of the invisible world is harder to reach than ever. It exposes the citizen to so great a variety of conflicting viewpoints that he finds it hard to make a choice. The prestige of science, the concern with a high standard of living, and the disappearance of all institutions of uncontested authority are the chief foes of faith in our present-day society. It is largely a matter of temperament whether we believe that matters will improve in the near future.

As a virtue, faith is strengthened and built up by self-discipline, and not by discussing opinions. Intellectual difficulties are by no means the most powerful among the obstacles to faith. Doubts are inevitable, but how one deals with them depends on one's character. The first of our four "articles of faith" well illustrates this situation. There are many sound reasons for accepting the rebirth doctrine. This is not the place to expound them, and I must be content to refer the reader to the very impressive "East-West Anthology" on Reincarnation which J. Head and S.L. Cranston have published in 1961 (New York, The Julian Press Inc.). Yet, although belief in rebirth is perfectly rational and does not conflict with any known fact, the range of the average person's vision is so limited that he has no access to the decisive evidence, which is direct and immediate experience.

The rebirth doctrine assumes at least two things: (1) that behind the natural causality which links together events in the world of sense there are other, invisible chains of a moral causality, which assures that all good acts are rewarded, all bad actions punished; and (2) that this chain of moral sequences is not interrupted by death, but continues from rebirth to rebirth. To the average person these two assumptions cannot be proved absolutely, conclusively and beyond the possibility of a doubt. However plausible they may seem on rational grounds, Buddhism teaches that they become a matter of direct experience only after the "superknowledges" (abhijna, abhiñña) have been developed.

The fourth "superknowledge" is the recollection of one's own previous rebirths, and the fifth the knowledge of the rebirths of other people, by which one "sees that whatever happens to them happens in accordance with their deeds." There are many well-authenticated cases of persons spontaneously remembering certain details of one or the other of their own previous lives, and these people obviously have an additional reason for belief in rebirth which is lacking in those who cannot recall ever having lived before. Full certitude on the issue is, however, given to those only who can, on the basis of the fourth jhana and by taking definite prescribed and disciplined steps on emerging from that jhana, "recall their manifold former lives," according to the well-known formula: "There I was, that was my name, that was my family, that was my caste, such was my food, this was the happiness, this the suffering which I experienced, this was the duration of my life-span. Deceased there I was born elsewhere and there had this name, etc." When a monk has practiced properly and successfully, "these things become as clear to him as if lit up by a lamp" (Visuddhimagga, xiii, 23).

Until that time comes, we cannot claim that we fully know the doctrine of karma and rebirth to be true. We take it partly on faith. And this faith of ours is maintained less by our dialectical skill as by the virtues of patience and courage. For we must be willing to wait patiently until we are spiritually ripe for the emergence of the super-knowledges, however far off that might seem to be. And secondly, we must be willing to take risks. Life nowhere offers a one hundred per cent security, and for our convictions least of all. Employed in gaining wealth a merchant must risk his property. Employed in taking life, a soldier must risk his own life. Employed in saving his soul, the spiritual man must risk his own soul. The stake automatically increases with the prospect of gain. Of course, we may be mistaken. I sometimes wonder what I would think if, on dying, I would not, as I now fondly imagine, wake up on the Bardo plane, but find myself confronted with Acheron and the three-headed Cerberus, or, worse still, were ill-treated with fire and brimstone in a Christian hell. The experience would, I admit, be rather disconcerting. All that I can say in the face of such uncertainty is that I am willing to take the consequences, and that I hope that my fund of boldness, audacity and good humor will not run out.

One has the choice to magnify intellectual doubts, or to minimize them. It seems not unreasonable that one should blame the difficulties of the teaching on one's own distance from the truth, one's own intellectual and moral imperfections. How can one expect to remember one's past lives, if at present one cannot even recall hour by hour what one did during one single day a mere month ago? If one hesitates to accept, as not immediately obvious, the doctrine that this world is the result of ignorance and of the craving of non-existent individuals for non-existent objects - is this not perhaps due to the very denseness of one's own ignorance, for which one can collect plenty of proofs all day long? Doubts are effectively overcome when one purifies one's own life, so as to become more worthy of knowledge. It is a condition of all learning that one accepts a great deal on trust, that one gives the teacher the benefit of the doubt. Otherwise one can learn nothing at all, and remains shut out from all truth. To have faith means to take a deep breath, to tear oneself away from the daily cares and concerns, and to turn resolutely to a wider and more abiding reality. At first we are, by ourselves, too stupid and inexperienced to see the tracks which lead to salvation. So we must put our trust in the Sages of the past, and listen intently to their words, dimmed by distance and the noise of the present day, but still just audible.

One last word about tolerance, without which faith remains raw and unsure of itself. It is a perpetual trial to our faith that we should constantly meet with people who believe differently. We are easily tempted to wish this irritant removed, to coerce others, if only by argument, and to annihilate them, if only by dubbing them fools. Intolerance for people of other faiths, though often mistaken for ardor, betrays nothing so much as doubts within oneself. We can, of course, always console ourselves by assuming that the others, in their own way, believe what we do, and that in the end it all comes to the same thing. But that does not always sound very convincing, and what we must, I am afraid, learn to do is to bear with their presence.

Vigor

Next to faith, vigor (Skr.: virya; Pali: viriya). Little need be said about the need for being energetic if one wants to achieve something. Without vigor, without strenuous effort, without perseverance, one obviously cannot make much progress. Everybody knows what "vigor" is, although a generation which made the fortune of the discoverers of "night-starvation" might wish that it had more of it.

The fact that faith and vigor are virtues does not, however, imply that they are good all through, and that, regardless of the consequences, they should be strengthened at all times. Excess is to be deprecated, even in virtues. All the five virtues must be regarded as one whole. Their balance and harmony is almost as important as the virtues themselves.2 They support each other to some extent, but they also stand in each other's way. The one must sometimes be used to correct the excess of the other. In this way, concentration must come to the rescue of the latent faults of vigor. When vigor and energy have it all their own way, tranquillity is in danger. We all know people with a large dash of adrenalin in their blood, who are always busy, perhaps even "madly efficient," but not particularly restful. Vigor by itself leads to excitement, and has to be controlled by a development of concentrated calm.

Similarly, faith alone, without wisdom, can easily become mere credulity. Wisdom alone can teach what is worth believing. This can be illustrated by Don Quixote, who in literature is perhaps the purest embodiment of faith, and whose actions demonstrate that too much faith, by itself, is not necessarily a good thing. Cervantes' novel gives a fine and detailed description of all the chief attributes of faith. Don Quixote vigorously, fearlessly, without complaining, and even serenely endures all tribulations because he wants to help others, all of them equally, according to their needs. When he dashes into the middle of the boiling lake, he reaches the very height of self-abandonment of which faith as such is capable. "And just when he does not know what will happen to him, he finds himself among flowery fields beautiful beyond those of Elysium." His faith has conquered the senses, it transmutes the data of common-sense experience, and the barber's basin becomes Mambrino's helmet. And yet, when we consider the intellectual basis of his faith, we find that it consists in nothing more than a belief in the truth and veracity of the Romances which describe the fictitious and not particularly edifying doings of the knight-errants of the past. This is the reason why his adventures form a sorry sight, why he is a caricature even of a knight of the Middle Ages, why, shorn of all common-sense, faith in this case becomes slightly pathological.

Mr. Blyth claims that "the Don Quixote of the First Part is Zen incarnate," that "the man who surpasses Hakuin, Rinzai, Eno, Daruma and Shakyamuni himself is Don Quixote de la Mancha, Knight Errant."

Zen, it seems, like all good things, can be abused. It is not very probable that, when the cloak of "Zen" is thrown over them, all donkeys do become tigers, all absurdities profundities. Irrationalism is not without its attractions, but can be overdone.

To suggest that one scripture, one conviction, one faith is as good as another, smacks rather more of the spiritual nihilism of our present age, than of the wisdom of Seng-t'san. I admit that I have always liked Don Quixote for saying that the "perfection" of madness does not consist in going "mad for some actual reason or other" but "in running mad without the least constraint or necessity."

But still I cannot help feeling that there is some difference, intangible perhaps, but nevertheless real, between the perfection of madness and the perfection of wisdom. Don Quixote's faith was a rather puerile one, because he had no judgment, and his vision was defective. Blyth himself admits in the end that Don Quixote "lacks the Confucian virtue of Prudence, the balance of the powers of the mind" (p.210).

I am not so sure about prudence, but the "balance of the powers of the mind" is certainly not only a Confucian, but also a Buddhist virtue, and a very essential one. Buddhaghosa, whom I am expounding here, leaves us in no doubt on this matter.6 What distinguishes a bhikkhu from a knight-errant is that he is essentially sober and calm, that his view of the world is sweetly rational, that he avoids violence in the pursuit of his aims, and that his estimate of his own role in the world does not greatly exceed his actual size in relation to the universe.

Mindfulness

A Buddhist owes his soberness to the cultivation of the third virtue of mindfulness (Skr.: smriti, Pali: sati). Whereas faith and vigor, when driven to excess, must be restrained by their counterparts, i.e., wisdom and tranquil concentration, the virtue of mindfulness does not share this disability. "Mindfulness should be strong everywhere. For it protects the mind from excitedness, into which it might fall since faith, vigor and wisdom may excite us; and from indolence, into which it might fall since concentration favors indolence. Therefore, mindfulness is desirable everywhere, like a seasoning of salt in all sauces, like the prime minister in all state functions. Hence it is said: 'The Lord has declared mindfulness to be useful everywhere, for the mind finds refuge in mindfulness and mindfulness is its protector. Without mindfulness there can be no exertion or restraint of the mind.' "

Although traces of it are not altogether absent in other religious and philosophical disciplines, in Buddhism alone mindfulness occupies a central position. If one were asked what distinguishes Buddhism from all other systems of thought, one would have to answer that it is the dharma-theory and the stress laid on mindfulness. Mindfulness is not only the seventh of the steps of the holy eightfold path, the third of the five virtues, and the first of the seven limbs of enlightenment. On occasions it is almost equated with Buddhism itself. So we read at the beginning of the Satipatthana Sutta that "the four applications of mindfulness are the one and only way (ekayano maggo) that leads beings to purity, to the transcending of sorrow and lamentation, to the appeasement of pain and sadness, to entrance upon the right method and to the realization of Nirvana."

What then is "mindfulness"? The Abhidharma, guided by the etymology of the Sanskrit term (smriti from smri, "to remember"), defines it as an act of remembering which prevents ideas from "floating away," and which fights forgetfulness, carelessness and distraction. This definition by itself, though correct, does not really make the function of this virtue very clear to us today. The theoretical assumptions which underlie the various practices summed up in the word "mindfulness" are too much taken for granted. What one assumes is that the mind consists of two disparate parts - a depth which is calm and quiet, and a surface which is disturbed. The surface layer is in perpetual agitation and turmoil.

The center, at the bottom of the mind, beyond both the conscious and the unconscious mind as modern psychologists understand it, is quite still. The depth is, however, usually overlaid to such an extent that people remain incredulous when told of a submerged spot of stillness in their inmost hearts. In most cases the surface is so turbulent that the calm of the depth can be realized only in rare intervals.

Mindfulness and concentration are the two virtues which are concerned with the development of inward calm. The principal enemies of spiritual quietude are: (1) the senses; (2) the movements of the body; (3) the passions, wants and desires; and (4) discursive thinking. They have the power to be enemies when: (1) they are not subjected to any discipline; and (2) when the ego identifies itself with what takes place on the surface of the mind, participating heartily in it, and the illusion arises that these activities are "my" doings, "my" concerns and the sphere in which "I" live and have my being. When thus busy with worldly things, we have neither strength nor freedom. In order to conquer these enemies of spiritual quietude we must: (1) withdraw the senses from their objects, as the tortoise draws in its limbs; (2) keep watch on our muscular movements; (3) cease wanting anything, and dissociate all wants from the ego; and (4) cut off discursive thinking.

By an effort of the imagination one must try to see oneself at rest, floating freely, with no force exerted on one's spiritual self. The practice of mindfulness then is a series of efforts which aim at maintaining this isolation. Mindfulness is the name given to the measures which we take to protect the patch of inner calm, which may at first not seem very large. One, as it were, draws a line round this domain and at its boundaries keeps watch on trespassers. The expectation is that conscious attention will disintegrate the power of the enemies, diminish their number, and dissociate them from the ego. However diverse in nature the numerous exercises which come under the heading of mindfulness may seem to be, they all have in common this one purpose, that of guarding the incipient and growing calm in one's heart.

First, as regards the sensory stimuli, there is the "restraint of the senses," also called the "guarding of the doors of the senses." For two reasons sense stimulation may disturb inner calm: (1) because it gives an occasion for undesirable states, like greed, hate, etc., to invade and flood the mind; (2) because attention to the sensory world, however necessary and apparently innocuous, distracts from the object of wisdom, which is the emptiness of dharmas. One cannot grasp what is meant by "restraint of the sense dominants," if one regards it as quite a natural thing that the mind should dwell on sense-linked objects. This is, indeed, most unnatural. In its natural purity thought abides in the calm contemplation of emptiness. The mind which sees, hears, etc., is a fallen mind.

The capacity of sense-experience to compel the mind to act in a certain way is greatly diminished if each sensory stimulus is examined at the point where it passes the threshold of consciousness. Attention, normally passive, involuntary and compulsive, is subjected to voluntary control. In the process of imposing some control on the senses one will be surprised to find how keen they are to function, how eager to find suitable objects with which to feed one's impulses and instincts, one's hopes and fears, one's interests and appetites, satisfactions and grievances. It is not so bad that one should see things, hear sounds, etc., but it is a threat to spiritual health when one gets interested and entranced, when one takes up what is seen and heard and seizes on it as a sign of what matters.

The practice of mindfulness is not confined to taking note of what enters the mind by way of the sense-organs. One also tries to determine what is allowed to enter, and to generally reduce the number of sensory impacts by restraining the use of the physical organ, for instance, when one walks with eyes directed only a few feet or yards ahead. In addition, by an effort of the will one refuses to co-operate with one's habitual impulses in building up a mere casual observation into a thing of moment to which one returns again and again. Finally the intruder is weakened and worn down by appropriate reflections. He is kept out of the heart and devalued - as trivial, as already passed, as nothing in particular, and by thinking that "this does not concern me at all, this means nothing to me, it is only a waste when salvation and Nirvana are considered."

Secondly, as regards the muscular movements of the body - an unquiet body is a concomitant of a disturbed mind, both its cause and symptom. It is important to mindfulness that one should consciously notice the position and movement of the body when walking, eating, speaking, etc., and suppress and correct those movements which are uncontrolled, hasty and uncoordinated. This practice can, it is true, not be carried out at all times. In London traffic, for instance, the unhurried and unflurried demeanor of the mindful has little survival value. Where, however, it can be applied, we come to cherish this exercise which pulls us together, sometimes to an amazing extent in an amazingly short time. Insignificant as it may seem, compared with the splendors of Buddhist art and metaphysics, this training is their indispensable foundation stone. It is by his dignified and self-possessed deportment that the bhikkhu is recognized. And, of course, we should not forget that the mindful attention to muscular movements includes the breathing practices, which are a most fruitful source of insight.

Where we have to face the disturbance of the passions and of stray thoughts in general, the defense of our inward calm becomes more difficult. Mindfulness itself turns into incipient concentration.

At this point one may ask whether the practice of the five cardinal virtues, from faith to wisdom, is at all likely to be furthered by writing articles about them. It is, of course, not an entirely useless undertaking to guard the traditional teaching from current misunderstandings, quite apart from the pleasure of putting fleas into peoples' ears, and fomenting discussions about the importance of faith, or the value of erudition. But what about the virtues themselves? Thomas a Kempis once said that he would rather feel compunction than know the definition of it. What matters to a Buddhist is that he should be strong in faith, vigor, mindfulness, concentration and wisdom, and what use to him is the knowledge of how they are defined? Detailed advice on how these virtues should be practiced, it is true, can never be given in articles written for the general reader. Such advice must always be addressed to one person at a time, must take their individual constitution into account, and can, therefore, be given only by word of mouth.

On the other hand, if mindfulness is a virtue, then the ability to recollect one's own virtues is also a feature of the Buddhist life. And how can one attend to the presence or absence of mental states in oneself if one is unable to recognize them for what they are? The Satipatthana Sutta recommends systematic meditation on the wholesome and unwholesome mental states which arise in the mind. To quote the Sutta, one knows, for instance: (1) when there is vigor that there is vigor; (2) when there is no vigor that there is no vigor; (3) how the vigor which did not exist came to be produced; and (4) how and under what conditions it will grow to greater perfection. Psychology is so vital to Buddhist instruction because one cannot know anything definite about the furniture of one's mind unless one is acquainted with the categories into which mental conditions can be analyzed.

A mindful man is well informed about his own mental condition. His capacity for introspection is highly developed. And his interest in his own mind will not really make him self-centered as long as he remembers that he has to deal with the rise and fall of impersonal processes. In addition, in the case of the higher mental states, rational clarity is imperative if constant self-deception and wasteful groping in the dark are to be avoided. In a new country a map is helpful so that one may know where one is. The manuals of mystical theology written by the practicing contemplatives of the Catholic Church are also rich in descriptions of the sublimer virtues.

But this is not all. Where the Buddhist virtues are described for a lay audience one must not omit to mention the all-important fact that the upper ranges of these virtues demand a reformation of the conduct of life which is greater than almost any layman is willing to undertake.

The higher mindfulness, and nearly the whole range of concentration and wisdom, presuppose a degree of withdrawal from the world which is incompatible with the life of an ordinary citizen. Those who are unwilling to achieve a radical seclusion from the world can practice these virtues only in a very rudimentary form. It is quite idle to pretend that they do not involve a complete break with the established habits of life and thought. Unless we make the sacrifices involved in withdrawing from the world, we are bound to remain strangers to the fullness of mindfulness, concentration and wisdom.

But if the monastic life is a necessary condition for these virtues, why talk about them at all? Partly because it is salutary, though painful, that we should see their absence in us, and partly because they constitute the subjective counterpart of the scriptures which we read. The Suttas describe the world as it appears on a spiritual level on which concentration and wisdom have come to maturity. The understanding of the scriptures is furthered by an understanding of the subjective attitude which corresponds to them. And so, although we are forced to go beyond the range of our immediate experience, and although the description tends to become more intangible as it rises to loftier heights, we will now, leaving aside the higher ranges of mindfulness, try to explain the traditional definitions of concentration and wisdom, as they are handed down to us.

Concentration

Concentration (samadhi) continues the work of mindfulness. It deepens our capacity to regain the peaceful calm of our inner nature. But here we are at once faced with the difficulty that in Buddhist psychology "concentration" occurs twice: (1) as a factor essential to all thought; and (2) as a special, and rather rare, virtue.

In its simplest form, concentration is the narrowing of the field of attention in a manner and for a time determined by the will. The mind is made one-pointed, does not waver, does not scatter itself, and it becomes steady like the flame of a lamp in the absence of wind. Without a certain degree of one-pointedness no mental activity at all can take place. Each mental act lasts, strictly speaking, for one moment only, and is at once followed by another. The function of concentration is to provide some stability in this perpetual flux, by enabling the mind to stand in, or on, the same object, without distraction, for more than one moment. In addition it is a synthetic quality (sam-a-dhi = syn-thesis), that binds together a number of mental states which arise at the same time, "as water binds the lather of soap."

Buddhaghosa stresses the fact that intellectual concentration is also found in unwholesome thoughts. The mind must be undistracted so that the murderer's knife does not miss, the theft does not miscarry. A mind of single intent is capable of doing what it does more effectively, be it good or bad. The higher degrees of this kind of concentration owe much to the presence of the "hunting instinct," and can best be observed in a stoat following a rabbit. Intellectual concentration is a quality which is ethically and spiritually neutral. Many scientific workers have an unusually high capacity for concentrated thought. Anyone acquainted with the "scientific humanists" who inhabit our big cities will, however, agree that their intellectual achievements are not conducive to either peace of mind or spiritual progress. When Sir Isaac Newton boiled his watch instead of the egg his landlady had given him, he thereby showed the intensity with which he focussed his mind on his intellectual task. But the result of his intellectual labors has been to cast a dark shadow over the spiritual radiance of the universe, and ever since, the celestial harmonies have become nearly inaudible. As H.W. Longfellow, in his poem on "The Arsenal at Springfield," has put it:

Is it, O man, with such discordant noises,
With such accursed instruments as these,
Thou drownest Nature's sweet and kindly voices,
And jarrest the celestial harmonies?

How then does concentration as a spiritual virtue differ from concentration as a condition of the intellect? Spiritual or transic concentration results less from intellectual effort than from a rebirth of the whole personality, including the body, the emotions, and the will. It cannot possibly be achieved without some discipline over the body, since we must be able to endure the prescribed posture, practice the prescribed breathing exercises, and so on. It is further built on a change of outlook which we can well describe as "ethical." Tradition is quite unambiguous on this point. Before spiritual concentration can be even approached, we must have stilled or suppressed five vices, which are known as the "five hindrances": sense desire, ill will, sloth and torpor, excitedness and sense of guilt, and doubt. Where these hindrances are present, where concentrated thought is fused with greed, the desire to excel, to get a good job, etc., there concentration as a spiritual virtue is not found.

In this sense physical ease and self-purification are the first two distinctive features of spiritual concentration. The third is the shift in attention from the sensory world to another subtler realm. The methods by which this shift is effected are traditionally known as the four trances (jhana) and the four formless attainments.

They are essentially a training in increasing introversion, achieved by progressively diminishing the impact of the outer stimuli. As a result of their successful withdrawal and renunciation the spiritually concentrated release the inward calm which dwells in their hearts. This concentration cannot be won, however, unless no attention is given to sensory data, and everything sensory is viewed as equally unimportant. Subjectively it is marked by a soft, tranquil and pacified passivity, objectively by the abstraction into an unearthly world of experience which lifts one above the world, and bestows a certainty greater than anything the senses may teach. The experience is so satisfying that it burns up the world, and only its cold ashes are found when one returns to it.

Wisdom

And so we come to wisdom (Skr.: prajna; Pali pañña), the highest virtue of all.

"Wisdom is based on concentration, because of the saying: 'One who is concentrated knows, sees what really is.'" Is concentration then an indispensable pre-condition of wisdom? The answer lies in distinguishing three stages of wisdom, according to whether it operates on the level of: (1) learning about what tradition has to say concerning the psychological and ontological categories which form the subject-matter of wisdom; (2) discursive reflection on the basic facts of life; and (3) meditational development. The third alone requires the aid of transic concentration, whereas without it there can be proficiency in the first two. And the wisdom which consists of learning and reflection should not be despised.

The main stream of Buddhist tradition has always greatly esteemed learning. Our attitude to the apple of knowledge differs from that of many Christians. On the whole, we regard it as rather more nourishing than baneful. The wisdom, which is the fifth and crowning virtue, is not the wisdom that can be found in the untutored child of nature, the corny sage of the backwoods, or the self-made philosopher of the suburbs. It can operate only after a great deal of traditional information has been absorbed, a great deal of sound learning acquired. The required skill in metaphysical and psychological analysis would be impossible without a good knowledge of the material on which this skill ought to be exercised. From this point of view learning is perhaps less to be regretted than its absence.

The second stage, after learning, is reflection, which is an operation of the intellect. Even the relative beginner can greatly increase his wisdom by discursive meditations on the basic facts of life. Finally, it is on the level of mental development (bhavana) that this meditational technique reaches its maturity, and then it does, indeed, require the aid of mindfulness and concentration.

"Wisdom" is, of course, only a very approximate equivalent of prajna. To the average person nowadays "wisdom" seems to denote a compound made up of such qualities as sagacity, prudence, a well-developed sense of values, serenity, and sovereignty over the world won by the understanding of the mode of its operation. The Buddhist conception of "wisdom" is not unlike this, but more precise. It is best clarified by first giving its connotations, and then its actual definition.

As for the connotations, we read in the Dhammasangani:14 "On that occasion the dominant15 of wisdom is wisdom, understanding,16 search, research, search for dharma;17 discernment, discrimination, differentiation, erudition, expert skill, subtlety, clarity,18 reflection, investigation,19 amplitude,20 sagacity,21 a guide (to true welfare and to the marks as they truly are), insight, comprehension, a goad (which urges the mind to move back on the right track); wisdom, wisdom as virtue, wisdom as strength (because ignorance cannot dislodge it), the sword of wisdom (which cuts through the defilements), the lofty (and overtowering) height of wisdom, the light,22 luster and splendor of wisdom, the treasure23 of wisdom, absence of delusion, search for dharmas, right view." From mere cleverness wisdom is distinguished by its spiritual purpose, and we are told expressly24 that it is designed "to cut off the defilements."

Now to the actual definition: "Wisdom penetrates25 into dharmas as they are in themselves. It disperses the darkness of delusion, which covers up the own-being of dharmas."26

What then does wisdom meditate about? Wisdom may be held to concern itself with three possible topics: (1) true reality; (2) the meaning of life; (3) the conduct of life. Buddhist tradition assumes that the second and third depend on the first. In its essence wisdom is the strength of mind which permits contact with the true reality, which is also called the realm of dharmas. Delusion, folly, confusion, ignorance and self-deception are the opposites of wisdom.

It is because ignorance, and not sin, is the root evil that wisdom is regarded as the highest virtue. A holiness which is devoid of wisdom is not considered impossible, but it cannot be gained by the path of knowledge, to which alone these descriptions apply. The paths of faith, of love, of works, etc., have each their own several laws.

As the unfaltering penetration into the true nature of objects, wisdom is the capacity to meditate in certain ways about the dharmic constituents of the universe. The rules of that meditation have been laid down in the scriptures, particularly in the Abhidharma, and a superb description can be found in the latter part of Buddhaghosa's Path of Purification. Mindfulness and concentration were, as we saw, based on the assumption of a duality in the mind - between its calm depth and its excited surface. Wisdom similarly assumes a duality between the surface and depth of all things. Objects are not what they appear to be. Their true reality, in which they stand out as dharmas, is opposed to their appearance to commonsense, and much strength of wisdom is required to go beyond the deceptive appearance and to penetrate to the reality of dharmas themselves.

4

Development of Buddhist Philosophy

EARLY DEVELOPMENT

The philosophical outlook of Earliest Buddhism was primarily negative, in the sense that it focused on what doctrines to *reject* more than on what doctrines to *accept*. This dimension has been preserved by the Madhyamaka school.

It includes critical rejections of all views, which is a form of philosophy, but it is reluctant to posit its own. Only knowledge that is useful in achieving enlightenment is valued.

The cycle of philosophical upheavals that in part drove the diversification of Buddhism into its many schools and sects only began once Buddhists began attempting to make explicit the implicit philosophy of the Buddha and the early Suttas.

After the death of the Buddha, attempts were made to gather his teachings and transmit them in a commonly agreed form, first orally, then also in writing (The Tripitaka).

In addition to collecting the Buddha's speeches and rules for monastic life (Vinaya), monks soon undertook to condense what they considered the essential elements of Buddhist doctrine into lists of categories, provided with extensive commentary. This process took shape from about the 2nd century BCE to probably the 2nd century CE.

Later Developments

Very soon after, additional teachings began to be added to the list of important Buddhist texts. Many of these altered and refined Buddhist philosophy.

Comparison with other Philosophies

- Baruch Spinoza, though he argued for the existence of a permanent reality, asserts that all phenomenal existence is transitory. In his opinion sorrow is conquered "by finding an object of knowledge which is not transient, not ephemeral, but is immutable, permanent, everlasting." Buddhism teaches that such a quest is bound to fail.
- David Hume, after a relentless analysis of the mind, concluded that consciousness consists of fleeting mental states. Hume's Bundle theory is a very similar concept to anatta.
- Arthur Schopenhauer's philosophy was very similar to Buddhism.
- Ludwig Wittgenstein's "word games" map closely to the warning of intellectual speculation as a red herring to understanding, such as the *Parable of the Poison Arrow*.
- Friedrich Nietzsche, although himself dismissive of Buddhism as yet another nihilism, developed his philosophy of accepting life-as-it-exists and self-cultivation as extremely similar to Buddhism as better understood in the West today.

ASANGA

Asanga (also called Aryasanga), born around 300 CE, was an exponent of the yogacara school of Buddhist philosophy. Traditionally, he and his brother Vasubandhu are regarded as the founders of this school.

Born the son of a Brahmin in Gandhara in northern India, Asanga was perhaps originally a member of the Mahiuasaka or the Mulasarvastivada school but later converted to Mahayana;

after many years of intense meditation, during which time some traditions say that he often visited Tushita Heaven to receive teachings from Maitreya-natha. He went on to write many of the key Yogacara treatises such as the Yogacarabhumi-Shastra, the Mahayana-samgraha and the Abhidharma-samuscaya as well as other works, although there are discrepancies between the Chinese and Tibetan traditions concerning which works are attributed to him and which to Maitreya-natha.

CANDRAKIRTI

Candrakirti was abbot of Nalanda University and a disciple of Nagarjuna and a commentator on his works. Candrakirti was the most famous member of what the Tibetans came to call the Prasamgika school of Madhyamaka.

As a result of Bhavaviveka's interpretation of Nagarjuna's view, a new school of Madhyamaka known as Prasangika ('Consequentialist'). Chandrakirti's works include the Prasannapada-a Sanskrit term, meaning *Clear Words'*-the highly acclaimed commentary on Nagarjuna's Mulamadhyamakakarika) and the Madhyamakavatara (his supplement to Nagarjuna's text) and its auto-commentary. The Madhyamakavatara is used as the main sourcebook by most of the Tibetan monastic colleges in their studies of emptiness and the philosophy of the Madhyamaka school.

DIGNAGA

Dignaga (5th century AD), was an Indian scholar and one of the Buddhist founders of Indian philosophical logic.

He was born into a Brahmin family in Simhavakta near Kanchi (Kanchipuram), and very little is known of his early years, except that he took as his spiritual preceptor Nagadatta of the Vatsiputriya school. This branch of Buddhist thought defended the view that there exists a kind of real personality independent of the elements or aggregates composing it.

Among Dignaga's works there is *Hetucakra* (The wheel of reason), considered his first work on formal logic, advancing a new form of deductive reasoning. It may be regarded as a bridge between the older doctrine of *trairupya* and Dignaga's own later theory of *vyapti* which is a concept related to the Western notion of implication.

Other works include *The Treatise on the Objects of Cognition* (*Alambana-parikca*), *The Treatise on Systems of Cognition* (*Pramana-samuccaya*), and *The Treatise on the Correct Principles of Logic* (*Nyaya-mukha*), produced in an effort to establish what were the valid sources of knowledge.

DOGEN

Dogen Zenji (19 January 1200–22 September 1253) was a Japanese Zen Buddhist teacher born in Kyoto, and the founder of the Soto school of Zen in Japan. He was a leading religious figure of his time, as well as being an important philosopher. *Zenji* is a title meaning "Zen master", while the name Dogen means roughly "Source of the Way".

Early Life

Dogen was born into a noble family. His father may have been Koga Michichika, a high-ranking minister in the imperial court, while his mother was likely the daughter of Fujiwara Motofusa, who had once been a regent in the court. Dogen's father died when Dogen was 3 years old, and his mother when he was 8, which strongly impressed Dogen with the Buddhist notion of impermanence.

Early Training

At the age of 13, affected by this early glimpse of impermanence and faced with the possibility of a career as part of the aristocratic Fujiwara family, Dogen decided to become a monk. Initially, he went to Mount Hiei, which was the headquarters of the Tendai school of Buddhism. Here, while studying the Buddhist sutras, he became possessed by a single question:

> *"As I study both the exoteric and the esoteric schools of Buddhism, they maintain that human beings are endowed with Dharma-nature by birth. If this is the case, why did the Buddhas of all ages—undoubtedly in possession of enlightenment—find it necessary to seek enlightenment and engage in spiritual practice?"*

This question was, in large part, prompted by the Tendai concept of "original enlightenment", which states that all human beings are enlightened by nature and that, consequently, any notion of achieving enlightenment through practice is fundamentally flawed.

As he found no answer to his question at Mount Hiei, Dogen left to seek an answer from other Buddhist masters. Dogen went to visit Koin, the Tendai abbot of Onjoji Temple, asking him this same question. Koin said that, in order to find an answer, he might want to consider studying Chan in China. Koin sent Dogen to Myoan Eisai in Kyoto, a leading Tendai monk who had been to China and brought back the practice of Rinzai Zen in 1191. In 1214, Dogen went to study with Eisai at Kenninji Temple, and—upon Eisai's death the following year—he continued his study under Eisai's successor, Myozen. In 1221, Myozen conferred Dharma transmission upon Dogen, acknowledging that he had learned the teachings. Two years later, Dogen decided to make the dangerous passage across the East China Sea to China to try to find an answer. His teacher Myozen accompanied him on the trip.

Travel to China

In China, Dogen first went to the leading Chan monasteries in Zhèjiang province. At the time, most Chan teachers based their training around the use of *gong-àn*s (Japanese: *koan*). Though Dogen assiduously studied the koans, he became disenchanted with the heavy emphasis laid upon them, and wondered why the sutras were not studied more. At one point, owing to this disenchantment, Dogen even refused Dharma transmission from a teacher. Then, in 1225, he decided to visit a master named Rujing, the thirteenth patriarch of the Caodong lineage of Zen Buddhism, at Mount Tiantong in Ningbo. Rujing was reputed to have a style of Chan that was different to the other masters whom Dogen had thus far encountered.

Under Rujing, Dogen realized liberation of body and mind upon hearing the master say, "Cast off body and mind". This phrase would continue to have great importance to Dogen throughout his life, and can be found scattered throughout his writings, as—for example—in a famous section of his "Genjokoan":

> *"To study the Way is to study the self. To study the self is to forget the self. To forget the self is to be enlightened by all things of the universe. To be enlightened by all things of the universe is to cast off the body and mind of the self as well as those of others. Even the traces of enlightenment are wiped out, and life with traceless enlightenment goes on forever and ever."*

Shortly after Dogen had arrived at Mount Tiantong, Myozen had passed away. In 1227, Dogen received Dharma transmission and *inka* from Rujing, and remarked on how he had finally settled his "life's quest of the great matter".

Return to Japan

Dogen returned to Japan in 1227 or 1228, going back to stay at Kenninji, where he had once trained under Eisai. Among his first actions upon returning was to write down the *Fukan Zazengi*, a short text emphasizing the importance of and giving instructions for zazen, or sitting meditation. However, tension soon arose as the Tendai community began taking steps to suppress both Zen and Jodo Shinshu, the new forms of Buddhism in Japan. In the face of this tension, Dogen left the Tendai dominion of Kyoto in 1230, settling instead in an abandoned temple in what is today the city of Uji, south of Kyoto. In 1233, Dogen founded the Kannon-dori-in in Uji as a small Centre of practice; he later expanded this temple into the Kosho-horinji Temple. In 1243, Hatano Yoshishige offered to relocate Dogen's community to Echizen province, far to the north of Kyoto. Dogen accepted due to the ongoing tension with the Tendai community, and his followers built a comprehensive Centre of practice there, calling it Daibutsuji Temple. During this period, Dogen would also periodically teach at Yoshimine-dera Temple in southern Kyoto. In 1246, Dogen renamed Daibutsuji, calling it Eihei-ji. This temple remains one of the two head temples of Soto Zen in Japan today, the other being Soji-ji.

Dogen spent the remainder of his life teaching and writing at Eiheiji. In 1247, the newly installed shogun's regent, Hojo Tokiyori, invited Dogen to come to Kamakura to teach him.

Dogen made the rather long journey east to provide the shogun with lay ordination, and then returned to Eiheiji in 1248. In the autumn of 1252, Dogen fell ill, and soon showed no signs of recovering.

He presented his robes to his main apprentice, Koun Ejo, making him the abbot of Eiheiji. Then, at Hatano Yoshishige's invitation, Dogen left for Kyoto in search of a remedy for his illness. In 1253, soon after arriving in Kyoto, Dogen died. Shortly before his death, he had written a death poem:

Fifty-four years lighting up the sky.

A quivering leap smashes a billion worlds.

Hah!

Entire body looks for nothing.

Living, I plunge into Yellow Springs.

Dogen's Zen

At the heart of the variety of Zen that Dogen taught are a number of key concepts, which are emphasized repeatedly in his writings. All of these concepts, however, are closely interrelated to one another insofar as they are all directly connected to zazen, or sitting meditation, which Dogen considered to be identical to Zen, as is pointed out clearly in the first sentence of the 1243 instruction manual "Zazen-gi": "Studying Zen... is zazen". In referring to zazen, Dogen is most often referring specifically to *shikantaza*, roughly translatable as "nothing but precisely sitting", which is a kind of sitting meditation in which the meditator sits "in a state of brightly alert attention that is free of thoughts, directed to no object, and attached to no particular content".

Oneness of Practice-enlightenment

The primary concept underlying Dogen's Zen practice is "oneness of practice-enlightenment". In fact, this concept is considered so fundamental to Dogen's variety of Zen—and, consequently, to the Soto school as a whole—that it formed the basis for the work *Shusho-gi*, which was compiled in 1890 by Takiya Takushu of Eihei-ji and Azegami Baisen of Soji-ji as an introductory and prescriptive abstract of Dogen's massive work, the *Shobogenzo* ("Treasury of the Eye of the True Dharma").

For Dogen, the practice of zazen and the experience of enlightenment were one and the same. This point was succinctly stressed by Dogen in the *Fukan Zazengi*, the first text that he composed upon his return to Japan from China: "To practice the Way singleheartedly is, in itself, enlightenment. There is no gap between practice and enlightenment or zazen and daily life". Earlier in the same text, the basis of this identity is explained in more detail:

"Zazen is not "step-by-step meditation". Rather it is simply the easy and pleasant practice of a Buddha, the realization of the Buddha's Wisdom. The Truth appears, there being no delusion. If you understand this, you are completely free, like a dragon that has obtained water or a tiger that reclines on a mountain. The supreme Law will then appear of itself, and you will be free of weariness and confusion." The "oneness of practice-enlightenment" was also a point stressed in the *Bendowa* of 1231:

> *"Thinking that practice and enlightenment are not one is no more than a view that is outside the Way. In buddha-dharma [i.e. Buddhism], practice and enlightenment are one and the same. Because it is the practice of enlightenment, a beginner's wholehearted practice of the Way is exactly the totality of original enlightenment. For this reason, in conveying the essential attitude for practice, it is taught not to wait for enlightenment outside practice."*

Koans

There has long been a debate about how Dogen may have felt about koans as they relate to Zen practice. During Dogen's time, koan work had been boiled down to near meaninglessness. All too often koan answers were simply memorized by monks who otherwise had no clear understanding of their meanings. Teachers also had the tendency to place too great an emphasis on koan work, claiming that koans were the most significant tool one must use to practice Zen.

This latter point is likely what provided Dogen with the most discomfort, since his vision of shikantaza being of the utmost importance was at odds with such a claim. However, despite Dogen's criticisms of koans, one cannot deny the fact that he references hundreds of them in his writings. Both his Mana Shobogenzo and Kana Shobogenzo are filled with koans and commentaries on them. It may be safe to say that Dogen's appreciation for koans was not an endorsement for their systematic presentation into Zen practice. They had a much more intimate quality to him, and were only able to be entered while one was actively engaged in zazen. To Dogen, zazen was what Zen is truly about. So koans, naturally, could only fully be appreciated when one practiced zazen.

Dogen was likely unopposed to the use of koans in Zen practice. He just had questions on how they were being used in his lifetime, and did not see them as something that outranks zazen meditation in importance.

Writings

Dogen's masterpiece is the aforementioned *Shobogenzo*, talks and writings—collected together in 95 fascicles—on topics ranging from monastic practice to the philosophy of language, being, and time. In the work, as in his own life, Dogen emphasized the absolute primacy of shikantaza and the inseparability of practice and enlightenment.

While it was customary for Buddhist works to be written in Chinese, Dogen often wrote in Japanese, conveying the essence of his thought in a style that was at once concise, compelling, and inspiring. A master stylist, Dogen is noted not only for his prose, but also for his poetry (in Japanese waka style and various Chinese styles). Dogen's use of language is unconventional by any measure. According to Dogen scholar Steven Heine: "Dogen's poetic and philosophical works are characterized by a continual effort to express the inexpressible by perfecting imperfectable speech through the creative use of wordplay, neologism, and lyricism, as well as the recasting of traditional expressions".

Legacy

Dogen's most notable successor was Keizan, founder of Sojiji Temple and author of the *Record of the Transmission of Light*, which traces the succession of Zen masters from Siddhartha Gautama up to Keizan's own day. Together, Dogen and Keizan are regarded as the founders of the Soto school.

FAZANG

Fazang was the third patriarch of the Buddhist Huayan school.

JINUL

Jinul (1158 – 1210) was a Korean monk of the Goryeo period, who is considered to be the most influential figure in the formation of Korean Seon Buddhism.

He was born at a time when the sangha was in a state of crisis, both in terms of its external reputation as well as on internal issues of doctrine. Deeply disturbed at the degree of corruption that had crept into the sangha, Jinul sought to establish a new movement within Korean Seon which he called the "samadhi and prajna society". This movement's goal was to establish a new community of disciplined, pure-minded practitioners deep in the mountains. Jinul eventually accomplished this mission with the founding of the Songgwangsa monastery at Mt. Jogye.

JIZȦNG

Jizang was a Chinese Buddhist monk and scholar who is often regarded as the founder of the Three Treatise School. He is also known as Jiaxiang or Master Jiaxiang, because he acquired fame at the Jiaxiang Temple.

Biography

Jizang was born in Jinling (modern Nanjing). Although his father had emigrated from Parthia, he was educated in the Chinese manner. He was quite precocious in spiritual matters, and became a monk at age seven. When he was young, he studied with Falang at the Xinghuang Temple in Nanjing, and studied the three Madhyamaka treatises (The Treatise on the Middle Way, The Treatise on the Twelve Gates, and The One-Hundred-Verse Treatise) which had been translated by Kumarajiva more than a century before, and it is with these texts that he is most often identified. He became the head monk at Xinghuang Temple upon Falang's death in 581. At age 42, he began travelling through China giving lectures, and ultimately settled at Jiaxing Temple, in modern Shauxing, Zhejiang province.

In 597, Yang Kuang, later Emperor Yang, the second son of Emperor Wen of the Sui Dynasty, ordered four new temples in the capital Chang'an, and invited Jizang to be in charge of one of them, called Huiri Temple.

Jizang accepted, despite the fame of Yang's harshness. Zhiyi, a respected figure of the Tiantai school, had accepted to become monk at another one of the new temples, and Jizang sought to visit him, but unfortunately he died before Jizang was able to meet him. He was, however, able to correspond with him regarding the Lotus Sutra. Later he moved to another new temple, Riyan Temple. When the Sui Dynasty was succeeded by the Tang Dynasty in 617, he gained the respect and support of the new emperor, Gaozu as well, and became head abbot of four temples. Between ages 57 and 68, he sought to make more copies of the Lotus Sutra so that more people could be familiar with it. He produced 2,000 copies of the sutra. He also made copies of some of his own commentaries. Jizang was a prodigious writer, producing close to 50 books in his lifetime. He specialized in commentaries on the three treatises as well as texts from other Buddhist traditions, such as the Lotus and Nirvana sutras. His students included Ekan, Korean by nationality, who brought the Three Treatise School to Japan.

Philosophy

The general outlook of the Madhyamaka school is that commitments or attachments to anything, including a logical viewpoint, lead to *dukkha* (suffering). In commenting on Buddhist treatises, Jizang developed a general methodology of *poxie xianzheng* ("refuting what is misleading, revealing what is corrective"), by-passing the pitfalls of asserting the truth or falsehood of certain propositions in a final or rigid sense, but using them if they pragmatically lead to the ability to overcome the commitment to dichotomy.

He noted that the tendency of many Buddhists to become committed to becoming unattached (*shunyata* or "emptying") is also itself a commitment that should be avoided. One can avoid this by engaging in the same deconstruction that allowed liberation in the first place, but applied to the false dichotomy between attachment and non-attachment (*shunyata shunyata*, or "emptying of emptiness").

Applying this to the traditional two levels of discourse inherited from the Madhyamaka tradition (the conventional, regarding everyday thoughts, and the authentic, which transcends this by analysing the metaphysical assumptions made in the conventional thinking), Jizang developed his *sizhong erdi* ("four levels of the two kinds of discourse"), which takes that distinction and adds metadistinctions on three more levels:

1. The assumption of existence is conventional, and the idea of nonexistence is authentic.
2. The commitment to a distinction between existence and nonexistence is now considered conventional, and the denial of this duality is authentic.

3. The distinction between committing to a distinction between existence and nonexistence is now conventional, and the denial of the difference between duality and non-duality is authentic.
4. All of these distinctions are deemed conventional, and the authentic discourse regards that any point of view cannot be said to be ultimately true, and is useful only so far as it is corrective in the above sense.

Thus, the attachment to any viewpoint is considered detrimental, and is a cause of life's suffering. To repudiate the misleading finality of any viewpoint, on any level of discourse, is thus corrective and helps overcome destructive attachment.

NAGARJUNA

Nagarjuna was an Indian philosopher, the founder of the Madhyamaka (Middle Path) school of Mahayana Buddhism, and arguably the most influential Buddhist thinker after the Gautama Buddha himself.

His writings were the basis for the formation of the Madhyamaka (Middle Way) school, which was transmitted to China under the name of the Three Treatise (Sanlun) School. He is credited with developing the philosophy of the Prajnaparamita sutras, and was closely associated with the Buddhist university of Nalanda.

History

Very few details on the life of Nagarjuna are known, although many legends exist. He may have been born in South India, probably near the town of Nagarjunakonda in present day Guntur District of Andhra Pradesh.

According to traditional biographers and historians such as Kumarajiva, he was born into a Brahmin family, but later converted to Buddhism.

This may be the reason he was one of the earliest significant Buddhist thinkers to write in classical Sanskrit rather than Pali or Buddhist Hybrid Sanskrit.

From studying his writings, it is clear that Nagarjuna was conversant with the Nikaya school philosophies and with the emerging Mahayana tradition.

If the most commonly accepted attribution of texts (that of Christian Lindtner) holds, then he was clearly a Mahayanist, but his philosophy holds assiduously to the canon, and while he does make explicit references to Mahayana texts, he is always careful to stay within the parameters set out by the canon.

Writings

There exist a number of influential texts attributed to Nagarjuna, although most were probably written by later authors. The only work that all scholars agree is Nagarjuna's is the *Mulamadhyamakakarika* (Fundamental Verses on the Middle Way), which contains the essentials of his thought in twenty-seven short chapters. According to Lindtner the works definitely written by Nagarjuna are:

- Mulamadhyamakakarika (Fundamental Verses of the Middle Way)
- úunyatasaptati (Seventy Verses on Emptiness)
- Vigrahavyavartani (The End of Disputes)
- Vaidalyaprakarana (Pulverizing the Categories)
- Vyavaharasiddhi (Proof of Convention)
- Yukticacmika (Sixty Verses on Reasoning)
- Catuhstava (Hymn to the Absolute Reality)
- Ratnavali (Precious Garland)
- Pratityasamutpadah]dayakarika (Constituents of Dependent Arising)
- Sutrasamuccaya
- Bodhicittavivarana (Exposition of the Enlightened Mind)
- Suhrillekha (To a Good Friend)
- Bodhisambhara (Requisites of Enlightenment).

There are other works attributed to Nagarjuna, some of which may be genuine and some not. In particular, several important works of esoteric Buddhism (most notably the Pancakrama or "Five Stages") are attributed to Nagarjuna and his disciples. Contemporary research suggests that these works are datable to a significantly later period in Buddhist history (late eighth or early ninth century), but the tradition of which they are a part maintains that they are the work of the Madhyamaka Nagarjuna and his school.

Traditional historians (for example, the 17th century Tibetan Taranatha), aware of the chronological difficulties involved, account for the anachronism via a variety of theories, such as the propagation of later writings via mystical revelation. A useful summary of this tradition, its literature, and historiography may be found in Wedemeyer 2006.

Lindtner considers that the Mahaprajnaparamitopadesa, a huge commentary on the Large Prajnaparamita not to be a genuine work of Nagarjuna. This is only extant in a Chinese translation by Kumarajiva. There is much discussion as to whether this is a work of Nagarjuna, with some original comments by Kumarajiva, or an original work by Kumarajiva based on the philosophy of Nagarjuna.

Philosophy

Nagarjuna's primary contribution to Buddhist philosophy is in the development of the concept of sunyata, or "emptiness," which brings together other key Buddhist doctrines, particularly anatta (no-self) and pratityasamutpada (dependent origination). For Nagarjuna, it is not merely sentient beings that are empty of atman; all phenomena are without any svabhava, literally "own-nature" or "self-nature", and thus without any underlying essence; they are *empty* of being independent. This is so because they are arisen dependently: not by their own power, but by depending on conditions leading to their coming into existence, as opposed to being. Nagarjuna was also instrumental in the development of the two-truths doctrine, which claims that there are two levels of truth in Buddhist teaching, one which is directly (ultimately) true, and one which is only conventionally or instrumentally true, commonly called *upaya* in later

Mahayana writings. Nagarjuna drew on an early version of this doctrine found in the Kaccayanagotta Sutta, which distinguishes nitartha (clear) and neyartha (obscure) terms—

By and large, Kaccayana, this world is supported by a polarity, that of existence and non-existence. But when one sees the origination of the world as it actually is with right discernment, 'non-existence' with reference to the world does not occur to one. When one sees the cessation of the world as it actually is with right discernment, 'existence' with reference to the world does not occur to one.

Nagarjuna differentiates between samvriti (conventional) and paramartha (ultimately true) teachings, but he seldom declares any to fall in this latter category; for him, even sunyata is sunya—even emptiness is empty. For him, ultimately:

nivrittam abhidhatavyam nivritte cittagocare।

anutpannaniruddha hi nirvanam iva dharmata।।

The designable is ceased when the range of thought is ceased.

For phenomenality is like nirvana, unarisen and unstopped.

This was famously rendered in his tetralemma with the logical propositions: X, not X, X and not X, neither X nor not X.

VASUBANDHU

Vasubandhu was an Indian Buddhist scholar-monk, and along with his half-brother Asanga, one of the main founders of the Indian Yogacara school. Vasubandhu is one of the most influential figures in the entire history of Buddhism.

Born in Gandhara in the fourth century, he was at first a Sarvastivadin when he initially studied Sarvastivadin Abhidharma, as presented in the Maha-vibhasa. Dissatified with those teachings, he wrote the *Abhidharmakoœa* in verse and his auto-commentary, the *Abhidharmakosa-bhasya*, an important summary and critique of the *Mahavibhasa* from the Sautrantrika viewpoint. He later converted to Mahayana and composed many other voluminous treatises, especially on Yogacara doctrines. Most influential in the East Asian Buddhist tradition was probably the *Trimsika*, the Thirty Verses on Representation-only and its companion *Vimsatika*, but he also wrote a large number of other works, including:

- a commentary to the *Mahayana-samgraha*
- the *Dasabhumikabhasya* (*Ten Stages Sutra*)
- *Catuhsataka-sastra*
- *Mahayana satadharma-prakasamukha sastra*
- *Amitayus sutropadesha*
- *Discourse on the Pure Land*
- *Vijnaptimatrata Sastra*.

Some modern scholars, notably Frauwallner, have sought to distinguish two Vasubandhus, one the Yogacarin and the other a Sautrantika, but this view should probably be rejected now on the basis of the anonymous *Abhidharma-dipa*, a critique of the *Abhidharmakoœa* which clearly identifies Vasubandhu as the sole author of both groups of writings.

WONHYO

Wonhyo (617-686) was one of the leading thinkers, writers and commentators of the Korean Buddhist tradition.

With his life spanning the end of the Three Kingdoms period and the beginning of the Unified Silla, Wonhyo played a vital role in the reception and assimilation of the broad range of doctrinal Buddhist streams that flowed into the Korean peninsula at the time. Wonhyo was most interested in, and affected by Tathagatagarbha, Yogacara and Hwaom thought. However, in his extensive scholarly works, composed as commentaries and essays, he embraced the whole spectrum of the Buddhist teachings which were received in Korea, including such schools as Pure Land, Nirvana, Sanlun and Tiantai (*Lotus Sutra* school).

He wrote commentaries on virtually all of the most influential Mahayana scriptures, altogether including over eighty works in over two hundred fascicles. Among his most influential works were the commentaries he wrote on the *Awakening of Faith*, *Nirvana Sutra* and *Vajrasamadhi Sutra*, along with his exposition on the meaning of the two hindrances, the *ijangui*. These were treated with utmost respect by leading Buddhist scholars in China and Japan, and served to help in placing the *Awakening of Faith* as the most influential text in the Korean tradition.

Wonhyo spent the earlier part of his career as a monk. In 661 he and a close friend-Uisang (625–702, founder of the Korean Hwaom school)-were travelling to China where they hoped to study Buddhism further. Somewhere in the region of Baekje the pair were caught in a heavy downpour and forced to take shelter in what they believed to be an earthen sanctuary.

During the night Wonhyo was overcome with thirst, and reaching out grasped what he perceived to be a gourd, and drinking from it was refreshed with a draught of cool, refreshing water. Upon waking the next morning, however, the companions discovered much to their amazement that their shelter was in fact an ancient tomb littered with human skulls, and the vessel from which Wonhyo had drinken was in fact a human skull full of brackish water.

Moved by the experience of believing a gruesome site to be a comfortable haven, and skull of mildewy water a refreshing drink, Wonhyo was astonished at the power of the human mind to transform reality. After this "consciousness-only" enlightenment experience, he left the priesthood and turned to the spreading of the *Buddhadharma* as a layman. Because of this aspect of his character, Wonhyo ended up becoming a popular folk hero in Korea. He was a colleague and friend of the influential Silla Hwaom monk Uisang, and an important result of their combined works was the establishment of Hwaeom as the dominant stream of doctrinal thought on the Korean peninsula. Wonhyo's twenty-three extant works are currently in the process of being translated into English as a joint project between Dongguk University and State University of New York at Stony Brook.

Wonhyo had a son, Seol Chong, who is considered to be one of the great Confucian scholars of Silla.

The International Taekwondo Federation pattern "Won-Hyo" is named in Wonhyo's honour. This pattern consists of 28 movements, and is the pattern for the green belt student.

BUDDHIST POLEMICS

Buddhist polemics revolve around the veracity and efficacy of doctrine and practice. It seems that from the very beginning Buddhists were involved in a struggle with non-believers to establish the *Truth*.

What we see is a process of ultraism in which each group, including the authors of the earliest texts, is inclined to denigrate those that had come before it. So the Pali suttas ridicule Jain and other non-Buddhist teachings, the Mahayana Sutras ridicule the Arahants, and so on. The thing that seems to be driving this process is a sequence of reform movements which seek to establish, or re-establish, norms of practice in line with a set of ideals which is actually common to all Buddhist schools. Alongside this reformist agenda is a strong conservatism which constrains Buddhists to accept texts as the word of the Buddha and therefore sacrosanct. The result is that a hierarchy of ideals is built up over time. In very early Buddhist texts (such as the Dhammapada, or Sutta Nipata) an Arahant (ie one who has achieved the goal, is enlightened, completely liberated from suffering) is seen as second to the Buddha only in the sense that he led them to the goal.

Their 'state' is ontologically undefinable, but is equivalent to that of the Buddha, ie both the Buddha and the Arahant have achieved Nirvana or final liberation. But even before the Mahayana came into being there were attempts to redefine the status of the Arahant as falling short of the goal, and capable of error. By the time the early Mahayana Sutras, such as the Lotus Sutra, the Arahant is portrayed as conceited and stubborn. The Perfection of Wisdom sutras, which span the entire development of the Mahayana, portray Arahants such as

Subhuti and Sariputra as being instructed by mythic Bodhisattvas, whereas the Pali suttas have these two being the ones giving instruction.

By the time the Vajrayana came into being there was already a considerable superstructure of doctrine and practice built up. But the Vajrayana was bound by the same constraints and so ended up adopting everything and trying to make sense of it. The Tibetans synthesised it all into a complex hierarchical system which has Hinayana, Mahayana, and various grades of Tantra as a towering stairlike path through which the spiritual aspirant must ascend in order to follow the Buddha. Somewhat ironically the highest levels of Tantric practice, such as Dzog Chen starts to resemble the simple mindfulness of the Pali Canon. Similarly in East Asian Vajrayana Kukai adopted a hierarchical structure for the various teachings, in which the Hinayana and Mahayana both rated as merely provisional teachings which were not effective in attaining enlightenment.

It is difficult to know what to make of this building of ever higher teachings, and more secret practices. If one accepts the Pali Canon as evidence (and most Buddhists would) then there is ample evidence that the so-called 'Hinayana' practices were efficacious. It is also clear that an Arahant was definitely one who had attained the goal set out by the Buddha. The differences between the Arahant Ideal (as the Mahayana designates the Hinayana goal), and the Bodhisattva Ideal (as the Mahayana designated itself) are not so much differences in goal or aim, as they are differences of emphasis-one emphasising the subjective, internal transformation of self; the other emphasising the altruistic, other regarding aspects of the teachings.

Theravada Criticised and Explained

The diversity of Buddhist thought has sometimes led to criticism of Theravada by other schools, although it is important to note that such criticism is far from universal, and that Buddhists of different schools often interact on terms of mutual respect.

Common critiques of Theravada made by Mahayana Buddhists are that Theravada monks aim to achieve enlightenment only for themselves, and that they lack compassion. However, supporters of Theravada emphasize that the Pali Canon does not recognize a self at all, and that providing help for others is actively practiced and encouraged in many monasteries. *Metta* (often translated as "loving kindness" or "good will") is an important aspect of Theravada Buddhism, it is also frequently practiced in meditation, and occurs in many sutras that are key to the Theravada tradition.

Also Buddhist monasteries in for example Thailand provide help to society in general in many different ways by such things as constructing (or financially supporting) hospitals, providing schooling, and in the recent past, even raising money to help pay off the country's debt to the IMF. Also monasteries in Theravada are very open for laypeople to come and visit and talk to the monks, and they do not charge money to monks for education and living-expenses, as is common in most Mahayana and Vajrayana monasteries, which helps those monks by giving them more opportunity for study and practice.

Theravada monks have sometimes been criticized for following their monastic rules blindly although, in fact, the rules give exceptions and allowances for several extreme situations, an example of which is saving another person's life. In Theravada the original Vinaya-rules are seen as guidelines for proper conduct, and the rules also allow for most proper conduct to take place. Inflexibilities and misunderstandings mostly occur when monks give precedence to some strict local (Thai, Burmese, Sri Lankan) standard over the actual precept of the Vinaya. The Buddha gave permission to the Sangha to not keep the minor and lesser rules if the Sangha (unanimously) sees fit to do so. Further he formulated the Four Great Standards, so the Vinaya could be applied (using the faculty of free thinking) to new situations which did not arise in the fifth century BC. Also the fact that many Theravada monks do not follow all the rules gives an indication of the flexibilty that is available for them.

Some other schools have also charged that Theravada practice is the slowest path to enlightenment, taking many eons to reach its goal. However, Theravada Buddhists see the Buddha and the ancient arhats as examples of practitioners who became enlightened in one lifetime. They believe Arahantship is the quickest way to full enlightenment, which is possible in one life. If one is willing to wait for aeons one can also take the Bodhisattva way, which is also recognized in the Pali Canon.

BUDDHIST SOCIALISM

Buddhist socialism is a political ideology which advocates socialism based on the principles of Buddhism.

Buddhist socialists have called for state provision of the Buddhist requisites of food, shelter, clothing and medicine, for the abolition or ameleoration of class distinctions, for campaigns for morality based on Buddhist traditions, and for workers and peasants to overcome the love of property.

People who have been described as Buddhist socialists include Buddhadasa Bhikkhu, S. W. R. D. Bandaranaike, U Nu and Norodom Sihanouk.

BUDDHIST SYMBOLISM

Buddhist symbolism appeared from around the 3rd century BCE, and started with aniconic symbolism, avoiding direct representations of the Buddha. Anthropomorphic symbolism appeared from around the 1st century CE with the arts of Mathura and the Greco-Buddhist art of Gandhara, and were combined with the previous symbols. Various symbolic innovations were later introduced, especially through Tibetan Buddhism.

Early Aniconic Symbols

Among the earliest and most common symbols of Buddhism are the stupa, Dharma wheel, and the lotus flower. The dharma wheel, traditionally represented with eight spokes, can have a variety of meanings. It initially only meant royalty (concept of the "Monarch of the Wheel, or *Chakravatin*), but started to be used in a Buddhist context on the Pillars of Ashoka during the 3rd century BCE. The Dharma wheel is generally seen as referring to the historical process of teaching the buddhadharma; the eight spokes refer to the Noble Eightfold Path. The lotus, as well, can have several meanings, often referring to the inherently pure potential of the mind.

The swastika was traditionally used in India by Buddhists and Hindus as a good luck sign. In East Asia, the swastika is often used as a general symbol of Buddhism. Swastikas used in this context can either be left or right-facing.

Other early aniconic symbols include the trisula, a symbol use since around the 2nd century BCE that combine the lotus, the vajra diamond rod and a symbolization of the three jewels (The Buddha, the dharma, the sangha).

The first hint of a human representation in Buddhist symbolism appear with the Buddha footprint.

The 32 Signs of a Great Man, and 80 Secondary Characteristics

Although the Buddha was not represented in human form until around the 1st century CE, the Physical characteristics of the Buddha are described in one of the central texts of the traditional Pali canon, the Digha Nikaya, in the discourse titled "Sutra of the Marks".

These characteristics comprise 32 signs, "The 32 signs of a Great Man", and were supplemented by another 80 Secondary Characteristics. These traits are said to have defined the appearance of the historical Buddha, Siddhartha Gautama and have been used symbolically in many of his representations.

The Mudras

The Mudras are a series of symbolic hand gestures describing the actions of the characters represented in only the most interesting Buddhist art.

PHILOSOPHICAL AREAS ADDRESSED IN BUDDHISM

Epistemology

Decisive in distinguishing Buddhism from what is commonly called Hinduism is the issue of epistemological justification. The schools of Indian logic recognize a certain set of valid justifications for knowledge, while Buddhism recognizes a smaller set.

Both accept perception and inference, for example, but for the orthodox schools (of Hinduism), the received textual tradition (e.g., the Vedas) is in itself an epistemological category equal to perception and inference (although this is not necessarily true for some of the non-orthodox schools, like Vedanta). Thus, in the orthodox schools, if a claim was made that could not be substantiated by appeal to the textual canon, it would be considered as ridiculous as a claim that the sky was green. Buddhism, on the other hand, rejected an inflexible reverence of accepted doctrine. As the Buddha said:

Do not accept anything by mere tradition... Do not accept anything just because it accords with your scriptures... Do not accept anything merely because it agrees with your pre-conceived notions... But when you know for yourselves — these things are moral, these things are blameless, these things are praised by the wise, these things, when performed and undertaken, conduce to well-being and happiness — then do you live acting accordingly. — the Kalama Sutta, Anguttara Nikaya III.65

Metaphysics and Phenomenology

Issues Arising from the Doctrine of Anatta

In earliest Buddhism and today still in Theravada and the Madhyamaka, any metaphysical essence or being underlying the play of phenomenal experience is rejected. No "soul" or permanent self was recognized, and the perception of a continuous identity was held to be an illusion.

Any feeling whatsoever, any perception whatsoever, any mental processes whatsoever, any consciousness whatsoever — past, future, or present; internal or external; blatant or subtle, common or sublime, far or near; every consciousness — is to be seen as it actually is with right discernment as "This is not mine. This is not my self. This is not what I am."

— the Anattalakkhana Sutta, Samyutta Nikaya XXII.59

From within the context of the Madhyamaka, we find Candrakirti:

"Self is an essence of things that does not depend on others; it is an intrinsic nature. The non-existence of that is selflessness".

— Bodhisattvayogacaryacatuhsatakamika 256.1.7

This anti-essentialist teaching, known as anatta, brought up many questions. If there is no atman or Brahman underlying the objects and events of the universe, how *could* they be explained? What gave them their existence? And if there was no "self", who makes the decisions we think we make, and what gets reincarnated?

Early Buddhist philosophers and exegetes created a pluralist metaphysical and phenomenological system in which all experiences of people, things, and events, can be broken down into smaller and smaller perceptual or perceptual-ontological units called dharmas.

These dharmas (roughly synonymous with "phenomena") were interpreted differently by different schools: some held they were real, some held only some were real, some held all were illusory, some held they were empty, some held they were intrinsically associated with suffering, etc.

Other debates in metaphysics and phenomenology include the issue of the Pudgala, or "person", which was inserted by the Pudgalavada school to replace the atman as that which transmigrates and that which carries the burden of karma from one life to another. Other schools made unsurprising objection to this. There were further sub-debates regarding whether the pudgala was real or illusory or something in between.

The Yogacara school, somewhat later, would later elevate the mind to act as a substitute for Brahman, much as the Pudgala replaces the atman. And the Tathagatagarbha (Buddha Essence) doctrine of Mahayana Buddhism would see the Buddha of those Tathagatagarbha sutras insisting that the *atman* (Self) lies at the very heart of the Buddha himself and of Nirvana (the two being One), as well as being concealed within the mass of mental/moral contaminants which blight all beings. In what claim to be the final Mahayana teachings of the Buddha, the eternal Self is distinguished from the five impermanent skandhas (constituents) which make up the non-Self or worldly ego, and the True Self is identified as the Dharmakaya of the Buddha in deathless Nirvana. Such doctrines saw a shift from a largely apophatic (negative) philosophical trend within Buddhism to a decidedly more cataphatic (positive) modus.

In many or all of these debates, some would point out the irony of pursuing questions which the Buddha of the *agamas/* Pali suttas was often prone to refuse to answer, on the grounds that they were non-conducive to enlightenment. The Buddha of the Mahayana, however, would on occasion take a different stand and speak of allegedly higher doctrines sui for the more advanced of his monks.

Dependent Origination

The original positive Buddhist contribution to the field of metaphysics is *pratityasamutpada*, which arises from the Buddhist critique of Indian theories of causality. It states that events are not predetermined, nor are they random, and it rejects notions of direct causation owing to the need for such theories in the Indian context to be undergirded by a substantialist metaphysics. Instead, it posits the arising of events under certain conditions which are inextricable, such that the units in question at no time have independent existence.

This being, that becomes.

From the arising of this, that arises.

This not being, that does not become.

From the ceasing of this, that ceases. — Samyutta Nikaya ii.

Ṗratitya-samutpada goes on to posit that certain specific events, concepts, or realities are always dependent on other specific things. Craving, for example, is always dependent on, and caused by, emotion.

Emotion is always dependent on contact with our surroundings. This chain of causation purports to show that the cessation of decay, death, and sorrow is indirectly dependent on the cessation of craving, and ultimately dependent on an all-encompassing stillness.

Nagarjuna, one of the most influential Buddhist philosophers, asserted a direct connection between, even identity of, dependent origination, anatta, and sunyata. He pointed out that implicit in the early Buddhist concept of dependent origination is the lack of any substantial being (anatta) underlying the participants in origination, so that they have no independent existence, a state identified as emptiness, or emptiness of a nature or essence (sva-bhava).

This element of Nagarjuna's thought is relatively uncontroversial, but it opens the way for his identification of samsara and nirvana, which was revolutionary.

Interpenetration

This doctrine comes from the Avatamsaka Sutra and its associated schools. It holds that all phenomena are intimately connected. Two images are used to convey this idea. The first is known as Indra's net.

The net is set with jewels which have the extraordinary property that they reflect all of the other jewels. The second image is that of the world text. This image portrays the world as consisting of an enormous text which is as large as the universe itself. The 'words' of the text are composed of the phenomena that make up the world. However, every atom of the world contains the whole text within it. It is the work of a Buddha to let out the text so that beings can be liberated from suffering. This idea was enormously influential on the Japanese monk Kukai in founding the Shingon school of Buddhism.

Ethics

Although there are many ethical tenets in Buddhism that differ depending on whether one is a monk or a layman, and depending on individual schools, the Buddhist system of ethics can always be summed up in the Eightfold Path.

> *And this, monks, is the noble truth of the way of practice leading to the cessation of suffering — precisely this Noble Eightfold Path — right view, right resolve, right speech, right action, right livelihood, right effort, right mindfulness, right concentration. — Samyutta Nikaya LVI.11*

The purpose of living an ethical life is to escape the suffering inherent in (unenlightened) worldly life. Although early Buddhism (Hinayana) is contrasted with later Buddhism (Mahayana) in that the latter emphasizes striving for the enlightenment of all (apparent) beings rather than simply oneself, in neither case can the motivation for ethical living be called 'selfish', because Buddhist doctrine holds the notion of a 'self' to be illusory.

Buddhist teachings claim that there is no real difference between ourselves and others; therefore one should attempt to increase the happiness of all living things as eagerly as one's own. This is why some Buddhists choose to be vegetarians.

EASTERN PHILOSOPHY

Eastern philosophy refers very broadly to the various philosophies of China, Japan, Korea, India, Iran (Persia), and to an extent, the Middle East (which overlaps with Western philosophy due to being the origin of the Abrahamic religions).

The usefulness of dividing philosophy into Western philosophy and other philosophies, in contrast to a notion that there can be one philosophy, not many, is open to challenge, partly because some see it as condescending to non-Western philosophies. To say this is not to deny that there are important traditions in philosophy that are intimately bound up with historical and geographical circumstances. At the same time however, there are examples of philosophers who are persecuted by the majority in their geographical circumstances and stand against the common opinions and practices of their specific time and place. Many claim that geographical and time notions of "Western" and "Eastern" philosophy is too vague and imprecise, committing the fallacy of over generalization.

When the term "philosophy" is used in an academic context, it typically refers to the philosophical tradition begun with the ancient Greeks that provided us with an abundance of manuscripts and archeological sites to study and research. The "Eastern philosophical" manuscripts and archeological sites are often overlooked in many North American and European universities, just as ancient "Western" and monotheistic claims are also overlooked in the last few decades, unlike in the early 1900's.

Philosophical and Religious Traditions

The following is an overview of the Eastern philosophic traditions listed in alphabetical order. Each tradition has a separate article with more detail on sects, schools, etc. rencyism.

Ayyavazhi

Ayyavazhi is the system of beliefs and philosophical system which is based on the teachings of Ayya Vaikundar and the scriptures Akilattirattu Ammanai and Arul Nool. The philosophy of this religion applies a common formula for the creationism of Human beings and Universe. It also says that what ever exists externally to human beings exist also internally. The dharma concept applied to Ayyavazhi primarily deviates into two. The social as well as spiritual conception. The format of mixing exclusivism and inclusivism in Ayyavazhi is unique and not found else where in the world. Unlike other dharmic religions the time conception in Ayyavazhi is linear projecting into a world of bliss, Dharma Yukam. The concept of personifying a foremost evil as Kroni, and the personification of the evil of the age as Kaliyan in Ayyavazhi were in contrast to other dharmic systems of philosophy.

The primary commandments (virtues) of Ayyavazhi is stated as Neetham.

1. Manu Neetham: How an individual should personify him or herself.
2. Raja Neetham: How an individual should be to the society or Nation.
3. Deiva Neetham: How an individual should be before God.

Buddhism

Buddhism is a system of beliefs based on the teachings of Siddhartha Gautama, an Indian prince later known as the Buddha, or *one who is Awake*-derived from the Sanskrit 'bud', 'to awaken'. Buddhism is a non-theistic religion, one whose tenets are not especially concerned with the existence or nonexistence of a God or gods. The Buddha himself expressly disavowed any special divine status or inspiration, and said that anyone, anywhere could achieve all the insight that he had. The question of God is largely irrelevant in Buddhism, though some sects (notably Tibetan Buddhism) do venerate a number of gods drawn in from local indigenous belief systems.

The Buddhist soteriology is summed up in the Four Noble Truths:

1. *Dukkha*: All worldly life is unsatisfactory, disjointed, containing suffering.
2. *Samudaya*: There is a cause of suffering, which is attachment or desire (*tanha*) rooted in ignorance.
3. *Nirodha*: There is an end of suffering, which is Nirvana.
4. *Marga*: There is a path that leads out of suffering, known as the Noble Eightfold Path.

However, Buddhist philosophy as such has its foundations more in the doctrines of:

- anatta, which specifies that all is without substantial metaphysical being,
- pratitya-samutpada, which delineates the Buddhist concept of causality, and

- Buddhist phenomenological analysis of dharmas, or phenomenological constituents.

Most Buddhist sects believe in karma, a cause-and-effect relationship between all that has been done and all that will be done. Events that occur are held to be the direct result of previous events. One effect of karma is rebirth. At death, the karma from a given life determines the nature of the next life's existence. The ultimate goal of a Buddhist practitioner is to eliminate karma (both good and bad), end the cycle of rebirth and suffering, and attain Nirvana, usually translated as *awakening* or *enlightenment.*

Chan/Zen Buddhism

Chan (*Chinese*) or Zen (*Japanese*) is a fusion of the Dhyana school of Mahayana Buddhism with Taoist principles. Bodhidharma was a semi-legendary Indian monk who travelled to China in the 5th century. There, at the Shaolin temple, he began the Ch'an school of Buddhism, known in Japan and in the West as Zen Buddhism. Zen philosophy places emphasis on existing in the moment, right now. Zen teaches that the entire universe is a manifestation of mind, and encourages the practictioner to confirm this for themselves through direct insight satori. Zen schools have been historically divided between those which encourage the pursuit of enlightenment as a sudden event (Rinzai), or as a fruit of "gradual cultivation" (Soto).

Zen practitioners engage in zazen (*sitting*) meditation, as other schools do, but Zen is noted for shikantaza (*just sitting*) as opposed to following the breath or mantra use. The Rinzai school is noteworthy for the use of koans, riddles designed to force the student to abandon futile attempts to understand the nature of the universe through logic.

Carvaka

Carvaka, also frequently transliterated as Charvaka or Carvaka, and also known as Lokayata or Lokyata, was a materialist and atheist school of thought with ancient roots in India. It proposed a system of ethics based on rational thought.

However, this school has been dead for more than a thousand years.

Confucianism

Confucianism, developed around the teachings of Confucius and is based on a set of Chinese classic texts. It was the mainstream ideology in China and the sinosphere since the Han dynasty and may still be considered a major underlying element of Far-East culture.

It could be understood as a social ethic and humanist system focusing on human beings and their relationships. Confucianism emphasizes formal rituals in every aspect of life, from quasi-religious ceremonies to strict politeness and deference to one's elders, specifically to one's parents and to the state in the form of the Emperor.

Neo-Confucianism

Neo-Confucianism is a later further development of Confucianism but also went much more differently from the origin of Confucianism. It started developing from the Song Dynasty and was nearly completed in late Ming dynasty. Its root can be found as early as Tang Dynasty. It has a great influence on the East Asia including such as China, Japan and Korea. Zhu Xi is considered as the biggest master of Song Neo-confucianism and Wang Yangming is the one of Ming's. But there are conflicts between Zhu's school and Wang's.

Daoism

Daoism, whose essence is centered around letting things take their natural course, is the traditional foil of Confucianism. Daoism's central books are the Dao De Jing, traditionally attributed to Laozi (Lao Tzu), and the Zhuangzi (Chuang Tzu). The core concepts of Daoism are traced far in Chinese History, incorporating elements of mysticism dating back to prehistoric times, linked also with the Book of Changes (Yi Jing or I Ching), a divinatory set of 64 geometrical figures describing states and evolutions of the world. Daoism emphasizes Nature, individual freedom, refusal of social bounds, and was a doctrine professed by those who "retreated in mountains". At the end of their lives-or during the night-Confucian officers often behaved as Daoists, writing poetry or trying to "reach immortality". Yet Daoism is also a government doctrine where the ruler's might is ruling through "non-action" (Wu wei).

Ancient Egyptian Religion

The Egyptian religion, embodied in Egyptian mythology, is a succession of beliefs held by the people of Egypt, as early as predynastic times and all the way until the coming of Christianity and Islam in the Greco-Roman and Arab eras. These were conducted by Egyptian priests or magicians. Every animal portrayed and worshipped in ancient Egyptian art, writing and religion is indigenous to Africa, all the way from the predynastic until the Graeco-Roman eras, over 3000 years. The Dromedary, domesticated first in Arabia, first appears in Egypt (and North Africa) beginning in the 2nd millennium BC. The temple was a sacred place where only priests and priestesses were allowed. On special occasions people were allowed into the temple courtyard.

Hinduism

Hinduism is generally considered to be the oldest major world religion and first among Dharma faiths. Hinduism is characterized by a diverse array of belief systems, practices and scriptures. It has its origin in ancient Vedic culture at least as far back as 3000 BC. It is the third largest religion with approximately 1.05 billion followers worldwide, 96% of whom live in the Indian subcontinent.

Hinduism rests on the spiritual bedrock of the Vedas, hence Veda Dharma, and their mystic issue, the Upanishads, as well as the teachings of many great Hindu gurus through the ages.

Many streams of thought flow from the six Vedic/Hindu schools, Bhakti sects and Tantra Agamic schools into the one ocean of Hinduism, the first of the Dharma religions. Also, the sacred book Bhagavad Gita is one of the most revered texts among Hindus. What can be said to be common to all Hindus is belief in Dharma, reincarnation, karma, and moksha (liberation) of every soul through a variety of moral, action-based, and meditative yogas. Still more fundamental principles include ahimsa (non-violence), the primacy of the Guru, the Divine Word of Aum and the power of mantras, love of Truth in many manifestations as gods and goddessess, and an understanding that the essential spark of the Divine (Atman/ Brahman) is in every human and living being, thus allowing for many spiritual paths leading to the One Unitary Truth.

Islamic Philosophy

The rise of Islam led to emergence of various philosophical schools of thought. Amongst them sufism established esoteric philosophy, mu'tazilah (inspired from Greek Philosophy) reconstructed rationalism while asharites cast significant impact on the non-reliability of reason and reshaped logical and rational interpretation of God, justice, destiny and universe.

Sufism is a school of esoteric philosophy in Islam, which is based on the pursuit of spiritual truth as a definite goal to attain. In order to attain this supreme truth, Sufism has marked *Lataif-e-Sitta* (the six subtleties), *Nafs*, *Qalb*, *Sirr*, *Ruh* (spirit), *Khafi* and *Akhfa*. Apart from conventional religious practices, they also perform Muraqaba (meditation), Dhikr (Zikr or recitation), Chillakashi (asceticism) and Sama (esoteric music and dance).

Al-mu'tazilah or Mu'tazilite is another controversial theological school of philosophy in early Islam. They called themselves Ahl al-'Adl wa al-Tawhid ("People of Justice and Monotheism").

They were the first who advocated free will and expanded the (western) rationalism in Islamic society. They also developed Kalam based on Greek dialectic. They ascended dramatically during 8th and 9th century due to support of intellectual and elites, but could not appeal to the masses. Later in the 13th century, they lost official support and most of their valuable works were destroyed.

Jainism

Jainism was founded by Mahavira, a teacher and religious leader who lived around the same time as the Buddha. The word *Jaina* comes from the title *Jina*, or victorious one, referring to those who have achieved victory over their own passions. Jainism teaches asceticism-acts of self-discipline, self-deprivation, and self-denial-as the way to enlightenment.

The original Jains were among the world's first monks, retreating from ordinary life to devote themselves to fasting and meditation. The Jain population is concentrated in India and has crossed 10 million. Jains are among the most prosperous of business communities in India.

Jewish Philosophy

Jewish philosophy is continually shaped by the Torah, Tanakh, Talmud, Midrash and Kabbalistic traditions. Much of philosophy (Hashkafa) is also considered in reference to mussar: self-improvement and education to attain a higher purpose-to become close to the Creator.

Philosophical discussions in the Talmud usually centre around legal issues, and the legal implications of having a particular philosophy. Midrash and Kabbalah follow a more overarching philosophical style which deal with issues such as ein sof-without end. The main feature is that the Eternal Creator is a given and that he is One and unique. Rambam (Maimonides) in is classic: Moreh Nevuchim (*Guide to the Perplexed*), clarifies this principal in Greco terms.

Legalism

Legalism advocated a strict interpretation of the law in every respect. Morality was not important; adherence to the letter of the law was paramount. Officials who exceeded expectations were as liable for punishment as were those who underperformed their duties, since both were not adhering exactly to their duties. Legalism was the principal philosophic basis of the Qin Dynasty in China. Confucian scholars were persecuted under Legalist rule.

Maoism

Maoism is a Communist philosophy based on the teachings of 20th century Communist Party of China revolutionary leader Mao Zedong. It is based partially on earlier theories by Marx and Lenin, but rejects the urban proletariat and Leninist emphasis on heavy industrialization in favour of a revolution supported by the peasantry, and a decentralized agrarian economy based on many collectively worked farms.

Many people believe that though the implementation of Maoism in Mainland China led to the victory of communist revolution, it also contributed to the widespread famine, with millions of people starving to death. Chinese Communist leader Deng Xiaoping reinterpreted Maoism to allow for the introduction of market economics, which eventually enabled the country to recover. As a philosophy, Deng's chief contribution was to reject the supremacy of theory in interpreting Marxism and to argue for a policy of seeking truth from facts.

Despite this, Maoism has remained a popular ideology for various Communist revolutionary groups around the world, notably the Khmer Rouge in Cambodia, Sendero Luminoso in Peru, and an ongoing (as of early 2005) Maoist insurrection in Nepal.

Shinto

Shinto is the indigenous religion of Japan, a sophisticated form of animism that holds that spirits called kami inhabit all things. Worship is at public shrines, or in small shrines constructed in one's home. According to Shinto practice, relationship with the kami that inhabit this world is foremost in a person's duties. The kami are to be respected, and in turn, they will return our respect. Shinto further holds that the "spirit" and "mundane" worlds are but one in the same. Purity is the most stressed of its tenants, with acts that create harmony pure, and those that are disharmonious to in the scheme of the universe considered impure. Shinto, as a faith, bears heavy influences from Chinese philosophies, such as Taoism, not to mention Buddhism.

Sikhism

- Simran and Sewa: These are the Foundation of Sikhism. It is the duty of every Sikh to practise Naam Simran (meditation on the Lord's name) daily and engage in Sewa (Selfless Service) whenever there is a possibility- in Gurdwara (Sikh place of worship); in community centre; old people's homes; care centres; major world disasters, etc
- The Three Pillars of Sikhism: Guru Nanak formalised these three important pillars of Sikhism:
- Naam Japna: – A Sikh is to engage in a daily practise of meditation and Nitnem (a daily prayer routine) by reciting and chanting of God's Name.
- Kirat Karni:-To live honestly and earn by ones physical and mental effort while accepting Gods gifts and blessings. A Sikh has to live as a householders carrying out his or her duties and responsibilities to the full.
- Vand Chakna:-The Sikhs are asked to share their wealth within the community and outside by giving Dasvand and practising charity (Daan). To "Share and consume together".
- Kill the Five Thieves: The Sikh Gurus tell us that our mind and spirit are constantly being attacked by the Five Evils – Kam (Lust), Krodh (Rage), Lobh (Greed), Moh (Attachment) and Ahankar (Ego). A Sikh needs to constantly attack and overcome these five vices; be always vigilant and on guard to tackle these five thieves all the time!
- Positive Human Qualities: The Sikh Gurus taught the Sikhs to develop and harness positive human qualities which lead the soul closer to God and away from evil. These are: Sat (Truth); Daya (Compassion); Santokh (Contentment); Nimrata (Humility); and Pyare (Love).
- Sikhism-Brief account of this religion.
- Sikh Beliefs-Brief outline of Sikh beliefs.

- Basic Tenets of the Sikhism:-A Summary of the most Important Beliefs and Tenets of Sikhism.
- Sikhism Primary Beliefs and Principles A more detailed account of Sikh beliefs with quotations from SGGS.

Zoroastrianism and Dualism

Zoroastrianism is the earliest known monotheistic religion, which originated in Iran. Zoroastrianism has a dualistic nature (Ahura Mazda and Angra Mainyu), with an additional series of six important angel-like entities called the Amesha Spentas. In modern Zoroastrianism they are interpreted as aspects or emanations of Ahura Mazda (the Supreme Being), who form a heptad that is good and constructive. They are opposed to another group of seven who are evil and destructive. It is this persistent conflict between good and evil that distinguishes Zoroastrianism from monotheistic frameworks that have only one power as supreme. By requiring its adherents to have faith and belief in *equally opposing* powers Zoroastrianism characterizes itself as dualistic.

Zoroastrianism may also be known as Mazdayasna ("Worship of Wisdom") by some of its followers after the Zoroastrian name of God, Ahura Mazda ("Divine Wisdom"). A modern Persian form is *Behdin* ("Good Religion/Law," see below for the role of *daena* Law). Zoroastrians may refer to themselves as *Zartoshti* ("Zoroastrians"), *Mazdayasni* ("Wisdom-Worshippers") and *Behdini* ("Followers of the Good Religion"), and *Zarathustrian*.

Arguments against the "Eastern Philosophy" Designation

Many have argued that the distinction between Eastern and Western schools of philosophy is arbitrary and purely geographic and to certain extent, Eurocentric. It crosses over three distinct philosophical traditions, Indian, Chinese and Persian philosophy which are as distinct from each other as they are from Western philosophy. It could be argued that the idea of some distinct "Eastern" philosophy as opposed to Western

Philosophy is simplistic to the point of absurd inaccuracy. Moreover, this artificial distinction does not take into account the tremendous amount of interaction within Eurasian philosophical tradition, and that the distinction is more misleading than enlightening. For example, Indian and Western schools of thought, with their robust mind-body conceptual dualism, share consequent tendencies to subjective idealism or dualism. Formally, they share the rudiments of Western "folk psychology" —a sentential psychology and semantics; for example, belief and (propositional) knowledge, subject-predicate grammar (and subject-object metaphysics) truth and falsity, and inference.

These concepts underwrote the emergence (or perhaps spread) of logic in Greece and India (In contrast to pre-Buddhist China). Other noticeable similarities include structural features of related concepts of time, space, objecthood and causation — all concepts hard to isolate within ancient Chinese conceptual space. It has also been suggested that the ancient Greek philosophers Pythagoras and Heraclitus were both influenced by ideas that originated in China.

The Perception of God and the Gods

Because of the influence of monotheism and especially the Abrahamic religions, Western philosophies have been faced with the question of the nature of God and His relationship to the universe. This has created a dichotomy among Western philosophies between secular philosophies and religious philosophies which develop within the context of a particular monotheistic religion's dogma regarding the nature of God and the universe.

Eastern philosophies have not been as concerned by questions relating to the nature of a single God as the universe's sole creator and ruler. The distinction between the religious and the secular tends to be much less sharp in Eastern philosophy, and the same philosophical school often contains both religious and philosophical elements. Thus, some people accept the metaphysical tenets of Buddhism without going to a temple and worshipping. Some have worshipped the Taoist deities religiously without bothering to delve into the philosophic underpinnings, while others embrace Taoist philosophy while ignoring the religious aspects. On the other hand, the followers of *Hare Krishna* sect in western countries give more emphasis to meditation and yoga and tend to ignore other traditional Hindu rituals.

This arrangement stands in marked contrast to most philosophy of the West, which has traditionally enforced either a completely unified philosophic/religious belief system (for example, the various sects and associated philosophies of Christianity, Judaism, and Islam), or a sharp and total repudiation of religion by philosophy (for example, Nietzsche, Marx, Voltaire, etc.).

Gods' Relationship with the Universe

Another common thread that often differentiates Eastern philosophy from Western is the belief regarding the relationship between God or the gods and the universe. Western philosophies typically either disavow the existence of God, or else hold that God or the gods are something separate and distinct from the universe.

The obvious exception here is the Greek and Roman pantheon of gods and goddesses during ancient times, which is very distinct from the influence of the Abrahamic religions, which teach that this universe was created by a single all-powerful God who existed before and only partially separately from this universe. Some aspects of the true nature and properties of this God would be incomprehensible to us as creations.

Eastern philosophic traditions generally tend to be less concerned with the existence or non-existence of God or gods. Although some Eastern traditions have supernatural spiritual beings and even powerful gods, these are generally not seen as separate from the universe, but rather as a part of the universe, just as Greek and Roman supernatural beings.

Conversely, most Eastern religions teach that ordinary actions can affect the supernatural realm.

The Role and Nature of the Individual

It has been argued that in most Western philosophies, the same can be said of the individual: Many Western philosophers generally assume as a given that the individual is something distinct from the entire universe, and many Western philosophers attempt to describe and categorize the universe from a detached, objective viewpoint.

Eastern philosophers, on the other hand, typically hold that people are an intrinsic and inseparable part of the universe, and that attempts to discuss the universe from an objective viewpoint as though the individual speaking was something separate and detached from the whole are inherently absurd.

Syntheses of Eastern and Western Philosophy

There have been many modern attempts to integrate Western and Eastern philosophical traditions.

German philosopher Georg Wilhelm Friedrich Hegel was very interested in Taoism. His system of dialectics is sometimes interpreted as a formalization of Taoist principles, but it also has similarities to the dialectical method used by Socrates as described by Plato.

Hegel's rival Arthur Schopenhauer developed a philosophy that was essentially a synthesis of Hinduism and Buddhism with Western thought. He anticipated that the *Upanishads* (primary Hindu scriptures) would have a much greater influence in the West than they have had. However, Schopenhauer was working with heavily flawed early translations (and sometimes second-degree translations), and many feel that he may not necessarily have accurately grasped the Eastern philosophies which interested him.

Recent attempts to incorporate Western philosophy into Eastern thought include the Kyoto School of philosophers, who combined the phenomenology of Husserl with the insights of

Zen Buddhism. Watsuji Tetsuro, a 20th century Japanese philosopher attempted to combine the works of Soren Kierkegaard, Nietzsche, and Heidegger with Eastern philosophies. Some have claimed that there is also a definite eastern element within Heidegger's philosophy. For the most part this is not made explicit within Heidegger's philosophy, apart from in the dialogue between a Japanese and inquirer. Heidegger did spend time attempting to translate the Tao Te Ching into German, working with his Chinese student Paul Hsaio. It has also been claimed that much of Heidegger's later philosophy, particularly the sacredness of Being, bears a district similarity to Taoist ideas. It may even be that Heidegger's philosophy might be read ultimately as an attempt to 'turn eastwards' in response to the crisis in Western civilisation. This however is only an interpretation. There are clear parallels between Heidegger and the work of Kyoto School.

The Twentieth century Hindu guru Sri Aurobindo was influenced by German Idealism and his Integral yoga is regarded as a synthesis of Eastern and Western thought. The German phenomenologist Jean Gebser's writings on the history of consciousness referred to a new planetary consciousness that would bridge this gap. Followers of these two authors are often grouped together under the term Integral thought.

Swiss psychologist Carl G. Jung's idea of synchronicity moves towards an Oriental view of causality, as he states in the forward to Richard Wilhelm's translation of the I Ching (Book of Changes). He explains that this Chinese view of the world is bases not on science as the west knows it, but on chance.

5

Buddhist Teachings

These are the basic teachings and concepts in Buddhism.

Karma: Actions have consequences; so our lives are conditioned by our past actions.

Rebirth: Consciousness continues after death, and finds expression in a future life.

Liberation from Karma: By following the Buddha's path one escapes the cycle of craving and suffering.

The Four Noble Truths: These are the essentials of Buddhism.

Enlightenment: The highest goal of life is to reach Enlightenment; a state of being that goes beyond suffering.

Dharma: The teachings and hence the way to nirvana.

The Core of Buddhist Teaching: At the heart of the Buddha's teaching lie The Four Noble Truths and The Eightfold Path which lead the Buddhist towards the path of Enlightenment.

Facing the Truth: The Buddha taught that the human tendency is to avoid the difficult truths of life and this in turn leads to suffering. By enabling the mind to be at peace through meditation a human being can confront reality and overcome hatred and craving.

Buddhism and Slavery

Slavery would seem to be incompatible with a fundamental

idea of Buddhism; that of freeing oneself of attachments: Thus the ideal community of the selfless arahants form an ideal, or a standard on which ethical and moral judgement of lay societies are based.

Thus such violations of human rights as slavery, torture, etc. could only be a movement in the opposite direction to the ideal, for these violations all result from strong attachment to the self of the violators of human rights. Wayne R. Husted, Damien V. Keown, Charles S. Prebish, Buddhism and Human Rights, 1998

Buddhist teachings don't explicitly forbid slavery, but the eightfold path says that engaging in trade in living beings is not a right form of livelihood. This appears to ban Buddhists from engaging in the slave trade.

...a lay follower should not engage in five types of business. Which five? Business in weapons, business in living beings, business in meat, business in intoxicants, and business in poison. Eightfold path

Other texts seem incompatible with many aspects of slavery itself.

For example, this quotation requires Buddhists to ensure that their workers and servants are properly treated:

In five ways should a master minister to his servants and employees:

by assigning them work according to their ability,

by supplying them with food and with wages,

by tending them in sickness,

by sharing with them any delicacies,

by granting them leave at times.

Sigalovada Sutta

Despite these texts there's no doubt that slavery was part of some Buddhist cultures, although many of these slaves were servants, rather than slaves of the sort traded across the Atlantic.

Richard Gombrich has argued that the Buddha did not intend to do away with slavery: Though it could well be argued that the Buddha made life in the world more worth living, that surely was an unintended consequence of his teaching. To present him as a sort of socialist is a serious anachronism.

He never preached against social inequality, only declared its irrelevance to salvation. He neither tried to abolish the caste system nor to do away with slavery.

While a famous sermon, the Sumanna-phala Sutta, stresses the practical benefits for a slave in leaving his servitude and joining the Order, in fact runaway slaves were not allowed to join the Order.

Moreover, though in ancient India there was no caste or other form of social ranking within the Order itself, the Order soon came to own (lay) slaves.

Richard F. Gombrich, Theravada Buddhism: A Social History from Ancient Benares to Modern Colombo, 1988

In fact the restrictions placed on monks required them to have some form of servant in monastic communities. So for example if monks were to obey the rule barring the cooking and storing of food, they would need somebody to do it for them. Some Buddhist commentaries warn that slaves are not allowed, unless they are called "called monastery servants (aramika) or legalisers (kappiya-karaka)".

Gombrich also notes that:

> *at one point the Vinaya commentary says in so many words that kings gave slaves to monasteries, and that they could not be ordained unless they had first been freed. Inscriptions record that people gave money for the specific purpose of maintaining monastic slaves-and offered the resulting merit to all living beings. Richard F. Gombrich, Theravada Buddhism: A Social History from Ancient Benares to Modern Colombo, 1988*

If granting endowments to maintain slaves at monasteries was considered meritorious, freeing them from slavery was considered even more meritorious. Thus the device of offering slaves to monasteries provided a two-fold way for the acquisition of merits. Rahula, Walpola (1956), History of Buddhism in Ceylon: the Anuradhapura Period, Colombo. Quoted in Gombrich

Some kings in Ceylon offered themselves to the monastic community "as slaves and then redeemed themselves, thus combining a symbolic gesture of total humility with extreme munificence".

In 9th century China Buddhist institutions are reputed to have employed 150,000 slaves, who were taken over by the Taoist Emperor Wu-tsung in 845 as part of his action against the Buddhist community.

In some parts of South East Asia Buddhist locations were a sanctuary for those fleeing more oppressive forms of slavery:

Where Buddhist monastic orders had claimed political retreats from state military power, their estates and temple complexes became sanctuaries where peasants sought the exemption from state conscription and corvee that 'slavery' to a privileged individual or institution provided. Gwyn Campbell, The Structure of Slavery in Indian Ocean Africa and Asia, 2004

Pagoda Slaves

In some Buddhist cultures a male slave would become free if their owner allowed them to become a Buddhist monk.

In Kampuchea a person could be made a 'Pagoda Slave' if they were found guilty of certain crimes-as could members of their family up to seven degrees removed. Pagoda slaves did domestic and maintenance work on temple sites. While pagoda slaves might have a relatively easy life for a slave they ranked very low on the social ladder and had an extra disadvantage:

Pagoda slaves, who were supposed to belong only to Buddha, could not be redeemed. Gwyn Campbell, The Structure of Slavery in Indian Ocean Africa and Asia, 2004

Because pagoda slaves could not be redeemed their children inherited slave status. Pagoda slaves were found mostly in what are now Burma and Thailand.

Pagoda slaves weren't only 'criminals' or the descendants of slaves; people could be given to monasteries for slave use.

Among Buddhist reformers of slavery was King Thibaw of Burma, a former monk. He paid 40,000 rupees in 1883 to buy the freedom of many slaves; 1,000 of those he freed are said to have become Buddhist monks and novices.

Slavery and Karma

Some writers think that slavery is justified by the doctrine of karma. They argue that people are born into slavery or become slaves because of their bad actions in a previous life. The way for a slave to progress towards salvation was to obey his or her owner, and do so willingly and without any bad feelings.

PURE LAND BUDDHISM

Pure Land Buddhism: Pure Land Buddhism offers a way to enlightenment for people who can't handle the subtleties of meditation, endure long rituals, or just live especially good lives.

The essential practice in Pure Land Buddhism is the chanting of the name of Amitabha Buddha with total concentration, trusting that one will be reborn in the Pure Land, a place where it is much easier for a being to work towards enlightenment.

Pure Land Buddhism adds mystical elements to the basic Buddhist teachings which make those teachings easier (and more comforting) to work with.

These elements include faith and trust and a personal relationship with Amitabha Buddha, who is regarded by Pure Land Buddhists as a sort of saviour; and belief in the Pure Land, a place which provides a stepping stone towards enlightenment and liberation. Pure Land Buddhism is particularly popular in China and Japan.

History: Pure Land Buddhism as a school of Buddhist thinking began in India around the 2nd century BCE.

It spread to China where there was a strong cult of Amitabha by the 2nd century CE, and then spread to Japan around the 6th century CE. Pure Land Buddhism received a major boost to its popularity in the 12th century with the simplifications made by Honen.

A century later Shinran (1173-1262), a disciple of Honen, brought a new understanding of the Pure Land ideas, and this became the foundation of the Shin (true) sect. Pure Land Buddhism took off in Japan when the monk Honen (1133-1212) simplified the teachings and practices of the sect so that anyone could cope with them. He eliminated the intellectual difficulties and complex meditation practices used by other schools of Buddhism. Honen taught that rebirth in the Pure Land was certain for anyone who recited the name with complete trust and sincerity. Honen said that all that was needed was... saying "Namu Amida Butsu" with a conviction that by saying it one will certainly attain birth in the Pure Land. The result was a form of Buddhism accessible to anyone, even if they were illiterate or stupid. Honen didn't simplify Buddhism through a patronising attitude to inferior people. He believed that most people, and he included himself, could not achieve liberation through any of their own activities. The only way to achieve Buddhahood was through the help of Amitabha.

The Shin Sect

A century after Honan, one of his disciples, Shinran (1173-1262) brought a new understanding of the Pure Land ideas. Shinran taught that what truly mattered was not the chanting of the name but faith. Chanting on its own had no value at all. Those who follow the Shin school say that liberation is the consequence of a person achieving genuine faith in Amitabha Buddha and his vow to save all beings who trusted in him.

TRANSFORMATION OF CONSCIOUSNESS INTO WISDOM

In the Chinese Consciousness-Only School of Buddhism, Buddhahood, characterized by the perfectly enlightened mind of True Suchness (bhutatathata) is understood as the final realization of a systematic and gradual path. Buddhahood is not a goal which is attained through the acquisition of a special conceptual understanding. Rather it is the end product of a fundamental internal transformation of all mental activity. In the language of Consciousness-Only, that process is referred to as the transformation of "consciousness" that has attachment to distinctions as its basic nature, into "wisdom" that is by its very nature totally free from attachment. "Wisdom", therefore, indicates a radically, qualitatively and totally different type of mental functioning. The purpose of this paper is twofold: 1) to delineate briefly the stages of transformation, and 2) after transformation is complete and Buddhahood has been realized, to indicate how the immanent aspect of Buddhahood utilizes wisdom tofunction in the world. Below we shall try to give a sketch of the prescriptions given by the School to rid oneself of the basic obstacles on the pathway to Buddhahood and to indicate briefly the manner in which one functions in the world after those obstacles have been removed.

The System of the Eight Consciousnesses

The Consciousness-Only School describes the mind as a system of seven active consciousnesses (vijnana) which all develop out of the eighth, or storehouse, consciousness. The latter is passive and contains the potentials, or "seeds" (bija) for the development and activity of the first seven consciousnesses. The seventh consciousness contains the sense of self or of ego individuality with which it defiles the first six consciousnesses. The sixth consciousness is a perceptual and cognitive processing centre, while the first five consciousnesses are the perceptual awarenesses of eyes, ears, nose, tongue and body.

Although with the emanation of these consciousnesses out of the eighth formal division is made among them, the distinction is totally based upon mental distinction. The eight are still basically "one." To use a simple analogy, let us think of a room with seven light-bulbs. You flick the light switch and seven distinct lights shine. Turn the switch off and the lights disappear. Yet there is just one electric current, and its source is comparable to the storehouse consciousness, or, as it is understood in the transformation of consciousness, to the enlightened mind. The system of eight consciousnesses, and the mental dharmas (caittas) which arise out of them and are dependent upon them, was developed as an important part of a pragmatic psychology of mind. The system can be used to describe in a manner which is accurate and practical both mental functioning and the specific techniques employed on the Path to the enlightenment of Buddhahood.

It provides a way to account for mental processes without recourse to the notions of a real, permanent self (atman) or of real, permanent external (and internal) objects (dharma). All actual and potential realms of experience are shown to be contained within the transformations of consciousness and appear as manifestations of the distinction-making mind.

Nevertheless, because of our attachment to and belief in the reality of self and the reality of the "objects" (dharmas) which we perceive and understand to be the external world, the true nature of ourselves and the world is obscured so that we are unaware of it.

The Types of Attachment

The basic obstacles which arise from the distinction-making character of consciousness are the division of the world into 1) subject, or one who grasps onto distinctions (the grasper), and 2) object, those distinctions which are grasped (the grasped). This distinction occurs on various levels and is reflected in each of the eight consciousnesses. The grasper corresponds to attachment to self and the grasped to attachment to dharmas. The former is often referred to as the obstacle of the afflictions and the latter as the obstacle of the knowable. These obstacles or attachments are of two types: 1) innate, and 2) distinguished or learned. The innate attachments are quite subtle and have existed from beginningless time as part of the human (or more generally, the sentient) condition.

The distinguished attachments, on the other hand, are coarser and arise from the distinction-making of our cognitive and perceptual processes. These attachments, the innate and distinguished attachments to self and the innate and distinguished attachments to dharmas, are the only obstacles to the realization of Buddhahood.

The Attachment to Self

The innate attachment to self is twofold. By taking the eighth consciousness, more specifically its "perceived portion," as its object, the seventh consciousness generates a continuous image of the eighth or storehouse consciousness as a real permanent self. Secondly, by taking the manifestation of the five aggregates (form, feeling, cognition, formation, and consciousness) as object, the sixth consciousness generates various non-continuous concepts of self.

The distinguished attachment to self belongs solely to the realm of the sixth consciousness and is much coarser in nature than the innate attachment of the seventh consciousness. The sixth consciousness either takes various aspects of the aggregates as object and conceives them to be the real self or independently generates self-concepts and takes them to be the real self. Such wrong conceptualization is often the result of misinformed religious or philosophical teaching.

The Attachment to Dharmas

The innate attachment to dharmas is also twofold. As the seventh consciousness takes the eighth consciousness as its object, it can also use it, more specifically its "perceived portion," to generate a continuous mental image of the eighth consciousness as dharmas.

Likewise, the sixth consciousness can take aspects of the aggregates and the perceptual faculties and their objects to be real dharmas; however, in contrast to the seventh consciousness, the functioning of the sixth consciousness in this manner is discontinuous.

The distinguished attachment to dharmas is exclusively an aspect of functioning of the sixth consciousness and is relatively coarse in its nature.

The sixth consciousness can either take concepts of the Hinayana Buddhist dharmas to be real or take the various objective categories or elements of non-Buddhist schools to be real. In other words, it mistakes its own concepts of an external reality for a real external reality.

The Five-stage Path of the Bodhisattva

Now that we have briefly outlined the nature of the obstacles to the realization of Buddhahood, we are in a position to discuss the Consciousness-Only School's prescriptions for their elimination. This is the gradual five-stage process known as the Path of the Bodhisattva. It begins with the birth of the intention to become fully enlightened (bodhicittotpada), which marks the entrance into the first stage, that of gathering provisions or Resources. It is followed by the stages of Application, Vision, Meditational Development, and culminates in the final stage which is Perfection, the perfect enlightenment of Buddhahood, the full realization of True Suchness.

The Stage of Resources

In the stage of developing his Resources, the Bodhisattva develops his deep faith in and understanding of the teachings of Consciousness-Only. During this period the Bodhisattva is merely able to subdue the rise in consciousness of the coarse, learned aspects of the grasper and the grasped, that is, of attachment to self and dharmas. In other words, he learns to see through and replace with dharmic analysis the learned conceptual analysis of perceiving and thinking about the world in terms of a real self and real objects. He does this by learning to prevent such concepts from arising and then snowballing into verbal and physical activities (the creation of karma). Thus he is able to utilize effectively the Consciousness-Only School's doctrinal framework in his everyday thinking and functioning in the world.

The Stage of Application

In the following stage, that of Application, concentration and insight are developed through preliminary meditational practices called the Four Aids to Penetration: Heat, Summit, Patience, and Highest Worldly Dharma. The Heat, Summit, and first two portions of the Patience Aid are practiced in meditations in which one enters into the first three dhyanas. The remainder of Patience and Highest Worldly Dharma Aids can only be practiced by entering into the fourth dhyana. During this gradual process not only is manifestation of the coarse, learned aspect of grasper and grasped subdued so that it no longer arises in consciousness, but the seeds of its manifestation, which are stored in the eighth consciousness, are completely destroyed. Since the seeds have been destroyed, they cannot sprout in dharmas; therefore, this coarse aspect of the attachment to self and dharmas can never again appear. It is the completion of this process that allows entrance into the third stage.

The Stage of the Path of Vision

Entrance onto the Path of Vision provides the first realexperience of True Suchness. It marks leaving the worldly flow and entering the flow of the Holy Ones. It corresponds to entrance onto the first of the "grounds" (bhumi) of the Path of the Bodhisattva, the Ground of Extreme Joy. It is at this point that the gradual transformation of consciousness into wisdom begins. This pure wisdom is the activity or functioning of True Suchness. The process of transformation is a gradual one and takes place as the Bodhisattva passes through the Ten Grounds of the Bodhisattva.

The Stage of the Path of Meditational Development

On the Path of Meditational Development (from dwelling on the first ground of the Bodhisattva through the final, tenth, ground) the wisdom, which first appeared on the Path of Vision, gradually eliminates the manifestations and the seeds of the manifestations of the innate attachments of grasper and grasped.

In passing through the first seven grounds, the Bodhisattva eliminates all the seeds of the subtle, innate attachment to self of both sixth and seventh consciousnesses (obstacle of the afflictions; the grasper). The single exception is the very subtle seeds of what is known as the spontaneous aspect of the obstacle afflictions. The Bodhisattva must preserve those seeds all the way up to the moment of realizing Buddhahood because they are the primary cause of the Bodhisattva's continued rebirth and, therefore, necessary for continued progress on the Path of the Bodhisattva.

The subtle, innate attachment to dharmas, (the obstacle of the knowable); the grasped) is also eliminated in gradual stages as the Bodhisattva proceeds through the ten grounds. On the final, tenth ground, the last, extremely subtle attachments to all known dharmas and their seeds,together with the above-mentioned seeds of the spontaneous aspect of the affliction obstacle necessary for rebirth, are completely eliminated. Then there can no longer ever be any kind of attachment, coarse or subtle, to self or dharmas, grasper or grasped. The obstacle of the afflictions and the obstacle of the knowable are completely eliminated.

The Stage of Perfection

Having outlined briefly the Path to Buddhahood and the stages in which the various obstacles to that enlightenment are eliminated, we are now in a position to discuss in greater detail the types of wisdom in terms of how they are used on the Path. As we have already seen, the distinguished or learned aspects of attachment to self and dharmas, grasper and grasped, are destroyed at the moment of entrance onto the Path of Vision. Their elimination clears the way for the appearance of a pure wisdom that has two components.

It is characterized as pure because of its complete lack of outflows (asraya), that is, the outward flowing of the mind and its attachment to various aspects of the conditioned world. Previous to this, the wisdom used as a guiding force in the meditational process was an impure, preliminary "applied" wisdom (prayogajnana) characterized by outflow. The first of the two components of the non-outflowing wisdom is called fundamental wisdom (mulajnana). It is characterized as non-distinction-making (nirvikalpa). In the process of its initial appearance, it naturally destroys the seeds of the distinguished attachment to self and dharmas. The destruction of the seeds and the appearance of the fundamental wisdom is a simultaneous and instantaneous process.

The second component of the non-outflowing wisdom is based on the first and for that reason is called subsequently attained wisdom (prsthalabdajnana). It is an expedient wisdom which operates in the world of distinctions. It analyzes the characteristics of dharmas, yet does not become attached to those characteristics as is the case with the preliminary "applied" wisdom, which has outflows. The subsequently attained wisdom reflects on the seeming characteristics of True Suchness and in this way is used to eliminate the seeds of learned attachment to self and dharmas. However, the mode of its functioning is gradual. It is employed in various meditational techniques to destroy the many separate aspects of the learned seeds.

The Functioning of Wisdom

Generally, wisdom functions in two ways. It acts to subdue the phenomenal activity of the mind (dharmas), and then, on a more fundamental level, it eliminates the seeds (bija), which are the source of that activity. Wisdom and distinction-making consciousness are like ice and water. As the water freezes, the ice appears; as the ice melts, the water appears. On the level of the phenomenal activity of the mind, the greater the attachment to distinctions, the weaker the functioning of wisdom; the stronger the functioning of wisdom, the less attachment to distinctions. For attachment to distinctions to be permanently eliminated, wisdom must operate with sufficient basis and power to supercede not only the manifestation of the distinctions but also their seeds, which are their basic cause. Another image often used to describe the process is that of light superceding darkness. If the light can not only fill the darkness but also fully and permanently penetrate the barriers to the light, then the darkness is permanently eliminated.

At the beginning of the Path, the power of wisdom is weak and the power of distinction-making consciousness is strong. In the first two stages of the path, those of Resources and Application, there is no manifestation of pure wisdom, wisdom characterized by complete lack of outflows. In order to clear the mind so that the seeds of pure wisdom can grow and finally become actualized, the Bodhisattva temporarily employs preliminary "applied" wisdom, which is characterized by outflows. That is, it tends to seek out the characteristics of mental objects, and by nature depends upon them for support. By treating True Suchness as a perceived characteristic of the mind, this provisional wisdom utilizes its own characterization of True Suchness as a support for meditation on the emptiness of the grasper and the grasped. In this way, the coarse aspects of the distinguished obstacles are eliminated and the other aspects of the distinguished and innate obstacles are subdued, that is, they are partially or fully prevented from rising into active awareness.

As an aid to this type of meditation, the Bodhisattva gradually decreases the extent of phenomenal activity produced by the seeds of the two obstacles by the use of resolution (adhimaksa), a special mental state, and of remorse (hri) and shame (apatrapa), both wholesome mental states. Resolution, remorse, and shame are all technical "dharmas," which are included in the One Hundred Dharmas of the Consciousness-Only School. Resolution is explained as that mental state which examines dharmas and comes to a decision about their natures. Employing resolution helps the Bodhisattva to see the conditioned, empty nature of all dharmas so that he will not become attached to them. Remorse and shame are the inner and outer recognition of one's own improper behavior and of a desire to change it.

With the successful completion of the first two stages, the balance shifts. The turning point is the entrance onto the Path of Vision. At that point wisdom no longer functions totally in dependence upon distinction-making consciousness. For the first time its non-outflow potential actually becomes operative as the basis for further progress on the Path. As we have already noted, the entrance onto the Path of Vision marks the initial experience of the nature of True Suchness. It is then fully realized as the Ten Grounds are passed through. With each step in the progressive elimination of the obstacles to Buddhahood, there is a corresponding step in the development of wisdom.

On the Path of Vision, fundamental wisdom instantaneously destroys the seeds of the distinguished attachment to grasper and grasped, while subsequently attained wisdom is used to eliminate gradually the various distinguished characteristics which are an obstruction to True Suchness. During this stage the preliminary "applied" wisdom does not operate.

On the first seven grounds of the Path of Meditational Development all three types of wisdom operate. The preliminary, "applied" wisdom, though characterized by outflows, functions because outflowing attachments are still present and practice is still intentional.

That is, it involves an act of will, signifying a tension between two competing aspects of mind. The subsequently attained wisdom is utilized in meditations with characteristics, whereas fundamental wisdom is employed in the meditations without characteristics.

Starting with the Eighth Ground and continuing to the realization of Buddhahood, outflows and the innate attachment to self are totally ended (except for that extremely subtle, spontaneous attachment necessary for rebirth). Because there is no longer any self, cultivation proceeds completely spontaneously. Since there is no longer any personal effort, the preliminary "applied" wisdom no longer functions (though its seeds are not totally eliminated until Buddhahood). All meditation is without characteristics and utilizes fundamental wisdom, while all actionsproceed spontaneously from the functioning of subsequently attained wisdom.

Development of the Four Types of Enlightened Wisdom

Fundamental wisdom and subsequently attained wisdom are classifications of wisdom, that is, the activity or functioning of True Suchness in terms of whether or not they act to distinguish the characteristics of dharmas. The Four Types of wisdom is another classification of the activity of True Suchness, in this instance, in terms of the functions which they inherit from the eight consciousnesses of which they are transformations.

'The first five perceptual consciousnesses are transformed into the Wisdom of Successful Performance; the sixth consciousness, the perceptual and cognitive processing centre, is transformed into the Wisdom of Wonderful Contemplation; the seventh consciousness, which ordinarily de-files the first six consciousnesses with self and self-related afflictions, is transformed into the Wisdom of Equality; and the eighth, the storehouse consciousness, is transformed into the Great Mirror Wisdom.

Both the Wisdom of Equality and the Wisdom of Wonderful Contemplation first begin to function on the Path of Vision. As attachment to the distinctions of the sixth and seventh consciousnesses diminishes, the power of these two types of wisdom increases. The functioning of the Wisdom of Equality is occasionally interrupted up through the Seventh Ground of the Bodhisattva when there are outflows (innate attachments) in the sixth consciousness that evoke the outflowing functioning of the seventh consciousness as support. This occurs because the seventh consciousness's attachment to grasper and grasped has not yet been fully eliminated.

The Wisdom of Wonderful Contemplation has two aspects, corresponding to understanding of the emptiness of self and of the emptiness of dharmas. They both function as long as there is no outflowing functioning of the sixth consciousness, which would naturally interfere. This type of wisdom is not active during the course of meditation without characteristics. (Meditation without characteristics becomes predominant on the Sixth Ground and is the exclusive type of meditation from the Seventh Ground on.)

On the first seven grounds, the progress which takes place has to do with the transformation of the sixth and seventh consciousnesses into their respective wisdoms. During this period, meditations with characteristics, which employ the sixth consciousness, are gradually phased out and replaced by meditations without characteristics. At the entrance onto the Eighth Ground, all outflowing activity of the seventh and sixth consciousnesses is permanently ended and the functioning of the Wisdoms of Equality and of Wonderful Contemplation proceeds spontaneously and without effort.

Both the Great Mirror Wisdom and the Wisdom of Successful Performance begin to function only at the moment of the realization of Buddhahood. The eighth consciousness must continue to exist upto that point as a receptacle of the wholesome outflowing seeds which allow the Bodhisattva to be reborn and to continue progress on the Path from the Eighth Ground to entry into Buddhahood. By the moment of entry, the eighth consciousness has become so pure that it can no longer serve as support for the seeds of outflowing dharmas, no matter how fine. Although from the Eighth Ground, the eighth consciousness continues to act as the supporting basis for the extremely subtle spontaneous affliction that the Bodhisattva purposely preserves as the vehicle of his continued rebirth in the world, in every other sense the eighth consciousness is undefiled and no longer the cause of rebirth. From the latter point of view, the Eighth Ground marks the beginning of the laying of the groundwork for the Great Mirror Wisdom.

The activity of the Wisdom of Successful Performance must await the appearance of the Buddha's pure non-outflowing perceptual faculties, because the faculties of a Bodhisattva, even after the Eighth Ground, are based on a body which is the result of the subtle seeds of affliction and, therefore, could not provide the proper support. This kind of wisdom is active only when attention is directed to the perceptual faculties. The groundwork for it is laid when the awareness of the faculty of pure form, an aspect of the perceiver portion of the eighth consciousness, no longer associates itself with the characteristics of perceived objects, that is, the dharmas arising from the perceived portion of the eighth consciousness. (This also marks the initial emergence of subsequently attained wisdom.)

The Four Types of Wisdom and Buddhahood

Having discussed when on the Path the Four Types of Wisdom arise, we can now describe their functioning after the full realization of True Suchness at Buddhahood. All seeds and all dharmas, the entire universe both potential and actual, are reflected without distortion in the Great Mirror Wisdom. Its awareness of True Suchness is the functioning of the fundamental component of this type of wisdom, while its awareness of the activity of seeds and dharmas (as an aspect of True Suchness) is the functioning of its subsequently attained component. The Great Mirror Wisdom is equated with that aspect of the functioning of the reward-body (svasambhogakaya) and pure land of the Buddha which has no purpose beyond what it is in itself.

The Wisdom of Equality understands the nature of the equality of self and other and of all beings. It appears as images of the Buddhas which are limitless. It is equated with that aspect of the reward-body (parasambhogakaya) of the Buddha that functions for the sake of others. More specifically, it is the mode of wisdom which the Buddha uses to teach the great Bodhisattvas. It is also called the great transformation body (nisyandakaya). As is the case with the Great Mirror Wisdom, both components of wisdom function here to include both True Suchness and "worldly" aspects in their understanding.

The Wisdom of Wonderful Contemplation understands withoutdistortion the individual and universal characteristics of all dharmas in both their True Suchness and worldly aspects. According to Master Kuiji, it "examines the merits and abilities of all beings and rains the great rain of Dharma to destroy the great net of doubts and to benefit all sentient beings. " (59:32b)

The Wisdom of Successful Performance operates as the countless transformation bodies of the Buddhas and as the lands both with and without outflows in which they teach living beings. It is exclusively concerned with those dharmas that are the dharmas of perception, that is, the transformation bodies of the Buddha and the phenomena which the faculties of those bodies perceive. Therefore, only the subsequently attained component of wisdom functions in relation to it.

In other words, the Buddha employs the Wisdom of Successful Performance to appear in his ordinary earthly body (and other transformation bodies) and to function perceptually within that body. He sees, hears, smells, tastes, and touches without any obstruction or distortion of feeling not only in the ordinary range of perception but in an unlimited manner, universally in time and space.

With the Wisdom of Wonderful Contemplation he knows clearly, without distortion or obstruction, all dharmas which are the objects of his perception and all other dharmas which are exclusively the objects of cognitive processes. In this way he knows the mental and physical condition of all beings and speaks and acts accordingly in all the various ways necessary to teach them most effectively.

AMITABHA

Amitabha in context: The Pure Land sect emphasises the important role played in liberation by Amitabha (which means Immeasurable Light) who is also called Amitayus (which means Immeasurable Life).

People who sincerely call on Amitabha for help will be reborn in Sukhavati-The Pure Land or The Western Paradise-where there are no distractions and where they can continue to work towards liberation under the most favourable conditions.

The nature of Amitabha is not entirely clear. Encyclopedia Britannica describes him as "the great saviour deity worshiped principally by members of the Pure Land sect in Japan." Another writer says "Amitabha is neither a God who punishes and rewards, gives mercy or imposes tests, nor a divinity that we can petition or beg for special favours". The mystical view of Amitabha regards him as an eternal Buddha, and believes that he manifested himself in human history as Gautama, or "The Buddha".

Amitabha translates as "Amito-fo" in Chinese and "Amida" in Japanese.

The Story of Amitabha

Once there was a king who was so deeply moved by the suffering of beings in the world that he gave up his throne and became a monk named Dharmakara.

Dharmakara was heavily influenced by the 81st Buddha and vowed to become a Buddha himself, with the aim of creating a Buddha-land that would be free of all limitations.

He meditated at length on other Buddha-lands and set down what he learned in 48 vows. Eventually he achieved enlightenment and became Amitabha Buddha and established his Buddha-land of Sukhavati.

His most important vow was the 18th, which said: "If I were to become a Buddha, and people, hearing my Name, have faith and joy and recite it for even ten times, but are not born into my Pure Land, may I not gain enlightenment."

Since he did gain enlightenment, it follows that those who do have faith and joy and who recite his name will be born into the Pure Land.

PURE LAND ESSENTIALS

Nembutsu: This means concentration on Buddha and his virtues, or recitation of the Buddha's name.

No special way of reciting the name is laid down. It can be done silently or aloud, alone or in a group and with or without musical accompaniment. The important thing is to chant the name single-mindedly, while sincerely wishing to be reborn in the Pure Land.

Scripture: The Pure Land scriptures include The Infinite Life Sutra, The Contemplation Sutra and The Amitabha Sutra.

Chanting: Chanting the name of Amitabha Buddha does not do anything at all to help the person to the Pure Land. Chanting is nothing more than an expression of gratitude to Amitabha Buddha and an expression of the chanter's faith. But it's not possible to do away with the chanting: Shinran wrote "the True Faith is necessarily accompanied by the utterance of the Name".

Faith: Shin Buddhists say that faith in Amitabha Buddha is not something that the believer should take the credit for since it's not something that the believer does for themselves. Their faith is a gift from Amitabha Buddha.

And in keeping with this style of humility, Shin Buddhists don't accept the idea that beings can earn merit for themselves by their own acts; neither good deeds, nor performing rituals help. This has huge moral implications in that it implies (and Shinran quite explicitly said) that a sinner with faith will be made welcome in the Pure Land-even more welcome than a good man who has faith and pride.

Popularity: The sect's teachings brought it huge popularity in Japan, since here was a form of Buddhism that didn't require a person to be clever, or a monk, and that was open to the outcasts of society.

It remains a popular group in Buddhism-and the reasons that made it popular 700 years ago are exactly the same ones that make it popular today.

UNDERSTANDING PURE LAND

Is this a new understanding of Buddhism?

On the surface Pure Land Buddhism seems to have moved a very long way from the basic Buddhist ideas, and it's important to see how it might actually fit in. The way to do this is to tackle each issue and see what's really going on.

Amitabha Buddha is treated as if he were God: On the surface, yes. But perhaps chanting Amitabha Buddha's name is not praying to an external deity, but really a way of calling out one's own essential Buddha nature. However some of Shinran's writings do speak of Amitabha Buddha in language that a westerner would regard as describing God.

The Pure Land appears to be a supernatural place: On the surface, yes. But perhaps the Pure Land is really a poetic metaphor for a higher state of consciousness. Chanting the name can then be seen as a meditative practice that enables the follower to alter their state of mind. (This argument is quite hard to sustain in the face of the importance given to chanting the name in faith at the moment of death-when some supernatural event is clearly expected by most followers. And the chanting is not regarded solely as a meditative practice by most followers. However gaps between populist and sophisticated understanding of religious concepts are common in all faiths.) There is no reliance on the self to achieve enlightenment.

On the surface, yes. But in fact this is just a further move in the direction that Mahayana Buddhism has already taken to allow assistance in the journey to liberation. And the being still has much work to do when they arrive in the Pure Land. (Shinran however taught that arriving in the Pure Land was actually the final liberation-the Pure Land was nirvana.)

MAHAYANA BUDDHIST TEACHINGS

The Consciousness-Only School

The starting point of the Consciousness-Only School is that everything is created from the mind as is "consciousness-only". Everything, from birth and death to the cause of attaining nirvana, is based upon the coming into being and the ceasing to be of consciousness, that is, of distinctions in the mind. Consciousness-Only doctrine is characterized by its extensive and sophisticated inquiry into the characteristics of dharmas. For if we can distinguish what is real from what is unreal, if we can distinguish what is distinction-making consciousness and not mistake it for the originally clear, pure, bright enlightened mind, then we can quickly leave the former and dwell in the latter.

Ch'an Master Han-shan (AD 1546-1623) has said, "When Consciousness- Only was made known to them (i.e., those of the Hinayana vehicles), they knew that [all dharmas] had no existence independent from their own minds. If one does not see the mind with the mind, then no characteristic can be got at. Therefore, in developing the spiritual skill necessary for meditative inquiry, people are taught to look into what is apart from heart, mind, and consciousness and to seek for what is apart from the states of unreal (polluted) thinking."

The founder of the Consciousness-Only School was the Bodhisattva Maitreya, who transmitted its teaching to the Venerable Asanga. He and his brother Vasubandhu were responsible for its early spread in India. The school was influential in Jung-Gwo (i.e., China) primarily because of the efforts of Tripitaka Master Hsuan-Tsang.

Asanga (Bodhisattva)

Together with his teacher the Bodhisattva Maitreya, Asanga was the founder of the Yogacara, or Consciousness-Only, School of Mahayana Buddhism.

The oldest of three sons, all called Vasubandhu, born in Purusapura (Peshwar) who were members of the Kausika family of Indian brahmins. All three became Buddhist Bhikshus. Asanga's youngest brother was known as Virincivatsa, while the middle brother was known merely as Vasubandhu.

Asanga was a man who was endowed with the innate character of a Bodhisattva. He became a Bhikshu of the Sarvastivada School, but afterwards he practiced meditation and became free from desire. Though he investigated the doctrine of emptiness, he could not understand it. He was about to commit suicide. Pindola, an Arhat, who was then in Eastern Purvavideha, having perceived this, came to him from that region and expounded the doctrine of emptiness peculiar to the Hinayana. He arranged his thoughts according to what he was taught and at once comprehended it. Though he had attained the doctrine of emptiness peculiar to the Hinayana, he, nevertheless, did not find comfort in it. Thinking that it would not be right to drop the matter altogether, he went up to the Tusita Heaven using the supernatural power peculiar to the Hinayana and inquired of Maitreya, the Bodhisattva, who expounded for him the doctrine of emptiness belonging to the Mahayana. When he returned to Jambudvipa, he investi-gated according to the methods explained to him and soon became enlightened. While he was engaged in investigation, the earth began to quake (of its own accord) in six ways. Since he understood the doctrine of emptiness, he called himself "Asanga", which means "without attachment". He afterwards often went up to the Tusita Heaven in order to ask Maitreya about the doctrines of the Mahayana sutras.

The Bodhisattva explained them extensively for him. Whenever he acquired any new understanding, he would come back to Jambudvipa and teach it to others. Most of those hearing him did not believe him. Asanga, Teacher of the Dharma, then prayed, saying, "I now intend to bring all beings to believe fully in the doctrine of the Mahayana. I only pray that you, O Great Master, come down to Jambudvipa to expound the Mahayana so that all beings may become fully convinced of its truth." Maitreya, thereupon, in accordance with his prayer, came down to Jambudvipa at night, flooding it with great rays of light, had a large assembly of those connected with the Dharma called in a lecture hall, and began to recite the Saptadasabhumi-sutra.

After having recited a passage, he would explain its purport. The seventeen bhumis were finished during the nights of four months. Although all were together in one and the same hall listening to the discourse, it was, neverthe-less, only Asanga, Teacher of the Dharma,, who had access to the Bodhisattva Maitreya, while the others could merely hear him from afar. At night, all together heard the religious discourse by Maitreya, while in the daytime Asanga, Teacher of the Dharma, commented once again, for the sake of others, upon what had been taught by the Bodhisattva. In this way all the people could hear and believe in the doctrine of the Mahayana. Maitreya, the Bodhisattva, taught Asanga, Teacher of the Dharma, to learn the "sunlight" samadhi. As he learned according to what he had been taught, he subsequently attained entry into that samadhi. After he attained entry into that samadhi, what he formerly could not understand all became intelligible. Whatever he heard or saw was never forgotten, his memory having become retentive, whereas he formerly could not fully understand the sutras of the Mahayana, such as the Avatamsaka, previously taught by the Buddha. Maitreya explained for him all these in the Tusita heaven; thus the Teacher of the Dharma became well-versed in them and remembered them all. Afterwards in Jambudvipa he composed several upadesa on the sutras of the Mahayana, in which he expounded all the teachings of the Mahayana taught by the Buddha. (Paramartha, "The Life of Vasubandhu", J. Takakusu, tr. [with some editing], pp. 273-275)

Vasubandhu (Bodhisattva) (fl. 4th cent. AD)

The second of three sons, born in Purusapura (Peshwar), India, into the Kausika family of Indian Brahmins. All three sons were called Vasubandhu and all three became Buddhist Bhikshus. His older brother was known as Asanga and his younger brother as Virincivatsa. He is known simply as Vasubandhu. In his youth he adhered to the Hinayana teachings of the Sautrantika School and wrote the Abhidharmakosa, perhaps the most well-known of all treatises on the Abhidharma. He was converted to the Mahayana by his older brother the Bodhisattva Asanga. After his conversion, he wrote many celebrated works on the Consciousness-Only School of the Mahayana, including the Twenty Verses on Consciousness-Only and the Thirty Verses on Consciousness-Only.

Vasubandhu's Conversion

"Asanga, teacher of the Law [Dharma], saw that his younger brother was endowed with an intelligence surpassing that of others, his knowledge being deep and wide, and himself well-versed in esoteric and exoteric doctrines. He was afraid that the latter might compose a sastra and crush the Mahayana. He was living then in the land of the Hero (Purusa-pura) and sent a messenger to Vasubandhu in Ayodhya with the following message: "I am seriously ill at present. You had better attend to me quickly." Vasubandhu followed the messenger to his native land, saw his brother and inquired what was the cause of his illness. He answered: "I have now a serious disease of the heart, which arose on account of you." Vasubandhu again asked: "Why do you say on account of me?" He answered: "You dot no believe in the Mahayana and are always attacking and discrediting it. For this wickedness you will be sure to sink forever in a miserable Life. I am now grieved and troubled for your sake to such an extent that my life will no long survive. On hearing this Vasubandhu was surprised and alarmed and asked his brother to expound the Mahayana for him. He then gave him a concise explanation of the essential principles of the Mahayana. Thereupon the Teacher of the Law (Vasubandhu), who was possessed of clear intelligence and especially of deep insight, became at once convinced that the truth of the Mahayana excelled even that of the Hinayana.

"He then fully investigated, under his brother, the principles of the Mahayana. Soon after he became as thoroughly acquainted with the whole as his brother was. When its meaning was already clear to him, he would meditate on it. From the beginning to the end everything was perfectly in accordance with the truth, there being nothing contradictory to it. For the first time he realized that the Hinayana was wrong and the Mahayana right. If there were no Mahayana, then (he thought) there would be no path (marga) and no fruition (phala) of the Tri-yana [Three Vehicles]. Since he formerly did harm by speaking ill of the Mahayana, in which he then had no faith, he was now afraid that he might fall into a miserable life on account of that wickedness. He deeply reproached himself and earnestly repented of his previous fault. He approached his brother and confessed his error, saying: 'I now desire to make a confession. I do not know by what means I can be pardoned for my former slander.' He said (further): 'I formerly did harm speaking ill (of the truth)

by means of my tongue. I will now cut out my tongue in order to atone for my crime.' His brother answered: 'Even if you cut out your tongue a thousand times, you cannot wipe out your crime. If you really want to wipe out your crime, you must find some other means.' Thereupon he asked his brother to explain the means of wiping out the offence. The latter said: 'Your tongue was able to speak very skillfully and effectively against the Mahayana, and thus discredit it. If you want to wipe out your offence, you must now propound the Mahayana equally skillfully and effectively.'" (The Life of Vasubandhu, J. Takakusu, tr., pp. 290-292)

A eulogy says:

It is difficult to practice two teachings at once.

He brought forth the secret meanings of the Compassion-ate Sage.

In awesome Shastras like piled up clouds,

Explaining the untransmitted doctrine,

Revealing the Consciousness-Only,

complete in both the Nature and Appearance Schools.

An eternal Dharma lamp,

He lights a million generations.

(Vajra Bodhi Sea #20, p. 2)

Hsuan-Tsang (Tripitaka Master) (596-664)

Great enlightened master, translator, and founder of the Consciousness-Only School in China.

"This Bhikshu's contributions to Buddhism have been exceptionally great. It can be said that from ancient times to the present, there has never been anyone who can compare to this Dharma Master in his achievements. His worldly name was Ch'a. His father was an official, but a poor one. Why did he end up a poor official? It was because he didn't take bribes. He wasn't after the citizens' money nor that of the government. He wasn't like people today who hold office and always feel they are earning too little money so that on top of their government salary they force the citizens to give them their hard-earned money as well. Dharma Master Hsuan-Tsang's father didn't want money. He remained a poor official all his life. Even though he was poor, he had a virtuous nature and because of that he had two sons who left the home-life, lectured Sutras, and were adept cultivators of the Way.

"Dharma Master Hsuan-Tsang left the home-life at the age of thirteen and commenced his study of the Buddhadharma. During those early years of study, if there was a Dharma Master lecturing a Buddhist text, no matter who the Dharma Master was or how far away the lecture was being held, he was sure to go to listen, whether it was a Sutra lecture, a Shastra lecture or a Vinaya lecture.

He went to listen to them all. Wind and rain couldn't keep him away from lectures on the Tripitaka, to the point that he even forgot to be hungry. He just ate the Dharma, taking the Buddhadharma as his food and drink. He did this for five years and then took the Complete Precepts.

"However, the principles lectured by the Dharma Masters he heard were all different. They all explained the same Sutras in very different ways--each with his own interpretation. And there was a big difference between the lectures of those with wisdom and those without wisdom. But Dharma Master Hsuan-Tsang had not yet really become enlightened, and he didn't have the Selective Dharma Eye, and so how could he know whose lectures to rely on? At that time he vowed to go to India, saying,

The Buddhadharma has been transmitted from India, and so there is certainly true and genuine Buddhadharma to be found in India.

Thereupon, he wrote a request for permission to go to India to seek the Dharma and presented it to the emperor. Emperor Tai Dzung of the Tang Dynasty did not grant his wish, but Dharma Master Hsuan-Tsang, who had already vowed to go, said, 'I would prefer to disobey the son of Heaven and have my head cut off than not to go and seek the Dharma.' And so he returned to the monastery and began to practice mountain-climbing. He piled chairs, tables, and benches together to simulate a mountain and practiced jumping from one piece of furniture to the next. This was his method of practicing mountain-climbing. From morning till night he leaped from table to chair. Probably there weren't any big mountains-- where he lived, and so he had to practice in the temple. All the young, old, and older novices wondered what he was up to, jumping on furniture all day long instead of reciting Sutras or cultivating. He didn't tell anyone that he was training to climb the Himalayas, and so most people thought he was goofing off. Eventually he trained his body so that it was very strong, and then when he was physically able, he started his trip through Siberia.

"On the day of his departure, when Emperor Tai-Dzung learned he intended to go even without imperial consent, the emperor asked him, 'I haven't given you permission and you still insist on going. When will you be back?'

"Dharma Master Hsuan-Tsang replied, 'Look at this pine tree. The needles are pointing toward the west. Wait until those needles turn around and face east. That is the time when I will return.'

He didn't say how many years that would be. And so he set out. At that time there were no airplanes, steamboats, buses, or trains. There were boats, but they were made of wood and not too sturdy. Besides, since he didn't have imperial permission, he probably could not have gotten the use of a boat anyway.

And so he travelled by land through many countries, from the Siberian area of the Russian border to India. He was gone for more than a decade. When he reached India, he didn't know the language at all. But bit-by-bit he studied Sanskrit and listened to many Dharma Masters lecture the Buddhadharma. Some people say this took him fourteen years. Others say it took nineteen. In general he went through a great deal of suffering and difficulty to study the Buddhadharma and then when he'd completed his studies, he returned to China.

"When his return was imminent, the needles on the pine tree turned to the east. As soon as the emperor saw that the pine needles were indeed pointing east, he knew that Dharma Master Hsuan-Tsang was coming back and he sent out a party of officials to the western gate to welcome him and escort him back. When they reached the gate, there indeed, was Dharma Master Hsuan-Tsang returning.

"Dharma Master Hsuan-Tsang then concentrated on translating the Sutras and other works that he had brought back with him. He translated from Sanskrit into Chinese. At the time when he was translating the Mahaprajnaparamita-sutra, within one single year, the peach trees blossomed six times. That was a sign of the auspiciousness of the Mahaprajnaparamita-sutra and its importance to all of us. The fact that it was being translated moved even the wood and plants to display their delight.

"Dharma Master Hsuan-Tsang translated a great many sutras. While in India, he bowed to the Buddha's sarira and bones. He saw where the Buddha in a previous life had given up his eyes, and went to the place where the Buddha in a previous life had practiced the conduct of patience, and went to the place where the Buddha in a previous life had given up his life for the sake of a tiger.

He also went to see the Bodhi tree under which the Buddha realized the Way. He went to all of those places celebrated in Buddhism. These pilgrimages are another indication of the extent of his true sincerity. While in India, whenever he met Dharma Masters, he never looked down on them, no matter how little they may have cultivated. He was extremely respectful. He wasn't the least bit arrogant or haughty. When he finished his studies, many Small vehicle Dharma Masters and masters of externalist ways came to debate with him, but none was able to defeat him.

Dharma Master Hsuan-Tsang is known as a Tripitaka Master (Tripitaka='Three Treasuries', 'Three Baskets'). The Tripitaka includes the Sutra Treasury, the Shastra Treasury, and the Vinaya Treasury. He was honoured with this title because he understood all three Treasuries without obstruction....

"As to his name, Sywan means 'esoteric and wonderful.' He was esoteric in the sense that none could really understand him. Dzang means 'awe-inspiring.' He was awe-inspiring in that he could do what others could not do. He was an outstanding person among his peers...." (HD 15-17)

The Master's name has also been transliterated as follows: Xuanzang, Sywan-Dzang, Yuan Chwang, etc.

6

Mahayana in Buddhism

Mahayana is one of two major branches of Buddhism, the other being Theravada. Mahayana originated in the Indian subcontinent of what is today northern Pakistan and spread to China during the first century CE where it was Sinicized and then spread throughout East Asia in its Sinicized form. The main countries in which it is practiced today are China, Japan, Korea and Vietnam.

From Mahayana developed the esoteric Vajrayana found mainly in Tibet and Mongolia, but also in adjacent areas of China, and even Buddhism in India Buddhism in Russia. The Vajarana school claims to encompass all previous schools. The most complete Mahayana Canon today is written in the Chinese language. In East Asia, Mahayana scriptures and terminology are traditionally written in Chinese characters and based upon classical Chinese. Two mainstream subsets of Mahayana Buddhism today are Amidism or Pure Land.

Mahayana is an inclusive faith characterized by the adoption of new texts, in addition to the traditional Pali canon, and a shift in the understanding of Buddhism. It goes beyond the traditional nontheist Theravada ideal of the release of suffering and personal enlightenment, to instead elevate the Buddha to a God-like status and to create a pantheon of quasi-divine Bodhisattvas that devote themselves to personal excellence, ultimate knowledge and the salvation of humanity and all other sentient beings (animals, ghosts, etc.). In Mahayana, the

Buddha became an idealized man-god and the Bodhisattva came to represent the universal ideal of excellence.

The fundamental principles of Mahayana doctrine were based around the possibility of universal salvation for all beings (hence "great vehicle") and the existence of Buddhas and Bodhisattva embodying transcendent Buddha-nature-the eternal Buddha Essence present but hidden in all beings-who strive to achieve such a goal. Mahayana also simplified the expression of faith for the common lay people by allowing salvation to be alternatively obtained through the grace of the Buddha Amitabha by having faith and devoting oneself in prayer to Amitabha. This devotional lifestyle of Buddhism is most strongly emphasized by the Pure Land schools and has greatly contributed to the success of Mahayana in East Asia, where spiritual elements traditionally relied upon prayer and mysticism.

Doctrine

Mahayana, in contrast to the Theravada school of Buddhism, can be characterized by:

- Universalism, in that everyone will become a Buddha;
- Enlightened wisdom as the main focus of realization;
- Compassion through the transferal of merit;
- Salvation-as opposed to liberation-supported by a rich cosmography, including celestial realms and powers, with a spectrum of bodhisattvas, both human and seemingly godlike, who can assist followers.

"Philosophical", Mahayana tends to focus on the first three characteristics (universalism, enlightened wisdom, compassion) without showing much interest in supernatural constructions, while "devotional" Mahayana focuses mainly on salvation towards other-worldly realms.

Universalism

Mahayana traditions generally consider that Buddhahood is not final. This is based on a subtle doctrinal distinction between the Mahayana and the early Buddhist schools concerning the issues of *nirvana-with-remainder* and *nirvana-without-remainder*. The early schools considered that nirvana-without-remainder always follows nirvana-with-remainder (Buddhas first achieve enlightenment and then, at 'death', mahaparinirvana) and that nirvana-without-remainder is final; whereas the Mahayana traditions consider that nirvana-without-remainder is always followed by nirvana-with-remainder – the state of sravakabuddhahood is not final, and is eventually succeeded by the state of Buddhahood, or total enlightenment.

This distinction is most evident regarding doctrinal concerns about the capability of a Buddha after nirvana (which is identified by the early schools as being nirvana-without-remainder). Most importantly, amongst the early schools, a samyaksambuddha is not able to directly point the way to nirvana after death. This is a major distinction between the early schools and the Mahayana, who conversely state that once a samyaksambuddha arises, he or she continues to directly and actively point the way to nirvana until there are no beings left in samsara. Because the views of early schools and Mahayana differ in this respect, this is exactly why the Mahayana do not talk about a bodhisattva postponing nirvana, and exactly why the early schools do.

For example, the early schools held that Maitreya will not attain nirvana while Gautama Buddha's teachings still exist. While the Mahayana schools hold that Maitreya will be the next Buddha manifest in this world and will introduce the dharma when it no longer exists, he is not postponing his nirvana to do so, and when he dies (or enters mahaparinirvana), he will likewise continue to teach the dharma for all time. Moreover, Mahayana argues that although it is true that for this world-system, Maitreya will be the next Buddha to manifest, there are an infinite number of world-systems, many of which have currently active Buddhas or Buddhas-to-be manifesting.

So, based on the doctrinal distinctions between the early schools and the Mahayana concerning the meaning of nirvana-without-remainder, we see two distinct views concerning the path of the bodhisattva, with the early schools stating that bodhisattvas postpone their own nirvana, whereas the Mahayana schools state that bodhisattvas attempt to reach nirvana as soon as possible, just as sravakas do, but with the motive to continue to effortlessly benefit all beings for all time due to the distinction of views regarding the ability of a Buddha after mahaparinirvana.

Because the Mahayana traditions assert that eventually everyone will achieve samyaksambuddhahood or total enlightenment, the Mahayana is labelled universalist, whereas because the Nikaya traditions assert that there are three routes to nirvana, which are distinct, they are considered not to be universalist.

Enlightened Wisdom

According to Mahayana, traditional Buddhism tends to focus on an ascetic, individual approach to the attainment of nirvana: suppression of desire, removal from the world, solitude. Its followers are sravakas and pratyekabuddhas.

The primary focus of Mahayana is bodhicitta, the vow to strive for Buddhahood or awakened mind (bodhicitta) both for oneself and for the benefit of all other sentient beings. Being a high-level bodhisattva involves possessing a mind of great compassion conjoined with insight into reality, realizing emptiness, and/or the tathagatagarbha.

With this mind the practitioner will realize the final goal of full enlightenment, or Buddhahood: an omniscient, blissful mind completely free from suffering and its causes, that is able to work tirelessly for the benefit of all living beings. Six virtues or perfections (paramitas) are listed for the bodhisattva: generosity, patience, meditation, morality, energy and wisdom.

Many "philosophical" schools and sutras of Mahayana Buddhism have focused on the nature of enlightenment and nirvana itself, from the Madhyamika and its rival, Yogacara, to the Tathagatagarbha teachings and Zen.

Compassion

Compassion, or Karuna, is the other key concept of Mahayana, and is considered the indispensable complement to enlightened wisdom. Compassion is important in all schools of Buddhism, but is particularly emphasized in Mahayana. It relies on the idea that excess acquired merit can be transmitted to others.

The bodhisattvas are the main actors of compassion, Avalokitesvara being foremost among them. Although having reached enlightenment, bodhisattvas usually make a vow to postpone entering into nirvana until all other beings have also been saved. They devote themselves to helping others reach enlightenment.

The Mahayana idea also that salvation is universal allowed for one to focus less on the release of personal sufferring and more on humanity's salvation, and is consequently described to be more compassionate and caring for the welfare of others than other traditions of Buddhism.

A comparison between Hinayana (earlier Buddhist traditions) and Mahayana made by the 10th century Tibetan author Jé Gampopa in *The Jewel Ornament of Liberation* follows:

'Clinging to the well-being of mere peace' signifies the lower capacity [Hinayana] attitude wherein the longing to transcend suffering is focused on oneself alone. This precludes the cherishing of others and hence there is little development of altruism. [...] When loving kindness and compassion become part of one, there is so much care for other conscious beings that one could not bear to liberate oneself alone. [...] Master Manjushriikiirti has said: 'A Mahayana follower should not be without loving kindness and compassion for even a single moment', and 'It is not anger and hatred but loving kindness and compassion that vouchsafe the welfare of others'.

Salvation

"Devotional" Mahayana developed a rich cosmography, with various supernatural Buddhas and bodhisattvas residing in paradisiacal realms. The concept of trinity, or trikaya, supports these constructions, making the Buddha himself into a transcendental god-like figure.

Under various conditions, these realms could be attained by devotees after their death so that when reborn they could strive towards Buddhahood in the best possible conditions. Depending on the sect, this salvation to "paradise" can be obtained by faith, imaging, or sometimes even by the simple invocation of the Buddha's name. This approach to salvation is at the origin of the mass appeal of devotional Buddhism, especially represented by the Pure Land.

This rich cosmography also allowed Mahayana to be quite syncretic and accommodating of other faiths or deities. Various origins have been suggested to explain its emergence, such as "popular Hindu devotional cults (*bhakti*), and Persian and Greco-Roman theologies, which filtered into India from the northwest" (Tom Lowenstein, "The vision of the Buddha").

Mahayana Scriptures

The Mahayana scriptures were written probably around the 1st century BCE. Some of them, such as the Perfection of Wisdom sutras, are presented as actual sermons of the Buddha that had been hidden. By some accounts, these sermons were passed on by oral tradition, as with other sutras; other accounts state that they were hidden and then revealed several centuries later by some mythological route. In addition to sutras, some Mahayana texts are essentially commentaries.

Among the earliest major Mahayana scriptures attested to historically are the Perfection of Wisdom (Prajna-Paramita) sutras, the Avatamsaka Sutra, the Lotus Sutra, the Vimalakirti Sutra, and the Nirvana Sutra.

The Mahayana sometimes divide Shakyamuni Buddha's teachings into three general categories, known as "turnings of the wheel of dharma (truth)": the Hinayana, the Prajna Paramita, and the Tathagatagarbha teachings.

The Mahayana canon further expanded after Buddhism was transmitted to other countries such as China and Tibet, where the existing texts were translated. New texts, such as the Platform Sutra and the Sutra of Perfect Enlightenment were explicitly not of Indian origin, but were widely accepted as valid scriptures on their own merits. Other later writings included the Linji Lu, a commentary by Chan master Linji Yixuan. In the course of the development of Korean Buddhism and Japanese Buddhism, further important commentaries were composed. These included, for example, in Korea, some of the writings of Jinul, and in Japan, works such as Dogen's Shobogenzo.

Origins

Mahayana as a distinct movement began around the 1st century BCE in the area around the Kushan Empire (now part of Pakistan) before it was transmitted in a highly evolved form to China in the second century CE. Mahayana's exact origin is unknown, however, a number of common elements and background are suggested by various scholars and theologians. The Abhidharma in the modern Theravada Pali canon and a Sarvastivada Abhidharma composed in Sanskrit that survives in both the Chinese and Tibetan traditions, has no common order of composition. This indicates that overall, Buddhism became increasingly fragmented and that this might have led to a widening distance between laity and sangha, who were increasingly preoccupied with theological speculation. The Mahayana movement, on the other hand, was ecumenical, reflecting a wide range of theology from both the Sthaviravada and Mahasanghika sects.. Moreover, those who believe that Mahayana sutras were invented during this period speculate that the process of reshuffling sutras in terms of relevance to various Abbhidharma eventually led to editing itself. This process slowly eroded the taboo regarding the composition of new sutras.

Another important element is the lay practice of stupa devotion, which was actively encouraged by Ashoka. According to Akira Hirakawa (A History of Indian Buddhism: From Sakyamuni to Early Mahayana), stupas — which were initially mere monuments to Gautama Buddha — increasingly became the place of devotion and of spreading Buddhism to the masses, the majority of whom were illiterate Hindus. On the inside wall of the stupa, pictures were drawn or sculpted depicting the life of Buddha and his previous lives as a bodhisattva. This has given rise to devotion to the trancendent omnipresent and always-present Buddha and the bodhisattvas, distinct from the purely monastic sangha.

Epigraphical Evidence

One of the first known mentions of the Buddha using the word Bhagavat or Bhagavan ("Supreme Lord") is a dedication on a relic vase inserted in a stupa in Gandhara, written in kharoshthi by an Indo-Greek meridarch (civil governor of a province) named Theodorus in the 1st century BCE: *"Theudorena meridarkhena pratithavida ime sarira sakamunisa bhagavato bahu-jana-stitiye"*:

"The meridarch Theodorus has enshrined relics of Lord Shakyamuni, for the welfare of the mass of the people" (Swat relic vase inscription of the Meridarkh Theodoros). The earliest stone inscriptions containing recognizably Mahayana formulations and a mention of the Buddha Amitabha were found in the Indian subcontinent in Mathura and dated to around 180 CE. Remains of a statue of a Buddha bear the Brahmi inscription: *"Made in the year 28 of the reign of king Huvishka,... for the Buddha Amitabha"* (Mathura Museum).

Such inscriptions in Indian proper (Mathura) are rather late and few (the next known one is dated to the end of the 3rd century), in comparison to the multiplicity of Mahayana writings transiting from Central Asia to China at that time, and the involvement of Central Asian Buddhist monks, suggesting the focus of Mahayana development was probably in the northwest.

7

The Four Noble Truths in Buddhism

Mankind, pondering and disputing, has been engaged for so long in trying to find an answer to the enigma of existence, and so many first-class minds have been devoted to the task, that had the problem been open to solution by the intellect alone we should certainly have been furnished with the definitive blueprint of our being, beyond all doubt or conjecture, many centuries ago.

From the time when prehistoric myth became merged into an attempt to give a rational account of the universe the questions, 'What is life? How did it originate? Has it a purpose, and if so, what is it?' have haunted the imagination; yet still for most people they remain unanswered.

Reason has offered a wide range of ingenious possibilities from the speculations of the Eleatics down to the more sophisticated theories of the modern epiphenomenalists, but so far it has failed to provide any reasonable explanation that is not open to equally reasonable objections. And whilst reason has failed, its alternative, supernatural revelation, has shown itself equally contradictory and inconclusive, and has suffered an even worse defeat.

Its historical record has weighed heavily against it because of the disastrous influence it has often exerted in human affairs. The private revelations of mystics, by their exclusively subjective nature, can never offer more than an insecure foothold for faith in those who have not directly shared them, and a doubtful faith is the father of fanaticism.

The record of man's speculative thought down the centuries has come to resemble a maze of tracks in a boundless desert. The tracks can be identified by their characteristics; they are the tracks of religion, of philosophy, and obliterating many of these, the more recent tracks of science. For the most part the tracks of religion go round in circles. Beginning as myth they continue as myth hardened into dogma, and so go over the same ground in endless repetition.

Other tracks wander along aimlessly, drawn in this direction and that by new theories, new discoveries and new contacts, their path variable as the wind. These are the tracks of philosophy, the imprints of man's restless, inquiring mind—a mind which, despite its courage and adventurousness, has only the old material to work over and so is reduced to combining ideas in endless permutations, seeking to reconcile the irreconcilable and always failing to reach an end. Then, superimposed upon these there are the imprints of scientific thought, which has invaded philosophy to an ever-increasing extent, but which at the same time discourages any concern with ultimate issues, or with questions of value and purpose. Time and again the older tracks of philosophy and religion are seen to have crossed one another, and where they met there are signs of a scuffle. Too often, there is blood on the sands of history.

So it has been ever since man emerged as an animal capable of abstract thinking. Now we have entered a phase in which supernaturalism has given way almost entirely to scientific knowledge, and the approach to the problem is somewhat different. Yet science has not brought us any nearer to the answers. The tracks of thought still remain indecisive, their beginning a mystery, their end a mark of interrogation. Present day knowledge with its unprecedented accumulation of facts concerning the physical universe and the constitution of living organisms, has provided philosophers with a vast stock of new material to take into account, but so far the result has only been to give the mind more than it can handle.

Far from clarifying the general picture, the effect has been to overcrowd the canvas. To correlate the various specialized branches of knowledge is a stupendous task, and one that is further complicated by the areas of uncertainty in each of them. The non-specialist is seldom in a position to be able to separate theory from established fact in the scientific disciplines, and this is particularly so in the case of those which relate to the life-processes, such as genetics and biochemistry, and are therefore the most relevant to the inquiry.

Besides this, the facts that science presents often seem to point to opposite conclusions. Despite the great advances that have been made in physics, technology is still working to a great extent with factors that are not completely understood, or even satisfactorily defined. There are, for example, certain radiations forming the basic structure of the universe which appear both as waves and as particles, although logically they cannot be both at the same time. It is not even certain whether the expression 'at the same time' has any meaning in a universe where events can hardly be said to be simultaneous at all, and where the image of a star seen from a distance of many thousands of light years may be nothing more than the ghost of something that ceased to exist in space before man appeared on the earth. Expanding knowledge tends to cut us adrift from the apparent security of empirical facts, and in many ways the nature of thought itself has been brought into question.

There are people who entertain the hope that at some time in the not-too-distant future we may be able to get final answers to questions that have tormented men for generations by feeding all the relevant data into an electronic brain. But that hope is founded on two very large assumptions: first, that all the necessary data will eventually become available, and secondly that man can devise a machine more capable than its creator. So far, the most advanced electronic computer has not been able to do more in the field of mathematics than a human mind can do. It only does it more quickly. Even there it adds nothing new; there have been abnormal human brains that could extract cube roots with the same speed and accuracy. If a new and basically different mode of thinking is needed it must be sought for elsewhere than in electronic machines.

Does this mean that we shall never know any more about the ultimate things than we do now? The conclusions to which science moves at present are, in regard to the older beliefs, chiefly negative. They tell us what is no longer believable, but do not suggest alternatives or encourage any positive inferences. Yet in the quest for truth science contributes something of greater value than the facts it provides. It offers a method of inquiry, a disciplined use of the facts at hand, which is more productive than the pursuit of random theories. It indicates a method by which the data of experience, no matter how limited they may be, can be taken as starting points for a journey into unknown territory, and how from a few observed facts a general principle can be deduced.

Furthermore, it includes as an important part of its method the readiness to discard whatever theory is found to be in disagreement with the observed phenomena, and this iconoclastic function of science points to a truth of the highest significance, namely, that in the search for reality what is most essential is not the gathering and tabulating of facts, but the understanding of those facts in their true relation to one another, and the preliminary stripping away of hitherto accepted ideas until we are left with nothing more than the bare bones of experience, but that experience of the most fundamental and universal kind. Science works on theories, certainly, but is prepared to abandon them when they fall flat; it does not build model cosmologies from selected materials.

This method, which has been responsible for everything we can claim to have derived from our knowledge of the physical universe, is the only profitable one to follow when we seek to enlarge our understanding beyond the world of immediate sensory perception. And it is towards the possibility of such an extension that the psychological sciences are now turning. There is an increasing recognition of the truth that the world of external phenomena is only a part—and by no means the most important part—of man's total experience. What goes on within ourselves, in our psychological responses and motivations, and also on the intuitive levels of the mind, is being given the same analytical scrutiny as that which is turned on the objective features of the universe. For the first time, scientists are making a serious study of the mental processes, conscious and unconscious. They are giving equal attention to the paranormal aspects of the mind, such as the phenomena of telepathy, clairvoyance and the recollection of previous lives. From this may develop an entirely new approach to the problem of being.

A new one, that is, so far as the West is concerned. But nothing in mental science, or in philosophy, is really new. More than six hundred years before the Christian era, the tracks of speculative thought had reached a stage of the utmost complexity, in India. There we find the familiar arguments of mysticism versus rationalism, of empiricism, pragmatism, logical positivism, the opposing views of 'eternalism' and 'annihilationism', and of so many intermediate doctrines that it can be safely said that later philosophers have been able to produce nothing that was not a duplication or variant of one or the other of them. When we examine the sixty-two *di.t.this* or theories regarding the nature of life and the universe, which were current in the time of Gotama Buddha and described by him in the Brahmajala Sutta of the Digha Nikaya, we find there the seeds of all later thought, the archetype of every idea that has appeared in philosophy between Plotinus and Kierkegard.

That some of them were the doctrines of established schools which had been in existence long before the birth of the Buddha is evident from the accounts of the Buddha's own search for illumination, for on renouncing the world the prince-ascetic Siddhattha first placed himself under two teachers from among the many sects that were already laying claim to ultimate knowledge. Those teachers, Alara Kalama and Uddaka Ramaputta, were not logicians but exponents of yoga. As such they had their philosophy, but its final vindication was to be sought in the subjective realm, in an intensified perception outside the scope of formal reasoning. By the practice of *jhana*, or mental absorption, they had in fact succeeded in raising consciousness to a higher power.

But great as were the achievements of these two eminent yogis, the ascetic Gotama did not find the full enlightenment he sought in their systems. Neither did he reach it by way of the extreme asceticism to which he turned later. He found, on the contrary, that an entirely new mode of approach was needed if he were to break through the tangle of conceptual thinking on the one hand, and sublimated consciousness on the other. By the traditional yogic methods, he had gone beyond the world of forms, but not beyond that of ideas or the mere suspension of ideas. He found that the degree of illumination these methods gave was far from that of absolute knowledge and liberation. Thrown back on his own resources, with no longer any guiding principle except what he might find within himself, he returned in thought to the original impulse of his quest.

Its beginning, significantly enough, lay in a very early experience he had known, of an intuitive kind. He had been sitting watching his father, the king, carrying out the ritual of the spring ploughing. His attention had been caught and held by the flocks of birds that followed in the wake of the plough; they were eagerly scratching in the newly-turned furrows for worms and insects. Driven by hunger, the all-demanding hunger that is ever present in nature, and excited by the sight of their living prey, birds of all kinds were quarrelling and fighting one another, a noisy, turbulent mass of feathered bodies, striking and tearing with beak and claw, unmercifully.

A common enough sight, and one that carries no special meaning for most people. But to the young Siddhattha, it had been a troubling experience. So indeed it should be to anyone who believes in an overruling power, a Creator, whose chief attribute is love. Birds—among the most delicate and beautiful of nature's offspring, creatures so light and ethereal that when man thinks of spiritual beings it is with the wings of birds and something of their morning ecstasy that he pictures them—

those same birds that have been the poet's inspiration and the nature lover's joy, at close quarters are seen to be fully as rapacious and as cruel towards smaller creatures and to their owns species as the most ferocious of the larger animals. By such a slight transformation the winged angel becomes the winged tiger.

Yet, as the young Siddhattha saw even then, it could not be otherwise. Birds had to satisfy the urge to live, and for their food they had to prey on others and compete with others. So it was throughout nature, and from whatever particular the generalization was drawn it expanded into the same universal truth. Not only is nature indifferent to cruelty and pain, but it actually imposes them upon all living creatures as the condition and price of their existence. To inflict or to suffer; or both to inflict and to suffer—that is the law of life.

The peculiar insights of childhood, which often have an extraordinary clarity and depth, are too commonly lost when we become submerged in the world's incessant and implacable demands. As we accumulate knowledge we lose percipience; we know the fact, but its true inner meaning is estranged from us. So, regardless of the moral indifference of nature, men build and try to maintain systems of ethics, in the comfortable belief that in some way they harmonize with natural law and an underlying principle of goodness, call it God or what you will. But while doing so they are walking a tightrope stretched across a mocking abyss of negation. Woe to him who looks into that dark gulf and tries to find there the features of an omnipotent, all-merciful ruler of the universe! If he sees anything of the sort it will be only in his imagination, the reflection of an idea instilled into him by tradition.

If he sees nothing, he risks losing his balance. Unless he is strong enough to face this void, it is better for the tight-rope walker to keep his gaze fixed elsewhere, on some defined point in the sphere of action, and trust solely to the labyrinth organs, his own interior instruments of balance. His innate sense of right and wrong must be his support. It is not always a trustworthy sense, but for most intelligent people today it is all that is left. As for the theologian, in order to remain on good terms with the birds, he has to forget their private lives and admit only the idealized convention; let the angels have their wings, but not the beak or claws.

To most thinking people now, there is no longer any question of reconciling theology with reality. Not many, however, have the courage to face the facts and say, with the Existentialists, that 'the universe is absurd, because there is no reason for it to exist—no God has created it to declare his glory or serve as a dwelling-place for his creatures—and because nothing in it has any specific function to fulfil. Man has no destiny or privileged position, and not even the consciousness, which he has of himself, can save him from the universal absurdity of all created beings.' That disquieting knowledge lies like a cancerous growth in the background of man's mind, driven inwards yet injecting its poison into all that he says and does and believes in. Rationalism, humanitarianism and all the other substitutes that have been devised in place of the spiritual life lost to mankind are all essentially meaningless in face of the futility man feels, his sense of utter helplessness in an alien world. The Egyptians found no difficulty in worshipping a dead god, but modern man can only worship life.

When Siddhattha arrived at the most critical point of his quest, when all the traditional paths had been followed to their uttermost limits and still the truth beyond all truths had not been found, he recollected his early experience and what it had revealed to him. He remembered too that it had led him to another experience, on a different level of consciousness. At that time he had delved for the answer to the problem into the deepest layers of his being, for he knew instinctively that what he was seeing in nature was a true reflection of his own condition as a living, sentient organism doomed, like all others, to unceasing conflict. Each of us stands alone with each one's destiny, yet in another sense each is deeply involved with all others. If the solution to the world mystery was to be found anywhere it must be in the fullest, most intimate understanding of one's own nature.

So he turned his mind back to that incident in early life which had shown him his true path, to the glimpse he had had of a knowledge he possessed before creed and tradition claimed him. After his Enlightenment, the Buddha described it in these words:

"I recalled how once I was seated under the shade of a jambu tree while my father, Suddhodana, was ploughing the royal furrow, and having put aside desires and impure states of mind, yet cognizing and reflecting in the bliss born of detachment, I attained the first mental absorption. Could it be that this was the way to realization? With that thought the clear consciousness came to me: 'Yes, indeed, this is the way to realization.'"

Now the first mental absorption (*jhana*) is reached by purifying and tranquillizing the mind, which can be done by the practice of *anapana-sati*, contemplation of the breathing. The state of tranquillity is accompanied by joy and rapture, and in this jhana refined and calmed thought-conception and sustained thought are still present though no longer engaged with a multitude of objects, but exclusively in the subject of meditation. Having risen from that Absorption, the mind will be calm and concentrated, and being no longer disturbed by desires of the more active kind, it becomes able to examine the factors of experience with detachment, and so enjoys a new clarity of perception. It is as though the rippled surface of a pool were to become smooth and still. When that happens two things follow: the surface reflects external things more accurately, and at the same time it becomes possible to see through the surface to the depths below.

This is only the initial stage of the jhanic consciousness, which is progressive; but it opens the way to the succeeding levels. In these, the second, third and fourth absorptions, consciousness becomes more and more refined as the sensations of joy, the bodily perceptions, the reflex-perceptions and the remaining elements of self-awareness are discarded step by step. When the ascetic, Siddhattha, seated under the Bodhi Tree, remembered his first jhanic experience, he at once applied himself to inducing it once more, starting from the point of the first jhana that he had reached spontaneously on that occasion. Then, having attained tranquillity, he went on to apply mental concentration to the analytical examination of his own interior world—the body, the mind and the mental objects.

The technique of making the mind tranquil, known as Samatha bhavana, is the prelude to the cultivation of direct insight, or *vipassana-bhavana.* It is in the latter form of meditation that the mind finally penetrates the Four Noble Truths and so comes to distinguish reality from illusion. The ultimate truth is then seen 'face to face'. From being descriptive truths, that are merely grasped intellectually, the Four Noble Truths become known and understood and felt as certainties, on a new level of realization. In a quite indescribable way they become *experienced,* just as we experience the sensations within our own bodies, our thoughts and emotions—indeed, with an even greater force and reality than these.

Thus it was by intuitive penetration that Siddhattha attained Buddhahood after all other means had failed. He stood outside the limitations of the consciousness centred in an illusory self and was able to see through and beyond the cosmic processes, past the boundaries of space and time. At last, after those six years of arduous, agonizing and fruitless austerities, he was able to say, "I discovered that profound truth, so difficult to perceive, difficult to comprehend, tranquillizing and sublime; *which is not to be grasped by mere reasoning,* and is visible only to the wise (Majjhima Nikaya 26).

The truth he had penetrated was the fourfold division of knowledge, the basis of all that is comprehended in the term *nanadassana,* insight-wisdom. Expressed as the Four Noble Truths, it comes first in the Buddha's teaching and summarizes everything that follows. Concerning the first declaration of these truths, the Buddha said:

"The Perfect One, O Bhikkhus, the Fully Enlightened One, has established at Isipatana the supreme Kingdom of Truth, which none can overthrow—neither ascetic nor Brahman nor heavenly being nor fiend, nor god nor anyone whomsoever in the universe—by proclaiming, pointing out, revealing, setting up, explaining and making clear the Four Noble Truths.

And what are these Four Noble Truths? They are the Truth of Suffering, the Truth of the Cause of Suffering, the Truth of the Cessation of Suffering, and the Truth of the Noble Path that leads to the Cessation of Suffering."

Now these truths, as we shall see, are something quite different from the usual bases of religious belief; so different, in fact, that it has been questioned whether Buddhism is a religion at all. It has been disputed whether it is a philosophy, a code of ethics, a religion or a science. The fact is that it contains all of these and transcends them. Superlatively, it is the science of the mind. The Four Noble Truths crystallize the uniqueness of Buddhism and of the Buddha, for as the Teacher said:

"So long, O Bhikkhus, as the absolutely true knowledge and insight as regards these Four Noble Truths were not quite clear to me, so long I was not sure whether I had attained that Supreme Enlightenment which is unsurpassed in all the world ... But as soon as the absolutely true knowledge and insight as regards these Four Noble Truths had become perfectly clear to me, there arose in me the assurance that I had attained to that supreme, unsurpassed Enlightenment."

DUKKHA NIRODHA GAMINI PATIPADA ARIYA SACCA (THE NOBLE TRUTH OF THE WAY TO THE CESSATION OF SUFFERING)

'And what, O Bhikkhus, is the Noble Truth of the way that leads to the cessation of suffering? It is the Noble Eightfold Path, namely, Right Understanding, Right Intention, Right Speech, Right Action, Right Livelihood, Right Effort, Right Mindfulness and Right Concentration.'

The fourth Noble Truth outlines the practical means by which Nibbana is to be realized; but before announcing it the Buddha cleared away certain misconceptions which were current at the time and which had proved a serious hindrance to the quest for truth. In the first discourse after his Enlightenment, that delivered to the five disciples who had deserted him when he abandoned the path of self-mortification, he explained that there are two extreme courses to be avoided: on the one hand, that of sensual indulgence, which is "base, low, vulgar, impure and unprofitable," and on the other, the practice of extreme physical asceticism, which is "painful, impure, vain and unprofitable." In contrast to these stands "The Middle Path, which the Enlightened One has discovered; the Path which enables one to see and to know, which leads to peace, to discernment, to full knowledge, to Nibbana. Free from pain and torture is this Path, free from lamentation and anguish; it is the perfect path" (Samyutta, 56).

From the standpoint of modern psychology the Buddha's condemnation of extreme ascetic practices goes deeper than appears in the actual words he used. In certain forms of yogic asceticism still practised today there is an element of pathological self-hatred, perhaps also a masochistic pleasure in the experience of pain. Whatever the motive may be, such practices result in an inordinate preoccupation with the body, which instead of releasing the mind only fastens it more securely to its physical base. Around these manifestations of inverted sensuality there tend to gather constellations of obstructive ideas, such as that of a soul or spirit-entity distinct from the body and warring against it, the belief that the flesh is the enemy of the spirit and therefore a fit object of hatred, for which the spirit must be continually devising fresh tortures to bring it into subjection. Much the same attitude is found in the flagellations, the hair shirts, the prolonged fastings and the courting of martyrdom in early Christian asceticism. The body was the ever-present enemy; but an enemy is someone important, especially when one cannot get away from him. By being so regarded the body took on an independent life, and that a malignant one. Very often it hit back, with unpleasant psychological consequences.

But Buddhism eschews violence, to oneself as much as to another. The body must be brought under control, certainly, but by different methods. It is not itself the seat of the passions, but only the vehicle for them. It is in the mind that the citadel of craving must be stormed, not in that poor ox, the body, which only obeys its driver.

The Noble Eightfold Path, therefore, is a way of life that begins with the mind and ends with the mind transcended. Its first requirement is Right Understanding, which means an intellectual grasp of the nature of existence. 'What now is Right Understanding? Truly, it is to understand suffering, the cause of suffering, the extinction of suffering and the Way to its extinction' (Digha Nikaya 22). Elsewhere it is explained that it also means the understanding of the law of moral causality, the roots of meritorious and demeritorious action. In the Samyutta Nikaya it is also said that 'When one understands that body, sensation, perception, the mental aggregates and consciousness are all impermanent (and hence subject to suffering and devoid of selfhood), in that case also one possesses Right Understanding.

'What now is Right Intention? Truly it is intention that is free from greed and lust, free from ill-will, free from cruelty.' It is of two kinds: Right Intention concerned with the things of this world, which expresses itself in good actions bringing good worldly results; and Right Intention directed towards the higher path of purification, which has Nibbana as its fruit.

'And what now is Right Speech? Truly it is to avoid lying, and adhere to the truth; to abstain from tale-bearing and to promote harmony instead of dissension; to abstain from harsh language and cultivate gentle, courteous speech; and to avoid vain, irresponsible and foolish talk, speaking always in reasoned terms on subjects of value, such as the Dhamma of the Enlightened One.'

'And what now is Right Action? Truly it is to avoid the taking of life, to avoid theft and misappropriation, to avoid sexual intercourse with women under the protection of father, mother, brother, sister or relatives, married women, women under the ban of the king, engaged women and women who are the temporary wives of others. Now avoidance of killing, of theft and sexual intercourse with the prohibited classes of women is called mundane Right Action; it results in good worldly results (in this life or another). But the turning away from these things, the complete rejection of them with a pure mind intent upon the Path to deliverance—that is called transcendental Right Action and has its results in the paths and the fruits of purification.'

'And what now is Right Livelihood? Truly it is to reject wrong means of livelihood and to live by right means.' Here, wrong livelihood means gaining a living by slaughter or any other way detrimental to the welfare of sentient beings.

'And what now is Right Effort? Truly it is the Four Great Efforts (*sammappadhana*): the effort to avoid, the effort to overcome, the effort to develop and the effort to maintain.' The first is the effort to avoid the arising of evil, demeritorious states that have not yet arisen; that is to say, the arising of attachment on the presentation of sense-objects to the consciousness, from which greed and sorrow result. The second is the effort to overcome evil and demeritorious states that have already arisen through such causes. The third is the effort to develop good and beneficial states of mind conducive to enlightenment. The fourth is the effort to maintain these states when they have arisen, by perseverance, energy and endeavour.

'And what now is Right Mindfulness? Truly it is the contemplation of the Body, of Sensations, of the Mind and of Mind-objects. There, the disciple dwells in contemplation of the Body, of Sensation, of Mind and Mind-objects, ardent, clearly conscious and attentive, putting away worldly greed and grief.' This refers to the Four Stations of Mindfulness which is described as 'the only way that leads to the attainment of purity, to the overcoming of sorrow and lamentation, to the end of pain and grief, to the entering upon the right path and the realization of Nibbana.' (Maha Satipatthana Sutta).

'And what now is Right Concentration? Truly it is the absorption of the mind, the fixing of the mind upon a single object; this is Right Concentration.' The objects of concentration are the Four Stations of Mindfulness, and its prerequisites are the Four Great Efforts. 'The practising, developing and cultivating of these things constitute the development of Concentration.'

Each of the eight sections of the Path has a very precise meaning, a meaning that is related logically to the Buddhist philosophical and psychological system as a whole. Thus, Right View is something more definite than simply 'having good thoughts.' It stands for an intelligent grasp of the realities of life, in outline if not in detail. At the other end of the Path we come to Right Concentration, which signifies the transcendental state of consciousness, in which the truths that were formerly apprehended only by the intellect, and imperfectly, become the object of direct intuitional experience. It is only when this is attained that Right View itself is perfected. The eight sections of the Path are not to be taken seriatim or progressively, but are to be cultivated together, for the perfection of one can come only through the simultaneous development of each. Just as in the case of the links comprising the formula of Dependent Origination, the members of the Eightfold Path do not stand in a solely temporal cause-effect relationship to one another; they are to be considered as mutually-supporting factors also. Right Concentration develops and lifts on to a higher plane the knowledge that started as Right Understanding, and so the end is adumbrated in the beginning.

The path is conventionally divided into three parts: Sila (Morality), Samadhi (Concentration) and Panna (Wisdom). Right Speech, Action and Livelihood belong to Sila. Right Effort, Mindfulness and Concentration to Samadhi, and Right Understanding and Intention to Panna. A detailed discussion of Buddhist ethics is not possible in the compass of this work; it is sufficient to note that morality in Buddhism springs directly from the central concept of its philosophical system, the ultimate non-reality of self. The 'bad' or unwholesome deed is one that is self-centred and self-regarding, and so governed by greed or lust, animosity and delusion. The 'good' and meritorious is that which is selfless and inspired by benevolence and insight. Buddhist morality is not an arbitrary code of behaviour, tenuously attached to a theological system of doubtful worth, and subject to the exigencies of time and circumstance; it is rooted in principles that are universal and undeviating because they belong not to the changing world of events but to the inner world of psychological motive, which is a constant of human nature.

Where do craving and attachment come to an end? The Buddha's reply was that they come to an end where they arise—in the contact between the organs of sense and their respective objects, the things seen, heard, smelt, tasted, touched and conceived in the mind. When sensations are observed as bare experience, as empty phenomena having no relation to an experiencing 'self' and without awakening the discriminative responses, desire for them is cut off at its source. A process of dissociation takes place. So, in 'Contemplation of the Body' bare attention is directed to the body, considering it impersonally as a compound of physical elements unattractive in themselves as for instance, a hair in a dish of food. By analysing its constituents and dispassionately noting their repulsive aspects, attachment to the body is weakened and sooner or later, according to the degree of concentration achieved, it is eliminated. The body, instead of being viewed as an inferior and inimical 'self' is in this way seen to be precisely what it is: matter in momentary process of decay and corruption, the product of physical laws and past kamma.

The subjects of meditation, or more properly mental cultivation (Bhavana) are of various kinds suitable for different temperaments, but they all have one object, the realization of the voidness of phenomena, the essential voidness of the observer and the thing observed, which can only be arrived at by intense mental absorption. Now this voidness (*sunnata*) becomes fully comprehended when the jhanas, or states of absorption, have themselves been transcended:

'No longer giving attention to that (jhanic) consciousness he should now advert repeatedly in this way: 'There is not', or 'Void, void', or 'Secluded, secluded', and so give his attention to it, contemplate it and strike at it with thought and with applied thought.' Thus, 'The Bhikkhu who is devoted to the defining of the four Great Primaries immerses himself in voidness and eliminates the perception of living beings. Since he does not entertain false notions concerning (different kinds of beings), because he has abolished the perception of such beings, he conquers fear and dread, delight and aversion; he is not exhilarated by agreeable things nor depressed by disagreeable ones; and as one having great understanding he either attains the deathless or secures for himself a happy rebirth.' (Vism. XI. 117.)

DUKKHA NIRODHA ARIYA SACCA (THE NOBLE TRUTH OF THE CESSATION OF SUFFERING)

The Buddha's Enlightenment was attained in three stages. In the first watch of the night he acquired the knowledge of previous states of existence, the memory of which arose as the fruit of intense mental absorption (*jhana*). In the second watch he obtained the knowledge of the manner in which beings pass from one state of existence to another in accordance with their deeds. At this point he had discerned the truths of suffering and of moral causality as it operates through kamma. At the conclusion of the last watch he penetrated to the knowledge of the underlying causes of existence, the process of Dependent Origination. He then understood both the origin of conditioned existence, with its root in craving and ignorance, and the means by which the process could be brought to an end.

And in the last watch of the night, out of compassion for living beings, by fixing his mind on Dependent Origination and meditating on it both in order of becoming and in order of cessation, at sunrise he obtained supreme Enlightenment. And then he uttered these words of triumph, such words as countless myriads of Buddhas have spoken in the past:

Vainly have I wandered through many births, seeking the builder of this house. Painful indeed is repeated birth. Now, O Builder of the house, you are seen! Never again shall you build. All your rafters are shattered, the ridge pole cast down.

My mind has attained the unconditioned; the cravings are extinguished. (Dhammapada Comm and Dhammapada vs. 153-4)

The house is the body; the builder is craving, passions are the rafters and the ridgepole is ignorance.

'For, through the complete fading away and extinction of craving (*tanha*), clinging to existence (*upadana*) is extinguished; through the cessation of clinging the process of becoming (*bhava*) is extinguished; through the extinction of becoming, rebirth (*jati*) is extinguished, and through the extinction of rebirth, decay and death, grief, lamentation, suffering, sorrow and despair are extinguished. Thus comes about the extinction of this entire mass of suffering.'

'And thereby comes the cessation and overcoming of bodily form, of sensation, perception, mental formations and consciousness; this is the cessation of suffering, the end of disease, the overcoming of decay and death.' (Samyutta Nikaya, 12)

The cessation of suffering is Nibbana, in Sanskrit Nirvana, a word formed from the negative prefix *nir* added to the root *va*, which has the original meaning 'to blow.' In its Buddhist sense Nibbana means the cessation of the process of becoming, as when a fire goes out from lack of fuel or because of ceasing to blow on it. The fire is the threefold conflagration of lust, ill-will and delusion; when it ceases to burn because the fuel is withheld, the life-affirming impulses come to an end and there is no more rebirth. As experienced by the Arahat during the remainder of his natural life term it is *saupadisesa-nibbana*—the state of Nibbana in which the mental and physical aggregates still exist, but are no longer associated with clinging. It is absolute peace, tranquility and fulfilment:

'No anguish is there for him who has ended his journey and is freed from all grief, who is emancipated in every way and has destroyed all attachments. There are no more wanderings (in sa.msara) for such a one, who like the earth, has no resentment, is firm in character like a city gatepost and as pure as a deep pool free from mud ... Calm is the mind, calm the speech and calm are the actions of him who, rightly understanding, is wholly liberated and at peace.' (Dhammapada, Arahatta-vagga)

When the Arahat reaches the end of his life, the final cessation of his life-process (*samuccheda-marana*), he attains *anupadisesa-nibbana*; that is, the absolutely unconditioned Nibbana in which none of the factors of individualized personality remain. It is not the annihilation of a being, because in the true sense no being has ever existed; there has been only a process. Nibbana is the cessation of the process, the extinction of the aggregates of clinging that formerly gave rise to the phenomenal life-continuum. It is the only state in which suffering cannot find a foothold.

In the Dhammacakkappavattana Sutta the Buddha declares:

> *'This, Bhikkhus, is the noble truth of the cessation of ill: the complete cessation, giving up, abandonment of that craving, complete release from that craving and complete detachment from it.'*

Here, in the basic statement of Nibbana from the Buddha's first Discourse, we have the psychological state presented in terms that are ethically meaningful; they relate to an attitude towards the world and towards the contents of sensory perception. But what of the *nibbanadhatu*—that is to say, Nibbana considered in its own nature?

In that, its ultimate aspect, it is defined as *asaokhata-dhatu*, the Unconditioned, because it is not subject to change or conditionality; it is unitary, in the sense that it is not compounded, as are all phenomenal things. But to give it a precise definition in positive terms is not possible. All the terms of reference we use in thought and communication are founded upon things and ideas belonging to the realm of conditionality, so that we have no means of formulating an idea that is not related, by comparison or contrast, to some other idea. The whole content of our experience is a complex of relationships.

Thought swings continually between the opposites—light and dark, heat and cold, good and bad. All these are relative values representing oppositions or degrees of contrast, none of which has any real meaning apart from that relatedness. Since nothing in the world of sense-experience has any character except in relation to something else, the only way to regard the sensible world is as a sphere of merely relative reality.

It is certainly real on one particular level of awareness, the one on which consciousness normally functions (although, it must be noted, its nature as to details is not altogether the same for any two individuals), but on other possible levels of consciousness it must of necessity be quite unreal perhaps even nonexistent. The physicist sees the universe in terms of electronic forces, the mathematician reduces it to mathematical formulae; and while both have to deal with the world as though it really is what it appears to the ordinary man, their picture of it on the level of their work is something quite different. They have to live simultaneously in a world of the senses, taking it to be just as their sensory faculties report it to be, and in another world of the intellect, in which they know that the sensory picture is not a true one.

The information we receive has a kind of validity, but in the ultimate sense the picture formed from it is a product of sensory legerdemain. The 'solid' objects we see and feel consist more of space than of matter. This fact is demonstrated by the structure of the smallest atom known, that of hydrogen. In the hydrogen atom the distance of the electronic orbit from the nucleus is, relative to its size, twice the distance of the earth from the sun a matter of 96,000,000 miles.

On comparison, 'solid' matter contains more space than our solar system. What we cognize through the senses, therefore is not the 'thing as it is' but a relative aspect of it—relative, that is, to our own particular mode of consciousness. To say that the physical world as it appears to us is unreal or false, because it exists as a fact in our consciousness, but to say that it is real, as an external and objective reality, is even further from the truth.

This being so, it is clear that any thinking about Nibbana must be done without concepts, if such thinking were possible. The fact that it is not possible has given rise to some unfortunate misunderstanding.

Because he consistently refused to give any positive definition of Nibbana, and also declined to commit himself on such points as whether the world is eternal or not eternal, and whether the Arahat continued to exist in Nibbana or not, the Buddha has been called an agnostic. His reply to such questions was that they were wrongly put. They are in fact based on misconceptions regarding the reality or non-reality of the objects discussed and the terms of reference used in respect of them. Any reply given in positive or negative form would be about equally misleading. If this life were 'being' in the true sense, Nibbana would be non-being—annihilation. But that is not the case.

On the other hand, if this life were utterly unreal it would amount to non-being, in which case Nibbana would be absolute Being. If anything, this comes somewhat nearer the truth; yet it is not quite true. This life is not 'non-being,' for, the experience of suffering is real; and Nibbana cannot be called Being because it is not characterized by any of the features which we associate with 'being', such as the awareness of individual identity. It is devoid of selfhood.

The other questions are open to similar objections; they are inadmissible because they refer to states and predicates that have no real validity. The Buddha refused to answer them not because he did not know, but because he did not wish to falsify. One important point, however, is very definitely maintained: there is no place in the system for a Creator-god. The Buddha expressly condemned the idea of an overruling power, as leading to fatalism and inaction.

The questions that are called 'undetermined' (*avyakata,*) as well as that concerning the 'undeclared' (*anakkhata*) nature of Nibbana, are placed in their correct perspective by the Buddhist recognition of two kinds of truth; that is to say, conceptual or relative truth (*sammuti-sacca*) and absolute truths (*paramattha-sacca*) Conceptual truth embraces the sphere of relativity, its validity being conditional upon accepted modes of relationship, and also to a great extent on the laws of semantics. Thus when the Buddha said: (*attahi attano natho*) 'Self is the lord of self' (Dhp 160), he was using the word 'self' (*atta*) in its indispensable semantic role, as a word without which no thought of phenomenal personality can be expressed. In somewhat similar fashion we are constrained to say 'It is raining,' although we should find it difficult to define whether by 'it' we mean a cloud, the sky, or the sum of meteorological conditions. The personality, since it is a compound of ever-changing aggregates, a current of transition, has no noumenal existence. In the ultimate (*paramattha-sacca*) view, it is descriptively a current of events in the space-time continuum; while beyond the realm of description it does not exist in any sense. It is a merely conventional reality. It is necessary to reiterate this point because upon it hangs not only the Buddhist view of life but the concept of the ultimate goal.

It follows that a question framed in terms of relative reality cannot be answered in the same terms to give an answer that embodies absolute truth. In the ultimate sense, *paramattha-sacca* cannot be expressed at all; even the analytical descriptions of phenomena are only approximations to it, arrived at by eliminating the cruder misconceptions belonging to relative truth. It is that kind of 'descriptive' *paramattha-sacca* which is contained in the Buddhist ethico-psychological system, the Abhidhamma, where states of mind are dealt with, unattached to any concept of a persisting entity, in a manner that foreshadowed the trends of present-day dynamic psychology. There we find thought without a 'thinker' and action without an 'actor', both thought and action being no more than aspects of the life-flux of consciousness, just as they are in the philosophy of Henri Bergson.

Nibbana cannot be described; it can only be realized. And in its realization the problems connected with it, and with the nature of being in general, are not so much answered, as found to have been really nonexistent all along. They are unreal constructions, born of the mistaken belief that ultimate truth can be understood through conceptual thinking bound to the realm, and the terms, of sense-data. It is for this reason that the brave attempts of philosophers, profound and intricate though they may be, have never succeeded in giving a final and completely satisfying account of reality.

Notwithstanding the essentially incommunicable nature of the nibbanic experience, however, there are a great number of descriptive words applied to it in the Pali texts—words that have easily-understood value meanings and which convey the ideal of release from samsaric conditions in non-philosophical language charged with the poetry of aspiration. Nibbana, besides being the Deathless is the Further Shore (*para*), the Ageless (*ajara*), the Happy (*siva*), the Permanent (*dhuva*) and so on. But finally and always it is *anakkhata*, the Undeclared, and *asaokhata*, the Unconditioned. Seeking for the cause of cause we find only effect. The final Nibbana is the point at which cause and effect become identical, and by cancelling one another out, annihilate space, time and all the categories of thought.

'O Bhikkhus, of all the states, compounded or uncompounded, Liberation is the best—namely, the expulsion of pride, the relief of thirst, the uprooting of attachment, the cutting off of the round of birth and death, the extinction of craving, emancipation, cessation, the going out of worldly desire.' (A. II, 34.)

There is no lack of positive affirmation as to the reality of Nibbana. It is found wherever the Buddha contrasts the timeless and unchanging *asaokhata-dhatu* with the world of birth, decay and death, as he does in these words from the Udana:

O Bhikkhus, there is an Unborn, Unmade, Unoriginated, Unformed. Were there not such a state, Unborn, Unmade, Unoriginated, Unformed, there would be no escape from that which is born, made, originated, formed. But since, O Bhikkhus, there is indeed this, state of the Unborn, Unmade, Unoriginated and Unformed, there is truly an escape from the born, made originated and formed.

It is in such assurances as this that the reality underlying the third of the Four Noble Truths—the cessation of suffering as a positive goal—is brought most vividly before the mind.

DUKKHA SAMUDAYA ARIYA SACCA (THE NOBLE TRUTH OF THE CAUSE OF SUFFERING)

If this life were the only one through which we have to pass, if death were the end of joy and grief, alike, the existence of pain would have no special significance. The problem would be restricted to the practical means of alleviating it, so far as that might be possible. At the same time there would be no place for moral values in a life which originated fortuitously and pursued its course through a series of meaningless events to an equally meaningless end. The abstract concepts of good and evil, right and wrong could be discarded in favour of whatever artificial and arbitrary standards happen to suit the needs of the moment. In such circumstances it is conceivable that compassion itself would not rank very high in the scale of human values; for, logically the highest achievement would be personified by the individual who was most successful in avoiding suffering himself, even though he did so by inflicting it on others.

But mankind on the whole has never accepted this view. Although the conditions of nature are of a kind that outwardly at least give very little reason for assuming a moral order in the universe, man in principle has always behaved as though there were in fact some absolute values to be taken into account. He has an innate conviction of the reality of right and wrong, and even in violating the law he has acknowledged it. It is this instinctive belief in moral order that prompts us to seek a cause, conformable to our notions of justice, for the ills that afflict the world of sentient beings.

Buddhism takes for granted a system of moral law which requires a continuation of the life-process. It is a continuation by way of cause and effect, the cause being *kamma*, or volitional actions, and the effect *vipaka*, the pleasant, unpleasant or hedonically neutral experiences that follow from them. The moral equilibrium is maintained by the operation of an impersonal law which produces good results from morally wholesome thoughts, words and deeds, and bad results from those that are morally unwholesome. The succession of lives which the term 'rebirth' signifies is not the reincarnation of a soul-entity. It is an individual current of relationships in a cause-effect continuum, expressed as 'That having been, this comes to be.' Identity from one birth to another derives solely from this causal relationship, as it does in a single life-course when the child becomes the adult, the adult the octogenarian; its analogy is that of milk turning to curd, and curd to cheese. It is the purely conventional 'identity' that is found in the different phases of the protozoan and the atom.

In teaching that there is continuity after death in the form of a succession of rebirths Buddhism does not stand alone, but in agreement with many of the oldest religious traditions of East and West. The difference—an ontologically important one—lies in its treatment of the phenomenal personality, in which no single element of the five aggregates survives, but all are incessantly renewed in accordance with the universal rule that where a cause has existed a result must follow from it.

The doctrine of rebirth in Buddhism is frequently criticized on two grounds: that it is inconsistent with the principle of *anatta* (soullessness), and that it is a dogma at the root of a system which claims to be undogmatic. In regard to the first objection, a proper understanding of identity by way of causal connection as it appears in biological, psychological and even purely physical processes shows that the Buddhist dynamic concept of personality is the true one, and that it does not preclude the kind of identity which we commonly accept when we speak of the 'self.'

The second criticism on closer scrutiny is found to be quite unjustified. Leaving aside man's intuitive feeling that some part of his subjective awareness, of his individualized cognitive experience, if not his total personality, will survive death, and also the more important consideration that if there is indeed any principle of justice and moral order in the cosmos it can be found only in a law of moral retribution extending beyond the present life, there is a great and increasing mass of evidence to show that rebirth is a reality, and that it is possible in certain circumstances (for instance in hypnotic trance) to remember previous lives. The doctrine of rebirth is far from being an unsupported assumption.

It is a truth which is accessible to us in two ways: by reason of its necessity on teleological grounds, and directly through personal knowledge or the evidence provided by others. The sole 'common sense' objection to it—that one cannot personally remember a previous existence—falls to the ground when we consider the limitations of memory and the various circumstances which may impede and inhibit it. So far as heredity and other genetic considerations affect the question, they are not at all inconsistent with rebirth as it is understood in Buddhism. On the contrary, they provide a necessary part of the process by which mental energy produces organic life out of inorganic matter, and at the same time preserves the identity of species. Much that is still obscure in biological processes, such as the actual means by which hereditary characters are transmitted through substance that has only chemical properties, requires an additional factor to make it explicable. So too does an allied group of phenomena, the type of behaviour in animals, and to some extent in human beings, which is called instinctual. The persistence of such characters, for which biology provides no adequate explanation, becomes more intelligible when it is related to the Buddhist concept of a rebirth-continuum. Life is the outcome of two orders of causality the physical and the mental, and in the Buddhist view the genetic patterns through which hereditary characters are transmitted are the physical media of the mental energy conditioned by past kamma.

It was in the light of this knowledge of the continuity of existence that the Buddha looked for the origin of suffering not only in the current life but in former states of being. He discovered it in a primordial urge, the thirst (*tanha*) for sentient existence:

"What now is the Noble Truth of the Cause of Suffering? Truly it is that Craving which gives rise to fresh rebirth, and conjoined with pleasure and lust, finds gratification now here, now there. It is of three kinds: sensual craving (*kamatanha*), craving for existence (*bhavatanha*) and craving for self-annihilation (*vibhavatanha*)."

Sensual craving, which is generated by contact of the organs of sense with their objects, is sixfold: craving for pleasurable sights, sounds, odours, tastes, tactile sensations, and mental impressions. These are known as the fields (*ayatana*) of sense-perception. The craving for existence takes three forms, corresponding to the spheres in which life manifests; that is, craving for existence in the sensual spheres (*kama-loka*), in the fine-material spheres (*rupa-loka*) and in the formless spheres (*arupa-loka*) or mental planes. The craving for self-annihilation is the group of desires that accompany the erroneous view that the aggregates of phenomenal personality constitute a soul, which is annihilated at death.

In another classification craving is considered under two heads: *va.t.ta-mula-bhuta-purima-ta.nha*, the primordial craving which is at the root of rebirth, and *samudacarata.nha*, craving manifested in conduct. The first is the craving which promotes and sustains the round of existences, as it appears in the formula of Dependent Origination. There, "Conditioned by ignorance (of the true nature of existence) arise the kamma-formations (*saokhara*); conditioned by the kamma-formations arises consciousness (in the special sense of rebirth-linking consciousness, the mental impulse which like an electric spark bridges one life-continuum to another); conditioned by consciousness arises mind and body (of the new life-sequence); conditioned by mind and body arise the six fields of sense-perception; conditioned by the six fields of sense-perception arises contact (between organ of sense and sense object); conditioned by contact arises sensation (*vedana*), conditioned by sensation arises craving; conditioned by craving arises grasping (confirmed and habitual craving), from grasping arises becoming (the life-impulse); from becoming arises birth once more and from birth come decay and death," thus closing the circle. The formula of Dependent Origination in this way summarizes the causal relations of three cycles, a past, a present and a future life, with craving as the motivating factor.

"Thus it is, Ananda, that craving comes into being because of sensation" (Maha Nidana Sutta). But for the sensation to exist there must already be mind and body, and that mind and body itself must have been brought about by prior craving, so that the sequence of cause and effect extends infinitely into the past. This is precisely the idea which Dependent Origination presents; it is a system of related conditions rather than of temporal sequence, and actually stands for two modes of causality, serial and contemporaneous. The divisions of past, present and future may be placed indifferently at either of the two points where a new arising takes place; that is, at 'mind and body' or at 'birth'. But the points at which it can be brought to an end are, as we shall see later, the two dominant psychological factors, 'craving' and 'ignorance', which are contemporaneous and mutually supporting.

The question of a First Cause does not enter into the Buddhist view of the cycles of becoming (Samsara), nor of the universe. When the process of incessant arising and passing away is seen as a complex of interrelated conditions, any theory of a primal cause becomes irrelevant. In the logic of causality there can be no absolute beginning, for each cause is seen to be the effect of a preceding cause. So a Creator God must himself have had a creator; if he had not, the argument for his existence on the basis of causality collapses. The idea that there must have been a beginning in the ultimate sense rests upon a defect in human understanding, as certain modern philosophers have pointed out. We are brought to the position stated in the *Visuddhimagga*, that:

"No God nor Brahma here is found,
Creator of Samsara's round;
Empty phenomena flow on
Subject to cause and condition."

From another standpoint it can be said that the act of creation is taking place from moment to moment, as in the Bergsonian system of creative evolution. The prime mover is the craving impulse, which may be regarded as the basic energy of the universe.

This does not mean that the universe in its present form had no beginning. It came into existence in accordance with natural law (*niyama*), but it did not originate out of nothing. It is not the first or only system of its kind, but is one of an infinite cyclic series, of which no beginning can be found. As one cosmic system comes to an end another one comes into being.

Science offers several tentative theories as to how the present universe began, the two most widely accepted being based on the expanding universe hypothesis and the steady state cosmology respectively. Its 'beginning' can be placed with a fair amount of certainty at about 5,000 million years ago. But whether it started with a tremendous cosmic explosion or in some other way, Buddhist cosmic analysis holds that the matter, or energy, of which it is formed, derives from that of a previous universe, and that it was set in motion by the kamma of the beings belonging to that former system. The evolution (*samvatta*) and devolution (*vivatta*) of world systems follow a course parallel to the process which governs sentient life. When a cosmic system comes to an end, the matter of which it was composed disintegrates and its atomic units become dispersed or compressed in space in a uniform distribution.

For aeons it lies dormant, but in course of time the suspended energy becomes active once more, and the physical laws of attraction and repulsion come into play. Clots of matter begin to form, and from them the island universes emerge and take shape. After a further lapse of time, organic evolution begins, and runs its course to the end of the cycle, when the cosmic structure again disintegrates and the entire process is repeated. In this fashion evolution and devolution follow one another in a ceaseless round, all the time bound up with the kamma, or volitional energy, generated by living beings. And since all willed action is motivated by desire it is in literal fact the force of craving that perpetually renews and sustains the process.

Concerning the genesis of craving, the *Abhidhamma-tthasaògaha* VIII.I says:

> *"Through ignorance a being fails to understand the impermanent and 'substanceless' nature of existence as it truly is. He enjoys the things of the world, taking them to be real and lasting, and so creates a craving for them. On account of his cravings he seeks to obtain one and avoid the other. This leads to the continuity of his life-process, a chain of struggle for living. His craving and grasping do not end with the destruction of the physical body, but keep the struggle on in another birth.*
>
> *His good and bad activities (*saokhara*) of one life determine the type of his birth, his mental disposition and all his resultant consciousness in the subsequent one. This gives rise to the mental and physical aggregates in the new life according to its own nature. Depending on the mental and physical aggregates he acquires the six fields of sense-cognition. Depending on the six fields of sense-cognition he gets contact with the object of sense. The contact produces sensation; the sensation gives rise to craving, and craving to grasping. Grasping continues the life-processes. It does not cease with the death of the being, but flows on in the next birth. Thus he starts a new life again; he becomes old and dies, experiencing all kinds of grief, lamentation, suffering, anxiety and despair. Perpetually he moves on and on in the round of birth and death so long as he is in the bondage of ignorance."*

Man's failure to comprehend the universe is due to the primal nescience (*avijja*) which to a greater or lesser degree governs all conceptual thinking. Since *avijja* is linked with *tanha* it deepens as the mental defilements caused by craving increase, lessening as they are reduced. It is an invariable rule in the Buddhist system of causal relations that two or more factors are required to produce a given result. As we have seen, in the genesis of a living organism the mental energy produced in a past life combines with the physical processes of biology to form a sentient being. Similarly, in the genesis of world systems the total thought-energy of beings from the past activates the physical substance of the universe to bring about a new cycle of evolution. All these processes, therefore, are partly mechanistic ones, to the extent to which they depend upon purely physical laws, and partly are subject to variability through their dependence on mental causes and the intervention of will. To will is to desire, and so desire is really the chief determining factor; if it were not present at all the automatic processes of nature would take control and the universe would run its course to the end as a lifeless mechanism.

The constant pattern of interdependence is shown in the arrangement of the factors in Dependent Origination, where those that are conditioned by past causes alternate with others that are subject to modification by the act of willing. Thus, in the section relating to past causes, Ignorance gives rise to volitional thought and action (*saokhara*), the Ignorance factor being a continuing influence on the thought and action. Then, at the time of death a thought-moment arises which constitutes the rebirth-linking consciousness, its nature being determined by the volitional thought and action which preceded it. So past kamma shapes future tendencies, the rebirth-linking moment of consciousness carrying these tendencies into a new life just as the germinal seed carries in its chemistry the pattern of the future plant—a pattern that may, however, be altered in some respects by subsequent events.

The new mind and body thus brought into being is naturally equipped with the sensory apparatus and the fields of sensory perception appropriate to it. From these come its contacts with the external world and the sensations accompanying them. So far, the connections have represented two belonging to the order of past causality, Ignorance and the Volitional Mental Formations, and five which are their resultants, from Rebirth-linking Consciousness to Sensations. These last five, therefore, are conditioned by the kamma of the past.

But at this point the element of free will comes into play, for while sensations are predetermined as to their nature, the mental responses to them are not. Although ordinarily the response to a pleasant object is desire, which may prompt some action, if the moral sense tells us that the action is a bad one, the will can prevent it. Even the desire itself can be reduced, suppressed and controlled by an act of will or by diverting attention to something else. Consequently, the dependent connections which follow from this point, that is, Craving, Grasping and Becoming are not predetermined. They represent the active side of the picture, in which man shapes his individual destiny.

It is necessary to stress this point because it is often mistakenly believed that the doctrine of kamma is fatalism. Nothing could be further from the truth; Buddhism emphasizes above everything else the moral responsibility of the individual and the power that is his to create his own destiny. So in the last two connections, birth (rebirth) and decay and death, we find summarized the future resultants of the causes generated in the Craving-Grasping-Becoming series.

Considered from the standpoint of temporal sequence, Dependent Origination is thus divided into three sections, relating to past, current and future life. These three have two major divisions: the active order of becoming (*kammavatta*), in which causes are generated, and the passive order (*vipakavatta*), which stands for the results of those causes. Ignorance and volitional mental formations belong to the active order, whilst Birth and Decay and Death belong to the order of passive resultants. The middle section, that which deals with the current life, includes both the passive and the active orders. The five links from consciousness to sensation are passive resultants; but the remaining three, craving, grasping and becoming, represent the active, and creative process.

Again, at the beginning, ignorance and volitional mental formations are a summary of the active and causal process in the past; at the end, decay and death summarize the passive resultant series as it follows in the future. Thus the circle closes on itself in perpetual, self-sustaining operation, a cause-effect complex, the links of which can be considered either as a temporal sequence or as existing concurrently in the form of mutually supporting factors.

Understood correctly, the process of Dependent Origination does not postulate either absolute causal determinism nor absolute freedom of will. It describes an interplay of conditions which is ultimately subject to the individual's freedom of choice between good and bad courses of action. It is by this choice—the anguish of decision, which is itself a form of dukkha that life imposes on all morally responsible beings—that each individual determines for himself and by himself the nature of his rebirth. Whether it shall be in a state above the human condition or in one below it, or, if it is a human rebirth, whether it shall be a happy or an unhappy one, depends entirely on the actions—of body, speech and mind—that are being performed here and now. It depends, in short, on the degree to which craving is brought under control. And, as we shall presently see, Buddhism offers a means whereby craving can be entirely eradicated, and the process of Dependent Origination brought to an end for good.

But before moving on to the third stage of the inquiry, which is concerned with the possibility of escape from the round of rebirths, another function of craving is worthy of notice: that is, the part it plays in organic evolution.

We have already noted that apart from the Buddhist interpretation, life appears to be devoid of ethical values and purpose. Yet in the evolving pattern of organic structures it seems to display a strong directional trend. From extremely simple unicellular organisms nature has evolved highly complex forms, equipped with delicate sensory apparatus and a brain capable of rational thought. But this has been accomplished only over a long period of trial and error involving many failures, and by employing methods that are both wasteful and productive of the most extreme suffering, such as would have been eliminated in a better designed plan. So on a general survey the system seems to be in a certain sense directed, yet at the same time blundering and inept. There is sufficient order to suggest a creator; but an omnipotent and benign Intelligence could certainly have accomplished the work in better style. Science fights shy of teleological theories and concentrates attention on the means by which natural effects are produced; and so we have hypotheses such as that of natural selection, backed up by the observed facts of genetics, bio-chemistry and kindred sciences, which go some way towards explaining the *modus operandi* of evolution but do not offer any suggestion as to the 'why' of the process. The moving force behind or within it remains a mystery, and the paradox of a plan, apparently well conceived as to its biological results but very badly executed, and without any purpose except that of evolution for evolution's sake, has come to be considered so insoluble as to discourage further speculation.

An entirely fresh light is thrown on the problem, however, by recent studies that have been made of the electrical activity in the brain, as registered by the electroencephalogram. These have established definitely that the neural impulses and the processes of cognition are associated with electrical impulses.

Now if the brain functions by means of electrical energy—or, what is equally likely, by some other form of energy that acts in the same way as electricity—and is able to move the mechanism of the electroencephalogram solely by impulses generated in the brain cells, we have strong reason for supposing that mental activity is capable of spreading from its source in much the same way as do radio waves. It is in fact a radiating energy comparable to others that are perceptible to us, such as light and sound, and others—imperceptible, such as cosmic radiations. This would at once explain such diverse phenomena as hypnotism, telepathy and various forms of extrasensory perception. But the possibilities it opens up become still wider when we apply the hypothesis to organic evolution, and clearer still when we connect it with the Buddhist concept of craving as an actual force, generated by the mind and capable of operating on and through the physical substance of the universe.

The psychology of behaviourism holds that desire, manifesting as the 'will-to-live,' is the basic motivating urge in all forms of life that have analyzable mental reactions. The desire may be unconscious, revealing itself in instinctive patterns of behaviour, or it may be fully present to the conscious mind. When it lies beneath the surface of consciousness it functions as the Freudian 'id' and the 'libido' of Jung; that is, as the energy resident in all instincts. It may also be called the primordial life-urge; but whatever name may be given to it, in reality it is the force of craving—precisely that *tanha*, which the Buddha declared to be the root cause of rebirth.

Every volitional act is motivated by some kind of desire; consequently, thought itself is practically inseparable from desire in the mind still dominated by ignorance. And it is the thought-impulse that radiates outwards in the last moment of consciousness which gives rise to another psycho-physical organism, thus renewing the sequence of cause and effect in a fresh life-continuum. Throughout the creative process the urge that maintains this perpetual renewal of energy is the desire to experience conscious life, 'seeking, now here, now there,' for satisfaction.

In the first stages of evolution the individualized yet impersonal currents of craving, generated in the past, operate upon the physical substance of the universe and out of inorganic matter give birth to the first single-cell protozoa. From there the life energy proceeds to build up and elaborate, by the familiar trial and error methods we have noted, more and more complex and specialized forms, the craving-impulse being transmitted through the currents of 'rebirth' and the laws of genetics by parallel and complementary processes. Wherever the necessary chemical constituents of life exist together with the suitable conditions, life in some form manifests itself; and this principle obtains, as Buddhism has always taught, throughout the innumerable worlds that exist simultaneously in the universe.

So out of material from various sources, we are able to construct a picture that is teleologically satisfying and fully in conformity with the known facts. To summarize: it was under the domination of the craving-urge that the rudimentary forms of life evolved into the complex structures of the higher animals and man. More and better sensory organs were needed to satisfy the unconscious craving for sense-experience, and so the vital urge worked through the processes of biological evolution to produce them. Life is not the work of a conscious creator, with his object fully in view; it is the result of a blind, groping force, transmitted from one living being to another in the course of rebirth. Hence the many 'mistakes' thrown aside in the course of evolution—animals, which, through over-specialization or some other cause, became unfitted to their environment and consequently died out.

Science as yet has no valid theory to account for the purposive factor in evolution, nor for the persistence of instinctive behaviour patterns in those birds and animals which perform quite complicated operations such as nest-building, seasonal migrations and so forth, without the necessity of learning. Neither can it decide the much-disputed question of whether acquired characters are genetically transmitted, many geneticists feeling compelled to deny it, against the evidence of observation, solely on the ground that no biological mechanism can be found answering to the requirements of such transmission. Here again Buddhist doctrine comes to the rescue, for it shows how both instinctive behaviour and acquired characters can be transmitted by the re-arising again and again of the same current of identity—that is, 'rebirth'—within the same species, the same ethnic or cultural group and even the same family. For whatever tendencies are acquired and cultivated in one life, whether of animal or human being, will make themselves apparent in subsequent lives, until some fresh impulse of kamma diverts the life-current into a new channel.

Buddhism teaches that the distinction between human and animal life is not one of kind, but of quality, Man is not a distinct and special creation; he merely represents the highest peak to which organic life has reached on this planet. Man alone has the power of moral choice, whilst animals are merely suffering passively the results of past activities dominated by lust, ill-will and delusion. In other words, they are the products of former bad kamma. Their individual life-currents remain on a low level until the particular mental tendencies that produced them have run their destined course. When the results of the bad kamma are exhausted some residual good kamma from a former human life, of which all beings have a latent unexpended potential (*katatta-kamma*), comes into play and the life-current emerges on a higher level once more. This process can be understood only by discarding the idea of an individual self-entity, call it soul or what one may, and thinking instead in terms of the current of 'becoming' which Buddhism insists is all that constitutes the rebirth-continuum. By thus bridging the gulf that appears to exist between the human and animal worlds, the Buddhist doctrine of rebirth and kamma gives to life that organic unity which scientific thought demands. At the same time it shows that the universe, despite its seeming purposelessness, is in reality the manifestation of moral and spiritual law.

Thirty-six streams of craving are recognized in Buddhist psychology; eighteen of them internal (*ajjhatta*), depending upon subjective concepts, and eighteen external (*bahira*), associated with subject-object relationships. But every type and degree of craving contributes to the sum total of the grasping which fastens living beings to the wheel of rebirth. This is especially true of the lower forms of craving connected with the unwholesome mental concomitants: lust, ill-will and delusion. So we find in the Aoguttara Nikaya (III, 33): 'Where so ever beings spring into existence, there their deeds will ripen; and wherever their deeds ripen there they will gather the fruits of those deeds, be it in this life, or be it in the next life, or be it in any future life.'

And in the Samyutta Nikaya comes the solemn affirmation:

> *'There will come a time when the mighty ocean will dry up, vanish and be no more. There will come a time when the mighty earth will be consumed by fire, perish and be no more. But yet there will be no end to the suffering of beings who, fettered by ignorance and ensnared by craving, are hurrying and hastening through this round of rebirths.'*

DUḲKHA ARIYA SACCA (THE NOBLE TRUTH OF SUFFERING)

The Buddha formulated the first truth in the following words, which run like a recurring theme through the Buddhist scriptures:

"What, Bhikkhus, is the Noble Truth of Suffering? Birth is suffering; decay is suffering; death is suffering; sorrow, lamentation, pain, grief and despair are suffering. To be separated from the pleasant is suffering; to be in contact with the unpleasant is also suffering. In short, the five aggregates of Existence connected with attachment are all suffering."

This is often interpreted as a fundamental attitude of pessimism, even of despair, in the Buddhist outlook. It does so appear, for instance, in the use Schopenhauer made of oriental ideas in his philosophy. There is a tendency to see it as being in opposition to the vigorous, life-affirming attitudes of the West.

If the first Noble Truth were the whole of the Buddha's message there would be ground for the objection. And if it is insisted that Buddhism should fit into one or other of the pessimistic or optimistic, life-denying or life-asserting categories of thought there would, on this truth alone, be little choice as to which it should be. But in the Buddhist view there is no justification for preferring one pole of thought to another; what is required is that the view of life should be objective, unbiased and realistic.

The first Truth is drawn from a critical examination, not only of the human predicament but of all aspects of the life of sentient beings. Its acceptance involves a correction and readjustment of the usual perspectives. It then appears as the recognition of a universal symptom, one that is normally disregarded only because it is a chronic condition. The Buddhist emphasis on it is the essential preliminary to diagnosis and treatment; it is the stage at which the physician tells the patient that he is ailing.

But it is not to be supposed that the first truth as formulated denies the existence of joy and laughter. It stresses the evils of life to counteract man's natural inclination to dwell on the pleasant and ignore and forget everything disagreeable—that psychological device by which the will to live is maintained despite the most discouraging experiences. At the same time it is a reminder that whilst at any given moment we may personally be enjoying what we call happiness there are incalculable numbers of sentient beings that are in misery, a reminder of which most people are continually in need. And in speaking of happiness it is useful to remember that while many people feel reluctant to admit the overwhelming preponderance of suffering in life, comparatively few are capable of true happiness on their own account. Their only refuge from reality is in pleasure.

The Buddha said that he himself had known both pleasure and pain in their most extreme forms. If life were unrelieved misery, no one would feel desire to continue with it, while if it were unalloyed happiness, there would be no need for the remedy which religion seeks to provide. It may be added that in a world of ideal happiness and security, one of the hypothetical Utopias that men have dreamed of and which, incidentally, each dreamer constructs according to his own peculiar ideas of perfection, so that scarcely any two of them have features in common, there would be no incentive for effort of any kind. It is only where the adverse conditions of the world, as we know it, prevail, where good and evil, virtue and vice are in perpetual conflict, that man's noblest endeavours could be born. It is only in such a world, in fact, that these opposites could exist at all. And so far as the Utopias are concerned, human beings exhibit such a diversity of tastes, inclinations and desires that it is rather childish to suppose that any ideal society, which must necessarily be uniform, could ever confer happiness on all its members.

We hear much today about anxiety-neuroses as a part of modern, urban civilization, and they are real enough, but there is another side of the picture as well. Man's nature, balanced between the primitive and the civilized, needs the alternation of states of consciousness. Even too much freedom from anxiety is alien to human nature, as the so-called affluent societies are beginning to show.

The increase in crime, and particularly juvenile delinquency, the outbreaks of racial persecution and revolt against the established order are due as much as anything to the fact that the affluent society gives too much leisure to those who do not know how to use it, too much security to those whose natures demand risk and excitement, and too much orderliness to those who can express themselves only in violence. All these conditions are unnatural to perhaps the majority of men; the teenage boy, who joins in mass hooliganism, converts the highways into racing tracks or plays chicken with automobiles and trains, is only giving outlet to the primordial urge to face danger and assert himself against it. His self-esteem cries out for the thrill of conflict and the hazards that a too protective society denies him.

For the most part, man is still a primitive fighting animal; if it were not so, war would automatically have been abolished long ago. Augustine of Hippo said that all men desire peace, but all desire it in their own way. He was only partly right; all men want peace, but they also want it to be a kind of war. That is the unrecognized, 'unadmitted' fact behind all the talk of world peace at international conferences and in intellectual humanist circles: in the realm of his unconscious, man craves for the triumphs and pains of conflict.

The unrelieved boredom of eternal heavenly bliss would not suit man as he is now constituted. If suffering did not exist he would be obliged to invent it. Recognizing this fundamental fact of human personality, Buddhism attaches no importance to heavenly states, for it acknowledges that while the elements of personality with all their necessary imperfections continue to exist, an eternity of happiness would be insupportable. Without its opposite, happiness would have no meaning.

It is a worthy aim to strive for the improvement of worldly conditions and the perfection of the welfare state; yet there is a point beyond which it cannot be carried without leading either to internal disruption or some form of totalitarianism. The notion that a perfect human society can be evolved has taken the place of the hope of heaven which formerly prompted men to labour for their own perfection; and it has already given birth to more persecution and suppression of liberty than ever came out of the Inquisition. A perfect society cannot be fashioned by man who is imperfect; and if such a society were possible, man as he is would not fit into it. The historian and the anthropologist know that this is so, but unfortunately the demagogues are stronger. In a world ruled by the most vociferous elements, political and commercial, the individual is given little opportunity to seek one's own salvation. The only self-development he knows is the process of acquiring information which today goes by the name of education.

The implications of the Buddhist truth of suffering are considerably more than appear in the bare words of the formula. That birth (or as Buddhism defines it, the perpetual process of arising) is painful, and that mental and physical decay, with their culmination in death, are unavoidable evils, is a self-evident fact. But their evil is not only in their actual occurrence; it extends beyond it, for at every stage of life, man is overshadowed by the thought of them, as he is by the threat of sickness, accidents, bereavements and other misfortunes of greater or lesser likelihood. Whatever attitude of disregard he may adopt towards these threats to his peace of mind, it can never be anything more than a very fragile shield against possibilities that are too disturbing to contemplate. These vicissitudes are inseparable from life, and one who tries to ignore them is the true escapist. To be positively life-affirming it is these facts above all others that we must be prepared to assimilate into our Weltanschauung.

The realistic philosopher of today has good reasons for his pessimism. His mechanistic universe has no place for human values, for hopes of individual fulfilment. He takes the same direct and disillusioned view of life as that presented in the Buddhist truth of suffering, but he knows nothing of the remedy.

For him there is no assurance of any higher truth, no relief from the oppressive actualities that surround him in a cosmos apparently hostile, or at best indifferent, to man and his aspirations. A certain pride in his heroic despair may sustain him, and yet in his heart he may envy those who can still make the choice of faith against reason, and like Kierkegard, believe in a religion that is impossible because it is impossible.

Buddhism accepts the scientist's comfortless picture of the universe, but with a difference. In the Dhamma, both a higher truth and the means of realizing it are present as vital and knowable facts, and it is this which lifts the realistic outlook into the realm of hope. The dialogue between Buddhism and scientific thought is only just beginning, and as it develops it may result in a number of new and significant interpretations.

So far as the ordinary man is concerned, the loss of faith in traditional religious systems has left a spiritual vacuum which can be filled only by preoccupation with material improvements, or else by the never-ending struggle for some cause or other—the kind of struggle in which so often what is right and just becomes imperceptibly twisted into injustice, and the means become unworthy of the goal. For those who have seen the pitfalls there is nothing left but a resigned submission to whatever the world may impose. Yet man cannot endure a life that is entirely without values; if they are not to be found in nature he is under a compulsion to create them artificially. This is seen even in science where, as Conant has pointed out, value judgments intrude themselves at every turn. When we are forced to apply these value judgments to life itself, it as disconcerting to find that while the general scheme is apparently as devoid of ultimate purpose as it is of moral imperatives, the pain and misery with which it is fraught having no discernible end to serve, it is just those unpleasant features that predominate in man's total experience. An optimistic philosophy on late nineteenth century lines is hardly conceivable today. Even the possibility of one that is pragmatically constructive becomes more remote as humanity drifts helplessly from triumph to triumph in the conquest of nature. In the grip of nuclear politics and on the verge of gaining possession of the moon, most people find it best not to ask themselves what the word progress really means.

Literature and the arts tend to reflect the same bleak mood as contemporary philosophy. It is true that after *The Waste Land*, T. S. Eliot came to terms with religion, and Aldous Huxley's brittle and erudite wit turned to syncretic mysticism, but the note that had been struck continued to echo in their work and that of others. A later school of writers tried to find a substitute for the lost religious spirit in political attitudinizing, producing a certain effervescence but scarcely anything of real depth or enduring value. For the most part, literature at present has little to offer to mitigate the unpleasant aspects of life that it presents.

Formerly, the stock lament of the poet that joy quickly turns to grief, and the Elizabethan dramatist's concern with the night side of the soul were bearable, because they contained no foreboding of a final oblivion. For the effectiveness of his soliloquy it was necessary for Hamlet to picture death as the bourn from which no traveller returns—but he had in fact just seen his father return from it. Thus there was sadness, and a great deal of sheer horror in classic tragedy, but not the chill at the heart, the twentieth-century shudder at the stark futility of life, which the nihilism of today has given us. When man felt that suffering had meaning he could endure it; his suffering then provided the great underlying fact of all the finest art and literature, the truth that gave it depth and meaning. It is in the tragic that we recognize man's being, his commitment to the total human situation and his identification with all involved in it.

"There are three kinds of suffering," the Buddha said. "They are intrinsic suffering of mind and body (*dukkha-dukkhata*), the suffering of the aggregates (*saokhara-dukkhata*) and the suffering of transience (*viparinama-dukkhata*) (Digha Nikaya 33). The statement is comprehensive, for it goes beyond the experiential modes of suffering into suffering as a cosmic necessity. Mental and physical suffering is the pain that is known in its most obvious form, but the 'suffering of the aggregates' lies in the state of disease, unrest and instability which is inherent in the arising and passing away of the momentary phases of existence, of which we are normally unaware, but which is present all the time. The suffering of transience comes from the impermanent nature of happiness; in the inevitability of its end, happiness, contains both the potentiality and realization of pain.

Of these three aspects of suffering it is the second alone that calls for a special understanding of the Buddhist world view. The aggregates here spoken of are the five *khandhas*, or groups, which constitute a living, sentient being. They are: *rupakkhandha*, the visible, tangible body of form, the physical aggregate; *vedanakkhandha*, the aggregate of sensations derived from the six sensory organs—eye, ear, nose, tongue, tactile organs and mind; *sannakkhandha*, the perceptions arising from these organs in contact with their objects; *saokharakkhandha*, the mental properties including intellection, imagination, memory and volition, and lastly *vinna nakkhandha*, which is the sum content of consciousness at any given moment. All of these aggregates are compounded, conditioned and impermanent; they are in a constant state of change—that is to say, of arising and passing away—so that there is nothing in the nature of a stable, persisting entity to be found in them.

Since they are no more than a flux of conditionality they cannot contain any self-existing, immutable core of personality; the conscious being is in reality a cause-effect continuum flowing through space and time, his existence in the moment of conscious awareness a cross-section of an eternal process. The suffering of the aggregate is inherent in their mutability; the process of coming to be which never attains the fulfillment of perfect being.

The problem of identity-in-change can be understood only by viewing identity as a relationship of cause and effect. So we find in the series of transformations undergone by the protozoa, which present no clear distinction between plant and animal life, a highly complicated pattern of individuality. It can hardly be said that a protozoan at one stage of its career is the 'same' protozoan as that which existed before or that which will exist subsequently. Yet the protozoa do not arise independently; each transformation is the consequence of those that preceded it, and each is dependent also on external conditions. The closer we get to the basic structures of life the more evident this principle becomes.

In the case of human personality we find, on analysis, no mental or physical constituents beyond these five aggregates; for this reason personality is devoid of anything that can be called a self-entity. The ego is a conditioned subjective phenomenon, the psychic life a series of mental events. All that goes to make up a human being is comprehended in the 'three signs' (*ti-lakkhana*) of all phenomena: impermanence (*anicca*), suffering (*dukkha*), and soullessness (*anatta*). By *anatta* (Skt: *anatman*, void of soul) is meant the absence of any permanent, unchanging essence of being.

At the same time it is these aggregates of personality, which arise by way of antecedent and coincidental conditions, both mental and physical, that are the cause of clinging to life. In their function of sustaining and perpetually renewing the life-urge they are called grasping aggregates (*upadana-kkhandha*). They are the grappling hooks with which beings fasten themselves, willingly, to suffering.

Like all other organisms, man is conditioned to respond to irritation, for the principle of irritability plays a leading role in organic evolution. It is not surprising, therefore, to find that there are forms of suffering which he enjoys, and that pleasure and pain, as forms of stimulation, overlap one another and at times become indistinguishable. Bodily excitement moves from pleasure to pain by excess; aesthetic stimulation likewise crosses the border between joy and sadness. The beauty of a sunset can disturb and trouble the mind, yet no one avoids it on that account. Masochism is regarded as abnormal, yet perfectly 'normal' people go to the theatre to have their hearts moved to pity and terror by a great tragedy. Apart from this, pleasure in its very essence is a source of pain. While it lasts it is a disturbance and an agitation; when it ceases it leaves us dissatisfied and filled with longing for its continuation or repetition. The individual's personal reactions towards the experiences he finds pleasurable also involve some degree of suffering, as do the hazards he encounters in seeking them. Those who have a strong inclination towards luxury and sensual pleasures suffer when they are denied them, and find it difficult to practice restraint in their enjoyment of them. Yet the consequences of unbridled self-indulgence are likely to be even more painful, and of longer duration, than the pains of self-restraint. And this does not apply only to the grosser physical pleasures, even the most refined intellectual or aesthetic pleasures can become an obsession, and immoderate surrender to them may take the form of a spiritual orgy, destructive in its psychological effects. From whatever point it is viewed, pleasure either involves suffering as part of its function as an irritant, or brings suffering about as its result. Considered in the ultimate sense, as an irritation, all sensation is suffering; its desirability or otherwise depends upon a purely subjective distinction.

Buddhism makes a further fourfold classification of dukkha into unmanifested, manifested, indirect and direct suffering. 'Unmanifested' suffering is that in which the suffering and its cause do not appear, as in the tribulation of mind accompanying anger, passion and lust; or where they are not visible externally, but take the form of inward physical pain. 'Manifested' suffering is that in which both the pain and its cause are visible, as in suffering under torture. 'Indirect' suffering is that which contains in itself, as do the sensual pleasures, seeds of subsequent pain, while direct suffering is the pain as immediately experienced.

In its cosmological aspect suffering has an existence independent of man's awareness, for, as we have seen, it is one of the three signs of being, the characteristics of all phenomena. Since everything in the universe is subject to arising and passing away, the three characteristics, Impermanence, Suffering and 'Essencelessness' are found in all compounded things, material and immaterial.

Matter is made up of four Great Primaries (*maha bhuuta*), representing the categories in which it manifests. For convenience they are defined as the 'elements' of solidity, cohesion, temperature and motion. Space is sometimes added as a fifth. For philosophic purposes this is an adequate description, denoting as it does the varied transformations as well as the functions of the atomic units (*kalapa*) of matter. These atoms and their components are in a continuous state of movement and change, a process in which energy assumes the sensible aspect of solid physical substance. That this is nothing more than an appearance is fully confirmed by modern physics, for as Bertrand Russell has pointed out, "In pursuit of something that could be treated as substantial, physicists analysed ordinary matter into molecules, molecules into atoms, atoms into electrons and protons. But now electrons and protons themselves are dissolved into systems of radiations by Heisenberg and into systems of waves by Schroedinger. The two theories amount mathematically to much the same thing. And these are not wild metaphysical speculation; they are sober mathematical calculations accepted by the great majority of experts."

Since matter has resolved itself into energy, whether it be as radiations or waves, all phenomena are seen as a succession of events in the space-time continuum, not as static entities. To be properly understood they must be observed as processes bearing the unitary characteristic of all forms of energy, that is to say, perpetual movement and transmutation. Here again the problem of individuality obtrudes itself, for like the protozoan the atom has no real identity from one moment to another in the phases of its hectic existence. The basic structure of the universe itself is energy, something which can only be described as an unceasing restlessness and agitation.

In analysing the five aggregates of personality the Buddha began with the gross components of the physical body and of all other matter as being made up of the four Great Primaries, enumerating and classifying them according to whether they are internal or external, existing in one's own body or in the objective world. Thus, solidity (*pathavi*), whether it be of one's own body or of external objects, is all of one order; it belongs to the same category of phenomena and is subject to the same laws of arising and dissolution wherever it is found. The same is true of the factors of cohesion, temperature and motion, all of which are found internally and externally. Each classification ends with the assertion: "Now, whether it be the internal element, or whether it be the external element, both are one in their nature. This, one should understand according to reality and true knowledge—that this element does not belong to me; this is not 'I', this is not my 'Self.'"

Wherever it may be found, physical substance is in fact of one kind in its fundamental structure. Instead of dividing matter into three classes, solid, liquid and gaseous, Buddhist cosmic analysis defines it by group characteristics, as *lahuta* (lightness, buoyancy), *mudita* (softness, plasticity) and *kammannata* (activity). Since in physics there is nothing that can be called absolutely solid, gaseous or liquid, but each partakes in some degree of the nature of the others, the Buddhist classification serves its philosophic purpose by referring all to the four Great Primaries. The purpose of applying the knowledge specifically to the body, and of establishing a universal principle embracing all matter is to disabuse the mind of any belief that the human body is a supernatural organism distinct from other, material objects, and to counteract the tendency to regard the body as the 'Self' or as integral to the self.

In like manner the Buddha deals with the four immaterial or mental aggregates. Sensation, perception, volitional activities and consciousness are all causally conditioned factors. Their 'life' consists of thought-moments (*cittakkhana*) which arise and pass away with inconceivable rapidity. The real term of a being's conscious existence is no longer than the duration of one of these point-moments of consciousness which are strung, as it were, on the thread of cause and effect to give the illusory sense of self-identity.

So, in the Buddha's summary, "All aggregates are transient; all aggregates are subject to suffering, all things are devoid of self-entity. Body is transient; sensation is transient; perception is transient; mental aggregates are transient and consciousness is transient. And that which is transient is (necessarily) involved in suffering; and of that which is involved in suffering and change one cannot rightly say, "This belongs to me, this is 'I', this is my 'Self'. Therefore, whatever constitutes bodily form, or sensation, or perception, or mental aggregates or consciousness, whether it be gross or subtle, exalted or low, far or near, one should understand according to reality and true knowledge, "This does not belong to me, this is not 'I', this is not my 'Self.'

In its fullest sense the word *dukkha* is to be understood as including all degrees of mental and physical uneasiness, from wild dissatisfaction to despair, mild discomfort to acute agony. The living organism, being impermanent in all its parts, is subject to that form of suffering which is inherent in its restless, ever-changing nature, the suffering that is inseparable from the process of coming-to-be which never reaches the state of true being. In the mental aggregates the characteristic of restlessness takes diverse forms, such as irritability, frustration, anger, worry, conflicting desires and emotions, all distressful states which are rightly to be understood as dukkha. Seen in this light, even what we know as happiness is not free from the dukkha of agitation. 'Happiness' exists only in contrast to its opposite mode of restlessness which we call 'sorrow.' Since pleasure and pain are merely relative states, neither of which can be experienced without its opposite, Buddhism denies the possibility of a perfect, unchanging and unalloyed happiness where the conditions of conscious life prevail. The reasons for this will become more apparent when we examine the second Noble Truth, which deals with the source and origin of suffering.

8

The Ethics of Buddhism

Yet to present the teaching of the Buddha as being solely and exclusively concerned with ethics could serve as a detraction from the real objective of the Buddha-Dhamma, which is to serve as a path or vehicle leading to Enlightenment. While conforming to the norms of Buddhist ethics is essential for this purpose this alone will not guarantee the elimination of ignorance (avijja), which is the real meaning of Enlightenment.

The tendency of some exponents of the Dhamma to represent Buddhism as just another ethical system is misleading, especially when put before a newcomer to the Dhamma who may not be able to distinguish between Buddhist ethics and the precepts of other ethical teachers, and may conclude that Buddhism has nothing new to offer. All religions inculcate some basic ethics, whether relating to individual or to social conduct.

Indeed the advocacy of an ethical system does not need a religious framework, and some: of the great ethical teachers of the world (e.g. Socrates or Confucius) did not feel the need for one. The religion-surrogates of the modern world, like Humanism, rationalism, or Communism, have all evolved their own norms of ethics, however inadequate we may consider them to be. Wherein, then, lies the uniqueness of Buddhist ethics? This question could be answered in many ways, but here we shall look at it from the standpoint of three criteria. First of all there are the ethical rules themselves. When we consider what actions are considered "good" and what are deemed to be "bad", it might appear that there is a great deal of agreement between the different ethical Systems. Such actions like killing, theft, sexual misconduct, and falsehood seem to be condemned universally. The differences emerge when we examine the question more closely, e.g. when we investigate the rationale for these rules, whether they are absolute or are relative to some other end, and so on. The rule against killing could be taken as an example. Many ethical systems proscribe only the killing of humans (i.e. murder), but Buddhism applies the rule to all sentient existence. Furthermore even in the case of humans, exceptions are sometimes allowed, e.g. for "holy" or "just" war. Buddhism admits of no such exemptions. In Buddhism the ethical quality of actions depends on the mental factors associated with their commission or even contemplation, and on the impact they have on the well-being of others. If action is committed with greed, aversion or delusion it is unwholesome (akusala), but the degree of moral reprehensibility (and karmic consequence) depends on a whole host of factors. Even an "accidental" killing could have adverse consequences if it was caused through negligence and unmindfulness, which is a kind of "Delusion" (moha). What has been said of the rule regarding killing, may also be extended to the other ethical precepts as well. Furthermore Buddhist ethics does not stop at the Five Precepts (panca siila), which provides only the very minimum for the proper conduct of lay persons.

The second criterion that could be adduced for the evaluation of ethical Systems relates to the motivation for adhering to the ethical rules of the system, religious or secular. In Buddhism the goal of ethical conduct is self-control, self-understanding, and self-development. It is an essential prerequisite for the training of the mind, the elimination of ignorance and the attainment of Enlightenment. Theistic religions usually require the adherence to their ethical precepts as a means to the union with God, whether in an abstract metaphysical sense or more directly as entry into a kingdom ruled by God, or even the enjoyment of pleasures in a heavenly paradise. In such a system the most important rule, precept or commandment is not usually an ethical one, but belief in, love of, submission and obedience to, and veneration of God. This is thus placed at the head of the Judeo-Christian decalogue, with the ethical rules coming subsequently. When we look at "secular" ethics, such as those embodied in legal systems, the objective is usually the avoidance of social conflict, the regularization of property rights, and the like. Of course, some secular laws (e.g. those relating to the so-called "victimless crimes") are more directly "moral" in nature, but these too usually are indirect social objectives. The pursuit of Buddhist ethics too leads to social harmony, but this harmony is achieved through individual perfection, rather than through the compulsory observance of legalistic rules. But because of the non-compulsive nature of Buddhist ethics, they are not intended to replace the laws of society, but neither are those of other ethical systems erected on religious and philosophical foundations.

The third aspect of the question relates to the way in which "good" and "bad" conduct results in appropriate consequences. This is the question of the "policing of the rules". Here two approaches may be distinguished. One is where some kind of trial and punishment (or reward) is instituted individually for each person. The supreme judicial authority could be God to the theist; or simply the normal judicial processes of society in the case of the secularist and the materialist. The second approach relies on the workings of an impersonal law (like the Law of Karma in its Buddhist and Hindu-Jam forms). The legal model of trial-and-punishment is best suited to the enforcement of the laws of society, such as are necessary for the preservation of the authority of the State and the well-being of society. When this model is used to evaluate personal moral conduct and behaviour, as in the theory of divine judgement, several curious features arise. One that could be mentioned is the doctrine of the "forgiveness of sins". According to this doctrine the exercise of divine grace could wipe out "sins" and negate the principle that actions bring their own reward. In such a system the ultimate factor which determines the destiny of an individual is not the scrupulous observance of the ethical rules of the system, but the element of blind faith in its dogmas.

In Buddhism the operation of the law of kamma (karma) is all-pervasive and universal. Its exact modus operandi is not detailed, and may not be immediately obvious. Unlike in some other versions of the karmic hypothesis, in Buddhism there is no mechanical equivalence between action and result (vipaka). As mentioned above the karmic quality of an act depends on a whole host of circumstances. In the accumulation of kammas, good and bad, the fruiting of some may be postponed or delayed while that of others could be immediate. What is certain is that the law of kamma makes divine authority, divine grace, etc. redundant.

Thus in spite of superficial similarities, Buddhist ethics differs from other ethical systems when analysed in detail. In the Noble Eightfold Path the elements corresponding to morality and ethics are Right Speech, Right Action and Right Livelihood. These three together constitute siila. The cultivation of siila normally proceeds alongside progress in the other two great constituents of the Path, namely mental training (bhavana) and wisdom-insight (panna). Because of the mutually supportive nature of the three components of morality, mental development and wisdom, it is difficult to argue about the relative importance of these three components. Nonetheless it has long been the generally accepted view that panna is both the threshold as well as the culmination of Buddhist practice, with the other two components of sla and bhavana being the chief means to the realization of this great objective.

The distinction between ends and means is very important in the understanding of the true place of ethics in Buddhism. For the ordinary person (putujjana) ethical conduct may appear to be an end in itself, but for the adept (sekha) it is a means to the realization of a greater end. Because of the Buddha's custom of proclaiming the Dhamma according the varied capacities of his listeners, there are diverse references to the importance of siila in the Buddha's discourses which at first sight might appear to be inconsistent or even contradictory.

This apparent inconsistency, however, disappears when the actual context is considered. By way of illustration we can consider two places in the Pali Cannon of Buddhism which seem to attach different degrees of importance to morality (siila) in the Buddha's system.

"The first of these comes from the Brahmajala Sutta. This is the first discourse in the Sutta Pitaka (the section dealing with Buddhist doctrines), and this exalted position accorded to it reflects its importance to the early Buddhists, perhaps to the Buddha himself. This discourse was occasioned by a report brought to the Buddha of derisive commuents made on him, his Doctrine and the Sangha by a wandering teacher called Suppiya, and the equally unfounded praise bestowed on him by Brahmadatta a follower of Suppiya. This had led to conflict between teacher and pupil, and disquiet amongst the followers of the Buddha. The Buddha commences the discourse by advising his followers to consider all statements made about him, whether favourable or unfavourable, in an objective manner, with equanimity and even-handedness, and then to reject what was wrong, whether it be unfounded blame or unfounded praise, and to point out these errors in a calm and reasoned manner.

The Buddha anticipated that much of the praise heaped on him would be for the wrong reasons: "It is in respect only of trifling things (appamattaka.m) or matters of little value (oramattaka.m), or mere morality (siilamattaka.m) that an unconverted man (putujjana) when praising the Buddha would speak". What is interesting from our point of view is that the Buddha considers the mere keeping of ethical rules to be a matter not worthy of any real praise. In this sutta the Buddha groups ethical rules into three categories. The first of these (the cula siila) contains the basic ethical precepts (like the "killing of living things") which are usually included amongst the Five Precepts laid down for the guidance of lay persons. The other two categories (the majjhima and maha siilas) contain, ethical rules of lesser importance or those specially laid down for monks. As against these "moralities", none of which is deserving of real praise, the Buddha describes those things that are deserving of real praise. These are the "things profound difficult to realize, hard to understand, tranquillising, sweet, not to be grasped by mere logic, subtle, comprehensible only to the wise". More specifically they turn out to be the realization of Right View (samma di.t.ti), and the refutation of wrong views, in which connection the Buddha outlines the famous list of sixty-two schools of thought, ranging from theism to materialism, which then as now, were the main contenders with the Dhamma. Even though the Brahmajala was mainly concerned with what was praiseworthy in a Buddha, it does provide a clear statement of the principle that wisdom-insight (panna) ranks above siila and bhavana in the accomplishments necessary for the realization of the Buddhist goal of Nibbana.

The second extract from the Dhama which we shall consider seems to paint a slightly different picture. This is probably the best known stanza in the Dhamapada, itself the best-known of the Buddhist books. This Stanza (No.183) with its usual translation is as follows:

Sabbapapassa akara.na.m, kusalassa upasamapda,

sacittapariyodapana.m eta.m Buddhana sasana.m

Not to do any evil, to do good,

To purify one's mind, this is the teaching of the Buddhas.]

The ethical import of this Stanza is obvious. It seems to claim that the Buddha's teaching is threefold: avoid unethical conduct, cultivate good deeds, and train one's mind. There is no question of the ethical purport of the first two postulates. "Training the mind" could also be interpreted as an ethical postulate, especially when we consider the Buddhist view that evil thoughts generated by an unguarded mind are karmically effective.

The last phrase of this Stanza is usually taken to mean that the three ethical postulates constitute the whole (or at least the most important part) of the Dhamma. However it could be taken to mean that these ethical principles are part of the teachings of the Buddha, and not necessarily the part that constitutes the Buddha's unique discovery.

In the Commentary to the Dhammapada it is stated that this and the two following Stanzas constituted the admonition (ovadagata) delivered by the previous legendary Buddhas to bhikkhus on the uposatha days.

In the explanation of the meaning of the terms in this Stanza, the Commentator says that "to do good" really means the "generation and development of skillful acts from ordination until the realization of the path of Arahat-hood", while "purifying the mind" means the elimination of the five "hindrances" which are obstacles to the realization of jhanic states during meditation.

All this is in keeping with the general purpose of these stanzas, which was to serve as exhortations to Bhikkhus on the uposatha day, and not to serve as a summary of the Buddha-Dhamma.

The uniqueness of Buddhist ethics lies in its many outstanding qualities. It is all-embracing and comprehensive without being impractical or impossible to follow. It is free from taboos relating to diet, dress, behaviour etc. which very often pass as ethical principles. It serves the needs of the worldling as well as those of the recluse. It is useful to the rich and to the poor; to the powerful as well as to the powerless. To conform to Buddhist ethics one need not have to be a "buddhist"; and it serves as a norm to measure the ethical standard of other teachings. But Buddhist ethics is only the threshold for those who wish to pursue the Buddha's path to Enlightenment and the end of all ill.

SOCIAL CRITICISM IN BUDDHIST ETHICS

Buddhism arose in India during a period of intense intellectual and social ferment. It was a period during which the authority of the Vedas had been placed in doubt, the concept of god as a supreme being and creator was in question, the hereditary restrictions on caste mobility were under attack, and the efficacy of Brahminical rituals was being challenged. The authors of the Upanishads had opened the door for various heterodox currents to emerge in society, and amongst the most significant of these were the Lokayatas who polemicized against religious charlatans, and the Nyayavadis whose rational epistemology created the foundation for intense philosophical debate and encouraged the investigation of the real world based on reason and logic, freed from the burden of superstition and irrational adherence to burdensome rituals. Various ideological sects competed for the attention and acceptance of the ruling elites and the public. The most important amongst these were the Jains and the Buddhists. Although each of the various sects made original and interesting contributions to philosophy, it was the early Buddhists who attempted to provide a unified philosophical system where ethical conduct and social criticism lay at the very core of their ideological system.

Although today, Buddhism is viewed as a religion by many of its followers, the early Buddhists sects were either strongly atheistic or agnostic. The atheists believed that rather than "God having created man in his own image" it was man who had created "God" in his image. In their view, the liberation of humanity was contingent upon humanity shedding the delusion that "God" existed.

Other parables from surviving Buddhist texts indicate agnosticism. For instance, there is a suggestion that Buddhist followers ought not to waste their time on unsolvable metaphysical questions such as "does god exist". The search to identify the "one true god" or to speculate on the nature of god was seen as an exercise in futility.

But the most frequently cited argument against god by the Buddhists was that if an omnipotent and omniscient being such as "God" truly existed, and who was also all good, there could not be the kind of dukkha (suffering) that was so widespread in the real world.

These shlokas (verses) from the Bhuridatta Jataka illustrates this point:

> *If the creator of the entire world they call "God" be the lord of every being, why does he order such misfortune, and not create concord?*

If the creator of the entire world they call "God" be the lord of every being, why let prevail deceit, lies and ignorance, why create such inequity and injustice?

If the creator of the entire world they call "God" be the lord of every being, then an evil master is he, knowing what's right did let wrong prevail!

Unlike religions that ascribed earthly miseries to human sinfulness that brought upon the wrath of a vengeful god who needed to be feared, Buddhism saw the root of human suffering in ignorance that could only be ended through the acquisition of wisdom. Rather than expect some supernatural entity to end human suffering, the Buddhists argued that it was in human hands to end their sorrows through conduct and action driven by knowledge and correct understanding of human nature and the physical world. Hence, the aspiration for knowledge (jigyasa) was seen as the answer to blind faith. Although the Buddhists were not alone in developing this view, the elaboration of this point of view became pivotal to early Buddhist philosophy.

Central to Buddhist philosophy was an understanding of human nature and what caused dukkha-i.e. human suffering. They saw human personality as constituting five attributes, i.e. body, feeling, perception, disposition and consciousness, and used this framework to develop their understanding of human suffering. Citing examples of conditions that led to human suffering, such as aging, sickness and death, or association with the unpleasant, (or separation from the pleasant), or the inability to get what one wished-they concluded that suffering was a condition of stress and conflict inherent within human existence and interaction with the world. They also connected suffering to the very impermanence of things. They observed how people lamented over the loss of a loved one, or experienced sorrow when something or someone that had once given them happiness became separated from them.

They noted that even human pleasures were not immune from suffering because they didn't last forever, and the loss of pleasure inevitably left people feeling deprived.

Seeing as how clinging to things (that were necessarily impermanent) was one of the primary causes of dukkha, they cautioned against excessive attachment. At the same time, they recognized a recurring and more general type of existential unease and anxiety (anicchha) that arises from the very transience of life, and our inability to control or comprehend all worldly phenomenon, which they characterized as viparinama-dukkha.

But the Buddhists did not see dukkha only emanating from the difficulties of an individual. They also saw suffering emerge on a much larger scale from hostile social conditions such as poverty, war, and social oppression which they described as dukkha-dukkha.

As a formula (char-mulya) for addressing these different types of suffering, the Buddhists advocated a four-fold scheme of (a) recognizing the problem i.e. suffering (dukkha); (b) identifying the cause of the suffering-such as craving stemming from ignorance (samudaya); (c) establishing the goal of ending the problem (nirodha)-i.e. the cessation of suffering (nirvana); (d) conducting life in a manner that was consistent with the cessation of suffering-following the right path or engaging in the right practice (marga).

Followers were thus goaded into developing both a sense of personal ethics and a social conscience:

> *"He who has understanding and great wisdom does not think of harming himself or another, nor of harming both alike. He rather thinks of his own welfare, of that of others, of that of both, and of the welfare of the whole world. In that way one shows understanding and great wisdom." Anguttara Nikaya-(Gradual Sayings)*
>
> *"By protecting oneself (e.g., morally), one protects others; by protecting others, one protects oneself." Samyukta Nikaya (Kindred Sayings)*

Human actions (kamma, kaama, or karma) in the Buddhist framework were to be judged based on both the intention or motive (chetanaa) and the consequences (vipaaka) of the action. Altruistic actions which helped in the establishment and promotion of a just society were encouraged in the dharmaniyama (moral duty code).

{The discourses, or suttas in the Digha Nikaya, illustrate how there was deep concern with the creation of social conditions favourable to the cultivation of Buddhist values and the expansion of social equity and justice. These views undoubtedly influenced the creation of a "welfare state" during the reign of emperor, Ashoka (B.C. 274-236)}

In their theories of causality Buddhists challenged the view that human destiny was unaffected by the ethics or morality of human actions. They countered the doctrine of amoral causation (akriyavaada) whose adherents argued that there was no merit in doing good and no demerit for doing evil. (An extreme expression of such thinking was seen in philosophers who denied all morality and saw no crime in the killing of any person.)

Realizing that such a world-view could lead to the rejection of moral distinctions and personal responsibility for ones actions, they argued strenuously against such beliefs. They also argued against the theory of Makkali Ghosha (or Ghoshala) who believed that human fate was predetermined, and therefore denied that human actions had any bearing on the results of things (ahetuvaada) and maintained that human intention and effort were essentially powerless in changing human destiny, and therefore advocated fatalism (niyati).

They also countered philosophers from the school of "absolute skepticism" who doubted everything and never committed themselves to any specific position in doctrinal debates. Philosophers from this school such as Sanjaya Belarthaputra (who was known as a theorist of endless equivocation or an equivocationist (amraavikkhepavaadin)) were criticized in the Brahmajaala Sutta (or Sutra) as "eel-wrigglers" who were incapable of taking a definitive stance on the vital philosophical questions of the day. Such skepticism was seen as emanating from both the fear of being in error and the lack of knowledge (or inability) to provide reasonable answers to question put forward for discussion. Such all-pervading doubt coupled with a cynical skepticism (vichikicchaa) was viewed as a serious mental hindrance, a fetter in the path to wisdom.

Other theories that contradicted the notion that human actions mattered were theories of accidentalism (ahetu-apachayavaada), theistic determinism (ishvaranimmaanavaada) and past-action determinism (purvaketavaada or purvekatahetu). All of these were opposed by the Buddhists. Accidentalism was an indeterminist theory which held that whatever was experienced was uncaused and unconditioned by human intervention. Theistic determinism was a determinist theory, which held that whatever was experienced was due to God's will or by plan of a "Supreme-Being". Past-action determinism was also a determinist theory, but it held the belief that whatever was experienced, whether pleasurable or painful or indifferent was entirely due to ones past actions (from a previous life), and ones present actions had no relevance.

The danger in each of these theories was highlighted in these words: "Thus for those who fall back on these three erroneous views as essential dogma, there is neither the will to do what is ought to be done, or not to do what is ought not to be done, nor necessity to do this deed or abstain from that deed. No moral improvement or intellectual culture can be expected from them."

Some of the theories in circulation at that time built on a germ of truth but generalized to the point of absurdity. For instance the accidentalists were correct only to the extent that certain things did indeed appear to happen by random chance or accident. But they failed to recognize that sometimes what may have seemed to be accidental was more due to inadequate understanding or improper or incomplete perception, and that other activities had a clearly discernible cause. To deal with the extreme generalizations of such theorists, they introduced a middle standpoint for their epistemology and ethics.

They thus rejected the theory admitting that everything exists (sabba atthii ti) and in permanence-i.e. the extreme of eternalism (sassatavaada), and its opposite which advocated that nothing actually exists (sabba natthii ti) i.e. nihilism (the denial of all reality in real-world phenomenon) or the extreme of annihilationalism (ucchedavaada). Related to their critique of the eternalist and nihilist philosophies was their rejection of both hedonism and self-mortification (attakilamathaanuyoga) which they viewed as painful, fruitless, unprofitable and ignoble.

Buddhist texts also expressed suspicion about claims by heretical teachers of being constantly "all-knowing" and "all-seeing" and in possession of "all-embracing knowledge-and-vision." Such claims were countered with arguments relating to the actual behaviour of such charlatans in different situations.

For instance, they wondered why such "all-knowing" and "all-seeing" spiritual teachers lost their way in an unfamiliar place or why they were unable to escape from trouble while countering a fierce animal such as dog, elephant, horse or bull. Moreover, if they were really omniscient, they wouldn't need to ask for people's names, clans, or the name of a village or market town or make enquiries about anything. That they did such things indicated that their knowledge was evidently limited just like that of any average worldly person (puthujjana).

Unlike religions that were based on revealed truth or the sanctity of every word in a holy textbook, the Buddhist belief system prescribed reasoning based on investigation as the means of determining ones dhamma, (or dharma as in Hindu practise). In a parable in the Kaalaama Sutta, followers of Budhism are advised not to accept any moral codes on the following ten grounds: (1) Vedic authority (anussava), (2) tradition (paramparaa), (3) hearsay or report (itikiraa), (4) textual authority (pittakasampadaa), (5) apparent agreebility of the view (sama o no garu), (6) authority of the holder of the view (takkahetu), (7) apparent logicality of the view (nayahetu), (8) the fact that the view is an accepted standpoint (aakaaraparivitakka), (9) inadequate reflection on reasons (bhabbaruupataa), or (10) the fact that the view agrees with one's own.

In this manner, the Buddhism developed a very sophisticated philosophical system in which social ethics were integrated with rational investigation of human nature, social organization and the physical world. Buddhist ideas and concepts left a powerful impression on other Indian philosophical and religious belief systems, and over time, many commonalities developed amongst the competing ideologies.

However, there were also certain problems with the Buddhist world view which prevented its complete acceptance by intellectuals committed to the scientific method. For instance, although the Buddhists rejected the theory of past action determinism, they did posit the existence of a soul which survived a person's death and carried with it the merits and demerits of a person's past lives.

Presumably this concept was essential to the Buddhist goal of encouraging right conduct but it was rejected by those who considered the soul as inseparable from the body and did not believe that the soul survived death. Those who rejected the concept of transmigration of the soul naturally couldn't accept the idea that human destiny had anything to do with merits and demerits accumulated in previous incarnations of the "soul". In their view, morality and ethics were entirely social constructs and had to be dealt with accordingly. The realists (such as the Nyayavadis) who shared the Buddhist concern for morals and ethics in society argued that while morals and ethics ought to be encouraged, they could only be enforced through societal laws and judicial codes.

Another problem facing the Buddhists was that in many ways, their views were too advanced for their times. Society had not yet developed to the point where education was universal, and knowledge of the real world sufficient to prevent superstitions and irrational beliefs from being completely abandoned by the masses. In an era where society had only limited control over nature, it was inevitable that sections of society would continue with beliefs in deities and supernatural phenomenon in the hope that they may be spared from natural disasters or that their crops might withstand attacks from pests and disease. Thus although the Buddhists had a very important and salutatory effect on Indian society, the most advanced Buddhist concepts could be understood and practised by only a minority in society.

Over time, the spirit of inquiry and rational investigation that had spurred the early Buddhist scholars towards dialectical thinking and critical social analysis became more and more replaced by narrow and literalist interpretations of the earlier texts. For instance, advice against accepting something that appeared "logical" without personal verification was taken to mean that logic could be rejected. Advice against wasting ones time on unsolvable metaphysical questions was also taken too literally and many Buddhist scholars remained aloof from the metaphysical debates pursued by other philosophical schools such as those of the Jains and the Nyaya Vaisheshikas. What they didn't anticipate was that some of these debates might lead to useful advances in mathematics or deeper understanding of human thought processes and new insights on human memory and psychology. These led to valuable advances in the interpretation of moods and emotions-thus benefiting Indian art, literature and music.

In addition, later Buddhist monks lapsed into some of the very things that had been attacked by the early Buddhists such as indulgence in unnecessary and elaborate rituals, belief in supra-natural phenomenon, and alienation of the priests from the masses. Activities such as meditation which were encouraged as a means to gaining wisdom became ends in themselves, and were turned into idealistic fetishes. Although Buddhist monks dutifully delivered sermons on right conduct and right action, they often failed to engage in relevant and timely social criticism- and did not always connect the textual suggestions to concrete practice. Intra-Buddhist disputes developed around less significant details, even as some of the most important ideas that had initially shaped the philosophy were pushed into the background. As a result Buddhism as it was practised came to be associated with idealism and inaction. Whereas the early Buddhists saw no merit in worshipping god or its images, later

Buddhism developed a pantheon of deities not very different from other Indian religions. Thus even as Buddhism had spread almost throughout Asia by the 5th-6th C AD, it gradually began to lose its distinct edge and liberating influence on much of Indian society. Within the Indian subcontinent, strains of Buddhism survived in Sri Lanka, Bengal, Bhutan, Sikkim, parts of Bihar and Nepal, and parts of Sindh, Punjab, Kashmir and Afghanistan. In parts of Orissa and adjoining regions (such as Chhattisgarh and Telengana), Tantric (and other) influences reshaped the practice of Buddhism. Yet, Buddhism continued to have an impact outside India and developed pockets of influence as far West as Syria, as well as in much of Central Asia (including what is now Uzbekistan, Tajikistan, Kyrgyzia, Kazakhstan) and Tibet. In the East, its influence was felt on virtually every nation including Burma, Thailand, Malaya and Indonesia, Laos, Cambodia, Vietnam, China, Korea and Japan.

As noted earlier, the vast literature of Buddhism (like much of Hindu or Jain literature) was not a literature of revelation and authority. Its essays on social ethics and moral responsibilities, its treatises on philosophy and science, its art and poetry were but pointers to a path to wisdom. This gave Buddhism both flexibility and adaptability. Owing to its non-hegemonic character and humanist appeal, Buddhism was adopted without coercion or force. It was also successfully fused with Hinduism in many parts of South East Asia just as elements of it had been integrated into Hindu practices in India. In China, it was integrated with Taoism and Confucian principles; in Japan with Shinto beliefs. For several centuries, within India and outside, several people followed multiple faiths and identified as both Buddhists and Hindus, or as both Buddhists and Tantrics, (or Buddhists and Taoists) and so on. During the Gupta period (and in other reigns), philosophers from various schools of thought received royal patronage and temple grants were conferred for the construction of Buddhist and Hindu monuments alike.

It is also important to recognize that the form of Buddhism that was embraced in each nation was often quite different. For instance, in Western and Central Asia, it was not the philosophical or intellectual aspects of Buddhism that were popularized, but rather, its personal moral codes. Buddhist prosletysers imbued their stories of the Buddha with examples of miraculous healing and super-natural compassion so as to win more followers.

While such tendencies were also to be seen as Buddhism travelled within India or outwards, in Burma, Sri Lanka and Thailand, Buddhism developed organizational structures that appear to have been much more resilient. It was perhaps realized that the development of Buddhist virtue would require leadership and constant interaction with the community. In these nations, Buddhism did not degenerate into the extremes of mysticism or retreatism that became commonplace in certain parts of India (such as in the foothills of the Western Himalayas). Burmese and Thai monks maintained a practical and benevolent connection with the community, and thus retained a measure of respect within the community. This also appears to be the case in Japan. In Korea, the emphasis on gaining wisdom was taken very seriously, and Buddhist monks took the lead in promoting mass literacy.

This propelled the growth of technologies associated with the production of paper, writing instruments, inks, and furniture. And unlike in India, (where due to Upanishadic influences, "inner" wisdom came to be favoured over outer wisdom), Buddhist concern for disseminating the writings of the Buddha had significant positive secular impact. In Korean (and other Eastern) Buddhism, there was the correct realization that a Buddhist mindset, or that a Buddhist society could not be constructed overnight. There was thus the emphasis on the (helical) upgradation of individuals and society towards greater "Buddhahood". This philosophical element was perhaps signficant in that it prevented the sort of philosophical stagnation that occurred in India, where followers too often sought immediate succuor, and thus not only became divorced from reality, but also lost sight of the strategic potential of the philosophy.

In addition, it ought to be noted that Buddhism in India also had to contend with strongly anarchic and ultra-democratic tendencies. Precisely because its philosophical structure emphasized the relative and changing nature of truth, different tendencies under the Buddhist mantle competed for leadership through argument and debate. Initially, this led to important advances in democratic practices within the Sanghas. But over time, it also led to clashes of egoes, hair-splitting and deadlock. While some Buddhist sects compromised and fused with other tendencies (even alien tendencies), others remained fiercely autonomous. To survive, Buddhism had to confront both the tendency to be co-opted, as well as the tendency to atomize.

However, the catastrophic demise of Buddhism in India was triggered by the onslaught of Islam which first obliterated the remnants of Buddhism in Central Asia, and then later in Afghanistan and India.

By and large, Buddhism survived only in those countries that escaped invasions by Islamic conquerors. As a gentle faith that encouraged its followers to abjure violence, it was perhaps unable to protect itself from iconoclasts and proselytizers who intended to enforce a new religio-political order. Accustomed to centuries of peaceful co-existence, India's Buddhists had not anticipated the need to develop viable strategies for self-defence that could have combated the violence of India's Islamic conquerors who virtually obliterated Buddhism from the land of its birth.

Yet, it also appears that (in large part) later Buddhism had deviated considerably from the rational principles outlined in the early texts. Monasteries often became isolated from mainstream society, and monks who focused exclusively on meditative practices and idealistic or esoteric philosophical speculation contributed little to social progress. Some have even argued that the monastic orders had degenerated into sheer parasitism and were becoming a heavy social drain. Consequently, value judgements on the demise of Buddhism and the rise of Islam in India need to be made with a measure of caution.

Nevertheless, it must be acknowledged that the ascent of Islam was concomitant with the eclipse of Buddhism, and since the influence of Buddhism was greatly dependant on the existence of the monastic orders, the destruction of monasteries and their conversion to mosques and institutions of Quranic learning simply lead to mass conversions to Islam.

In the long term, this could have had the effect of stunting India's future intellectual development, since the destruction of important institutions of Buddhist learning also led to a notable decline in the opportunity (and social sanction) to study secular subjects such as logic and epistemology (which were also taught at Buddhist universities-such as Bhagalpur).

It might also be observed that the destruction of Buddhist centres of learning coincided with the destruction of extremely valuable textual materials-which could have been potentially rediscovered, and revived or reinterpreted by future generations of Indians so as to achieve a society that was more thoughtful and learned. Islamic texts did not offer anything comparable in terms of causality or epistemology. Nor did they offer the psychological, sociological, or moral insights that had been developed under the ambit of Buddhism. Nor was there any comparable stress on seeking knowledge or constantly updating ones understanding of nature and human society.

One can, therefore, only speculate as to the full consequences of this profound sociolgical and cultural loss (and discontinuity).

But East of India, Buddhism did survive, and in countries such Korea, Thailand and Burma, it continued to enjoy a loyal popular following. Philosophical innovations also took place, and as noted earlier, Buddhist scholars in China, Korea and Japan offered their own commentaries and somewhat individual interpretations of Buddhist concepts and formulations outlined in later (5-7th C.) Indian texts. And although the sacking of monasteries and centres of learning (such as Nalanda and Vikramshila in Bihar) led to records of the original Buddhist texts being permanently destroyed, it has been possible to reconstruct some of them from translations that survived outside

India such as in Thailand and Tibet. Notwithstanding the virtual erasure of Buddhism in India, it is possible to infer from these reconstructed texts and other archaeological records (and surviving monuments and artifacts) that Buddhism had a very powerful impact in shaping the destiny of India, and in triggering a social and cultural renaissance that would take Indian and other Asian civilizations to a higher level of social, cultural and material development.

THERAVAADA BUDDHIST ECONOMIC ETHICS

The economic ethics of Theravaada Buddhism, especially attitudes toward wealth, poverty, charity, and labor cannot be understood without understanding something about Buddhist soteriologies (i.e., theories of how a person achieves enlightenment). The earliest Buddhist soteriology was summarized in the Four Noble Truths: (1) suffering exists; (2) the cause of suffering is craving (attachment); (3) there is a way out of this suffering; and (4) this way is the Eightfold Path. This Eightfold Path consisted of three types of activity: (1) moral conduct; (2) mental discipline; and (3) wisdom. Moral conduct in turn included three of the eight components of the Path: (a) right conduct; (b) right speech; and (c) right livelihood, each of which involved various prescriptions for behaviour, attitudes, and mental dispositions.

Early Buddhist soteriologies must also be understood by examining the major concepts of karma, *anaatman*, nirvana/ sa.msaara and *pratiitya-samutpaada* (dependent coorigination) to see how they helped define such soteriologies. Karma, for example was understood to apply to all actions including moral ones and implied that a person's present situation was the result of past acts, thoughts, and feelings in this life and previous ones. It also taught that the effects of a person's actions carry on beyond the present life into future lives. Therefore, meritorious acts in the present life will result in rewards in future lives. Karma thus can be conceived of as a Buddhist basis for justice in the sense that through it each individual received what he or she deserved in life based upon past actions.

This of course included the economic realm with the implication that one's economic position (i.e., wealth) was the result of one's actions in this or previous lives-with good ethical actions leading to a better position in terms of wealth and bad ethical actions leading to a worse position. In this way, karma offered a rational explanation for social, economic, and political inequalities while also implying that economic justice *already* was achieved, i.e., persons economically have what they deserve, at least to start off. Karma thus contributed to a strong sense of morality as conditioning one's existence and to a stress on individual responsibility rather than social forces as the cause of one's present situation.

In addition to karma, the Buddhist concepts of nirvana and sa.msaara were also central to understanding Buddhist soteriologies and had important implications for views toward poverty and wealth. In early Theravaada Buddhism, for example, nirvana and sa.msaara were viewed as far apart-nirvana being the "unborn" and "unbecome"-and defined in terms of what sa.msaara was not. The soteriological goal was to escape sa.msaara through escaping craving, and to do this through practicing the Eightfold Path. Only when a person had escaped sa.msaara could they attain nirvana, whether nirvana was conceived of as an ethical state or also as a metaphysical one. The implication for early Theravaada Buddhist believers was that to attain nirvana right ethical behaviour was a key. Another implication was that since sa.msaara had little value, economic activities (which generally were associated with the realm of sa.msaara) could never have genuine religious significance.

The concept of *pratiitya-samutpaada* was a third major concept that helped determine Buddhist soteriology. It did so by pointing to the interdependence of all things and actions. In ethical terms, this implied that although the individual was ultimately responsible for his own karma, since all sentient beings are connected and since compassion is a virtue, helping one's fellow sentient beings also had value, including help of a material nature. Thus there was a strong moral basis for giving and not withholding material or spiritual assistance to others.

Finally, the concept of *anaatman* implied that since no eternal unchanging *aatman* (self) existed, there was no reason to withhold giving to others, or to hoard wealth, since there was no "I" that needed to be protected or defended more than others. Yet, the idea of *anaatman* also held a potential paradox. That is, if there was no self, then what individual or personal moral obligation could exist? Could ethics even be possible if there was no self? The most common early Theravaada Buddhist answer to this was that whether there was a self or not, karma continued to exist and wrongful moral actions led to negative karma while right actions led to positive karma. Thus the nonexistence of self did not imply that actions and their results, or ethical responsibility, could not exist.

The above discussion highlights the correspondence between the key concepts of Theravaada Buddhism and attitudes toward wealth, poverty, and ethical action. Based upon this, in the earliest Buddhism most kinds of economic behaviour of monks (e.g., labor, agricultural production, and possession or accumulation of wealth outside of one's robe and begging bowl) were proscribed, and monk economic ethics were mainly negative. With the passage of time, however, some Vinayas were relaxed. Individual monks were allowed to keep money, and monasteries were allowed to sell or use for profit goods donated to them, as well as lend out money and collect interest-as long as the profits went to the benefit of the Three Treasures, i.e., the sangha, the Buddha, and the Dharma. Economic activities undertaken by individual monks for personal profit, however, as well as monk labor (whether it involved agriculture or commercial activities), continued to be proscribed. In contrast to these early monk economic ethics, early economic ethics for the laity appeared clearly different since they allowed the laity to hold wealth and even praised the creation of wealth through diligent work following one's chosen or given occupation. However, lay economic ethics also stressed the avoidance of craving or attachment to such wealth and that it must be shared with the sangha and with family and friends. In addition, early lay economic ethics praised the value of labor and devotion to most secular occupations (with some exceptions).

Such a more lenient attitude toward lay accumulation of wealth and labor was not simply the result of monks trying to ensure their own material support from the laity. It was also the result of a clear and consistent logic in the early Buddhist view of reality that what had ultimate value for both monk and laity was the individual attainment of enlightenment. Although best pursued as a monk, such attainment of enlightenment was also possible for lay people. As a result, economic ethics, whether for monk or for laity, ultimately were directed toward furthering this goal of enlightenment. For both, the key to achieving this goal was overcoming craving. As the laity needed to earn their living, accumulating wealth was allowed and even encouraged as long as too much craving was avoided. Since the monks were on a different point in the path toward nirvana and required stricter discipline, it was considered better for them not to accumulate or hold wealth at all. This system required that the laity support the sangha in order to allow individual monks to devote themselves to their own enlightenment, but also so that they could teach the Dharma to the laity and give knowledge and understanding which furthered the process of laity enlightenment. Through giving to the sangha (*daana*), the laity earned merit which would help them receive better karma; by avoiding economic activities in favor of meditation and teaching, monks spread the Dharma and contributed to the overall supreme goal of maximum progress toward enlightenment for all.

Lay economic ethics taught in early Buddhism thus focused upon three areas: (1) accumulating wealth through hard work, diligence and setting certain restrains on one's own consumption; (2) choosing and pursuing the right occupation (i.e., avoiding occupations such as killing animals, trade in weapons, and the like); and (3) sharing wealth honestly acquired with family, friends and the sangha. Such merchant-type values in early Buddhist lay ethics contrasted sharply with the economic ethics of Brahminism, which reflected the patriarchal clan-based ethics of an agricultural society.

Support for this influence of merchant-class values upon early Buddhist lay ethics can be found in early Buddhist suutras and stories which refer to lay wealth in a way which tends to assume a certain amount of wealth already being held, and in the strong emphasis upon giving and receiving rather than the high value put in Brahmin ethics upon sacrifices. The influence of merchant-class ethics is also apparent in the three main themes of such suutras and stories: (1) diligence and honesty in acquisition of wealth; (2) restrain of one's own consumption in order to accumulate wealth; and (3) reinvestment of this wealth to produce more wealth, merit and happiness for self and others.

The best-known early suutra which exhibits these themes was the *Singaalovaada Sutta* or *Admonition to Singaala*, sometimes referred to as the Buddhist laymen's Vinaya. In it an ethic of diligent accumulation of wealth through hard work, restrained consumption, and reinvestment of profits into one's business is stressed, as in the following passage:

The wise and moral man
Shines like a fire on a hilltop
Who does not hurt the flower.
Such a man makes his pile
As an anthill, gradually.
Grown wealthy, he thus
Can help his family
And firmly bind his friends
To himself. He should divide
His money in four parts;
On one he should live,
With two expand his trade,
And the fourth he should save
Against a rainy day.

What is particularly interesting about this passage is that it urges that only a fourth of all one's wealth should be consumed for daily living while the other three-fourths should be saved, most of it to be reinvested in one's trade. This reflects a merchant-based mentality which while perhaps not ascetic in the same sense as the so-called Protestant ethic, does put a strong emphasis on saving and reinvestment. The suutra goes on to give specific advice on how to avoid squandering this accumulated wealth by avoiding such things as idleness, bad friends, addiction to intoxicants, roaming the streets at odd hours, frequenting shows, and indulging in gambling.

Other early suutras emphasize strongly the virtue of nonattachment to wealth as the foundation of all morals in society. This can be seen in both the *Cakkavatti-Siihanaada* and *Kuu.tadanta Suttas*, in which the generosity of a righteous king for the destitute becomes the basis for the establishment of virtue and prosperity in lay society. At the same time, a lack of such generosity was presented as the beginning of a steady expansion of vice and evil and a steady decay of society. Suutras such as the *Mahaa-Sudassana Sutta*, moreover, by stressing the impermanence of all wealth and worldly possessions, no matter how great their extent, reinforced the value of nonattachment to wealth.

With the passage of time, the lay virtue of generosity and giving only became more and more predominant. This was reflected in the many stories in the suutras of unbridled generosity leading to good karma and spiritual advancement. At the same time, while suutras pointed out the dangers of wealth in terms of creating craving, poverty was never advocated for the laity, but was viewed as a "suffering in the world for a layman."

Yet even though giving became the supreme lay virtue, there was a subtle difference between the earlier suutras, in which giving to both the poor *and* the sangha was urged, and later suutras, in which giving to the sangha was the main theme. In this way *daana* (giving to the sangha) became the central concept of lay economic ethics. By giving to the sangha, the individual not only furthered his own soteriological quest and karma, but benefited society and contributed to the betterment of others' karma through supporting the educational act of spreading the Dharma.

The concept of *daana* along with the concept of karma also contribute to a certain set of ideas about economic justice in Theravaada Buddhist economic ethics. On the one hand, the notion of karma has been used to argue *in favor* of an idea of justice existing in Theravaada Buddhist economic ethics, as follows:

Such equality before the law of kamma resembles the West's notion of procedural justice... there is equality of opportunity in the sense that the law of kamma treats all evenhandedly in rewarding virtue and punishing vice, and the determining essence of virtue (the attitude of nonattachment) is presumably an equal possibility for all.

Economic inequalities existing in society thus can be viewed as the result of past karmic acts and do not violate a sense of justice but in fact confirm it.

On the other hand, the concept of karma can also be used to argue *against* an idea of justice in Theravaada Buddhism. This is possible through emphasizing an interpretation of karma which implies that the way to nirvana is through a slow accumulation of individual merit effected by religious giving and individual acts of compassion rather than an interest in effecting social justice in the Western sense of an equitable distribution of wealth:

> *... The law of kamma, with its all encompassing explanation of existing inequalities, tends to do away with Buddhist perplexity over the plight of the poor. Buddhist emphasis on the virtue of charity tends to outweigh interest in justice and so ethical reflection is shifted away from evaluation of the existing distribution of wealth.*

What both of the above arguments share is a tendency to regard the issue of economic justice as one involving the need for greater economic equality and redistribution of wealth from the rich to the poor. This of course is only one interpretation of justice. If accepted, however, there is little clear evidence in Theravaada Buddhism supporting redistribution of wealth, except for the idea of *daana*, which implied redistribution of wealth *to the sangha* and not necessarily to the poor, and the idea of *karu.naa*, which implied more individually-based acts of compassion toward one's fellow sentient beings rather than an overall program for social change.

Support for an idea of economic or social equality in the form of an economically or socially classless society also never seems to have been envisioned in early Theravaada Buddhism, at least for the laity. Instead, clear differences in social, economic, and political levels seem to be assumed, a fact reflected in the lack of a clear prohibition against ownership or use of slaves either by layman or temple (though slave trading was proscribed). In addition while within the early sangha a large degree of economic and to some degree political equality existed, this equality was never extended beyond the sangha to a prescription for society as a whole. Moreover even within the sangha, there was a class structure in the sense of different levels of spiritual development and seniority which were acknowledged and affected how different monks were treated. Thus equality in early Theravaada Buddhism seems to have been primarily a spiritual ideal viewed in terms of equal *potential* for all to achieve spiritual enlightenment. This conclusion is supported by the fact that in contrast to Brahminism, almost all classes of people could and did enter the early Buddhist order of monks.

Early Theravaada Buddhist economic ethics and ideas regarding social and economic inequality were also strongly affected by various viewpoints of the proper relationship between the sangha and the state or king. Although the earliest Buddhism tended to view contact with the king as something to be avoided like a poisonous snake, and kings were labeled among other disasters that might occur to a person, by the time of King A"soka and afterward, Buddhism began to develop a close relationship with the state in most places where it existed, including India and Ceylon, and later Southeast Asia, China, Japan, and Tibet. This relationship was based upon the idea of the Cakravartin king, or the ideal enlightened king who carried out the Dharma in society and supported the sangha, in return for which he received the sangha's spiritual protection and legitimization. The story of King A"soka of course seems to provide a major historical context for this ideal, and the stone edicts left by his rule point to the close and mutually beneficial relationship between him and the Buddhist sangha. These edicts refer to social policies which have been referred to by some scholars as a type of ancient "welfare state" in that various facilities for the poor, sick, and indigent were constructed by the state, in addition to state support for the sangha. Yet a closer reading of these edicts themselves makes clear that A"soka never intended to change the fundamental economic and social structure of his society. Instead, he focused his social activism more upon spreading the Dharma through charitable works for the poor, sick, and imprisoned, religious giving to the sangha, and encouraging meditation and proper treatment of one's father and mother, teacher, relatives, slaves and servants, priests and ascetics, and animals.

>From the historical example of A"soka and other instances of sangha/state cooperation, early Theravaada Buddhism developed and evolved its own concept of the ideal relationship between sangha and state which, as two recent scholars have termed it, was a "purposeful political strategy of adjustment and accommodation" toward the state reflecting a "distinctly Buddhist understanding of the possibilities for social change" through "gradual reform with emphasis on religious education." In other words, here was established the typically Buddhist amelioratory approach to social change that would continue to affect both Theravaada and Mahaayaana traditions later on. In this approach, the role of the enlightened king or state was to formulate specific laws for society based upon general ideas and principles given by the Buddha. At the same time, the political role of the sangha was to teach the Dharma to the king and support the state by obeying the laws of the land (and not

challenge the given economic distribution and social structure). In this way, while ideas about social and economic justice did seem to exist in early Theravaada Buddhism, they existed in the form of particular ideas about karma, *daana* and the state/ sangha relationship which were clearly different than most current Western ideas about justice. Yet, this should not be surprising since current Western ideas are themselves a product of a long evolution of concepts, and although related to their predecessors in Judeo-Christian ethics and Roman law, are still clearly different from them.

In conclusion, wealth and labor had value in early Theravaada Buddhist ethics, but a value ultimately smaller than that given to the pursuit of enlightenment for the monk and gaining merit through *daana* for the laity. Wealth was never an evil in itself, either for laity or monk, but was to be welcomed as the result of past merits, as long as one never became attached to it. Giving was the way to avoid such attachment and for the laity such giving increasingly became giving to the sangha (*daana*), rather than directly to the poor or reinvesting into one's secular business. Moreover, in contrast to the Calvinist with his God of predestination, the Theravaadist layman never was assured of his salvation, and constantly had to work to earn it through the creation of additional merit through additional *daana*. This led to an emphasis on investment in *daana* over investment in one's secular business, with the ultimate consequence for the Theravaada Buddhist that his "proof of salvation" was found "not in accumulating and creating new wealth, but in giving it away in the form of *daana*." As a result, a type of Protestant asceticism emphasizing the accumulation of wealth which was then invested into one's secular business and (according to Weber) contributed to the development of modern capitalism in the West, never was encouraged in the Theravaada tradition once the idea of *daana* became dominant. Some scholars go even further and argue that this very tradition of *daana* is an important reason for the slower development of modern capitalism in countries with a strong Theravaada tradition.

9

Buddhist Meditation

Meditation refers to any of a family of practices in which the practitioner trains his or her mind or self-induces a mode of consciousness in order to realize some benefit....

Meditation is generally an internal, personal practice and most often done without any external involvement, except perhaps prayer beads to count prayers. Meditation often involves invoking or cultivating a feeling or internal state, such as *compassion*, or *attending to a specific focal point*. The term can refer to the state itself, as well as to practices or techniques employed to cultivate the state.

There are dozens or more of specific styles of meditation practice. People may mean different things when they use the word, 'meditation'. Meditation has been practiced since antiquity as a component of numerous religious traditions, especially in monastic settings.

A 2007 study by the U.S. government found that nearly 9.4% of U.S. adults (over 20 million) have practiced meditation within the past 12 months, up from 7.6% (more than 15 million people) in 2002.

Since the 1960s, meditation has been the focus of increasing scientific research of uneven rigor and quality. In over 1000 published research studies, various methods of meditation have been linked to changes in metabolism, blood pressure, brain activation, and other bodily processes. Meditation has been used in clinical settings as a method of stress and pain reduction.

The word *meditate* stems from the Latin root *meditatum*, i.e. to ponder. In the Old Testament haga, means to sigh or murmur, but also to meditate. When the Hebrew Bible was translated into Greek, haga became the Greek *melete*. The Latin Bible then translated haga/melete into *meditatio*. The use of the term *meditatio* as part of a formal, stepwise process of meditation goes back to the 12th century monk Guigo II.

Apart from its historical usage, the term *meditation* was introduced as a translation for Eastern spiritual practices, referred to as *dhyana* in Buddhism and in Hinduism, which comes from the Sanskrit root *dhyai*, meaning to contemplate or meditate.

The term "meditation" in English may also refer to practices from Islamic Sufism, or other traditions such as Jewish Kabbalah and Christian Hesychasm. A recent edited book about "meditation", for example, included chapter contributions by authors describing Buddhist, Christian, Hindu, Islamic, and Taoist traditions. Scholars have noted that "the term 'meditation' as it has entered contemporary usage" is parallel to the term "contemplation" in Christianity.

It is difficult to trace the history of meditation without considering the religious context within which it was practiced. Data suggest that even at prehistoric times older civilizations used repetitive, rhythmic chants and offerings to appease the gods. Some authors have even suggested the hypothesis that the emergence of the capacity for focused attention, an element of many methods of meditation, may have contributed to the final phases of human biological evolution. References to meditation with Rishabha in Jainism go back to the prehistoric age with the Acaranga Sutra dating to 500 BC. Some of the earliest written records of meditation date to 1500 BC in Hindu Vedantism. Around 500-600 BC Taoists in China and Buddhists in India began to develop meditative practices. In the west, by 20 BCE Philo of Alexandria had written on some form of "spiritual exercises" involving attention (prosoche) and concentration and by the 3rd century Plotinus had developed meditative techniques.

The Pali Canon, which dates to 1st century BCE considers Indian Buddhist meditation as a step towards salvation. By the time Buddhism was spreading in China, the Vimalakirti Sutra which dates to 100CE included a number of passages on meditation, clearly pointing to Zen. The Silk Road transmission of Buddhism introduced meditation to other oriental countries, and in 653 the first meditation hall was opened in Japan. Returning from China around 1227, Dogen wrote the instructions for Zazen.

The Islamic practice of Dhikr had involved the repetition of the 99 Names of God in the Qur'an since the 8th or 9th century. By the 12th century, the practice of Sufism included specific meditative techniques, and its followers practiced breathing controls and the repetition of holy words. Interactions with Indians or the Sufis may have influenced the Eastern Christian meditation approach to hesychasm, but this can not be proved. Between the 10th and 14th centuries, hesychasm was developed, particularly on Mount Athos in Greece, and involves the repetition of the Jesus prayer.

Western Christian meditation contrasts with most other approaches in that it does not involve the repetition of any phrase or action and requires no specific posture. Western Christian meditation progressed from the 6th century practice of Bible reading among Benedictine monks called Lectio Divina, i.e. divine reading. Its four formal steps as a "ladder" were defined by the monk Guigo II in the 12th century with the Latin terms *lectio*, *meditatio*, *oratio*, and *contemplatio* (i.e. read, ponder, pray, contemplate). Western Christian meditation was further developed by saints such as Ignatius of Loyola and Teresa of Avila in the 16th century.

By the 18th century, the study of Buddhism in the West was a topic for intellectuals. The philosopher Schopenhauer discussed it, and Voltaire asked for toleration towards Buddhists. The first English translation of the *Tibetan Book of the Dead* was published in 1927.

Secular forms of meditation were introduced in India in the 1950s as a Westernized form of Hindu meditative techniques and arrived in the United States and Europe in the 1960s. Rather than focusing on spiritual growth, secular meditation emphasizes stress reduction, relaxation and self improvement. Both spiritual and secular forms of meditation have been subjects of scientific analyses. Research on meditation began in 1931, with scientific research increasing dramatically during the 1970s and 1980s. Since the beginning of the '70s more than a thousand studies of meditation in English-language have been reported. However, after 60 years of scientific study, the exact mechanism at work in meditation remains unclear.

The historical Buddha Siddhartha Gautama is said to have achieved enlightenment while meditating under a Bodhi tree, after which The Buddha returned to the world where he founded the monastic way of life and taught the dharma, or truth, in order to liberate all living beings. Monks live a life of poverty, chastity, prayer, and meditation. The daily routine of a monastery differs from place to place, as does the sort of meditation practiced there. There are literally hundreds of specific Buddhist meditative methods.

Buddhist meditation is fundamentally concerned with two themes: transforming the mind, and using it to explore itself and other phenomena. The traditional goal of Buddhists is, as a part of The Noble Eightfold Path, reaching enlightenment, which means liberation from the bonds of delusion and suffering. Meditation is also practiced for health benefits, which have been observed using the scientific method.

Classically, Buddhists have characterized Buddhist meditation as the cultivation (bhavana) of calm abiding, known as shamatha, with the subsequent development of vipassana, or special insight into the nature of reality.

Anapanasati, or watching the breath, has been practiced since the time of The Buddha, and is still practiced in Zen, Tibetan, and Theravadan Buddhism, as well as a part of multiple secular mindfulness programs in Western medicine. In this type of meditation one simply turns the attention to each breath. Anapanasati has been shown to improve one's ability to sustain one's attention to a particular stimuli as well as improving executive functioning and slowing the natural aging process of the brain.

Gampopa, a Tibetan sage, wrote about ten stages (bhumis) which one ascends gradually on his or her path to full enlightenment, "Generally, bodhisattvas of the ten bhumis have the same realization while in meditative absorption. If explained particularly, differences occur during in the post-meditative state. At the first bhumi, one realizes the meaning of entering into the all-pervading Dharmadatu. Through that, one achieves the sameness of oneself and others."

The state of meditative absorption mentioned above by Gampopa is also known as Dhyana, Mahamudra or Dzogchen as mentioned in the paragraph below, and, in Hinduism, as union of the Atman (Self) with the formless, omnipresent Brahman. For more information on this meditative state of union with the all-pervading and nondual in cultures around the world. For additional information on Buddhist nondualism in particular.

Meditation in Tibetan Buddhism grew up as an integral part of religious life, alongside other practices like mantra recitation, study of sacred literature, hand mudras, prostrations, and so forth. All Tibetan schools share the traditional preliminary practice of Ngondro. After ngondro one begins either with Dzogchen in the Nyingma school or with Mahamudra in the Kagyu. There is a fairly wide consensus among lamas of both the Nyingma and Sarma schools that the end state of dzogchen and mahamudra are the same, that is, to awaken to the sky-like nature of mind.

The repetition of a phrase, a mantra, is common in Buddhism and especially in Tibetan Buddhism. In Tonglen, which originates from Tibetan Buddhism, one takes on the suffering of others on the in-breath and radiates total happiness and well-being to others on the out-breath. Through a practice known as Tummo, meditators in Tibetan traditions have caused steam to rise off a wet and very cold towels, which would have killed people who have not yet developed the meditation.

Metta, or cultivation of compassion and loving-kindness is common to the Tibetan and Theravada lineages of Buddhism. In this practice one generates strong feelings of love and the desire for others to have happiness. This practice has been studied by the scientist Richard J. Davidson, who has shown that it modulates areas of the brain previously linked to empathy, emotion, and theory of mind.

FIXING THE MIND WITH TIBETAN MEDITATION

A tremendously important part of all Buddhist philosophy is the emphasis it places on meditation as the way to salvation. In the west we have access to so many different systems that it can be very confusing to know where to start. We not only have all the many Buddhist forms available to us but there are the systems to be found in yoga, Hinduism, Theosophy, Spiritualism, Taoism, New Age etc. etc. This is not a bad thing. The Tibetan Buddhists themselves have thousands of meditation techniques. Each has a different objective and different styles suit different types of personality. But from a Buddhist perspective the ultimate goal of all meditation is to travel beyond the 'I' into the great immensity called Nirvana.

Benefits of Meditation

To practice even a little meditation can bring great benefit to you. From a practical standpoint you will gain greater vitality, mental alertness and health but most importantly you will gain the inner treasure of peace. This in turn will inevitably improve your relations with others, hopefully increase your compassion and make you a better and more stable person. On a more subtle level you are making tremendous progress spiritually and may bring yourself great merit that will serve you well in future lives. And your progress will become even more advanced when you perceive meditation not as a means of self gain but as something that is of benefit to all beings. When meditation becomes a form of service for the sake of all beings then you have put your foot on the bodhisattva's road.

A Tibetan Buddhist respects the various meditation techniques of the different systems within and outside their own tradition. As with most meditation practices the Tibetans advise that it is best to practice meditation in a quiet place during the morning when the mind is very clear and alert. The meditation experiment that follows is a traditional and widespread Tibetan technique used to fix the concentration. Although it is in itself very simple some the Tibetan adepts used variations on this method to develop the most advanced systems.

THE ROLE OF MEDITATION

Right Concentration is most often associated with meditation. In Sanskrit and Pali, the word for meditation is *bhavana*, which means "mental culture." Buddhist bhavana is not a relaxation practice, nor is it about having visions or out-of-body experiences. As explained by the Theravadin scholar Walpola Rahula,

The Buddhist bhavana, *properly speaking, is mental culture in the full sense of the term. It aims at cleansing the mind of impurities and disturbances, such as lustful desires, hatred, ill-will, indolence, worries and restlessness, sceptical doubts, and cultivating such qualities as concentration, awareness, intelligence, will, energy, the analytical faculty, confidence, joy, tranquility, leading finally to the attainment of highest wisdom which sees the nature of things as they are, and realizes the Ultimate Truth, Nirvana."* [Walpola Rahula, *What the Buddha Taught* (Grove Press, 1974). Bhavana really involves all parts of the Eightfold Path, but the particular role of Right Concentration has to do with the dhyanas.

THE FOUR DHYANAS (OR JHANAS)

The Four Dhyanas, Jhanas, or Absorptions are the means to experience directly the wisdom of the Buddha's teachings. In particular, through Right Concentration we can be freed from the delusion of a separate self. In the first dhyana, passions, desires and unwholesome thoughts are released. A person dwelling in the first dhyana feels rapture and a deep sense of well-being. In the second dhyana, intellectual activity fades and is replaced by tranquility and one-pointedness of mind. The rapture and sense of well-being of the first dhyana are still present. In the third dhyana, the rapture fades and is replaced by equanimity (upekkha) and great clarity.

In the fourth dhyana, all sensation ceases and only mindful equanimity remains. In some schools of Buddhism, the fourth dhyana is described as pure experience with no "experiencer." Through this direct experience, one perceives the individual, separate self to be an illusion.

THE FOUR IMMATERIAL STATES

In Theravada and probably some other schools of Buddhism, after the Four Dhyanas come the Four Immaterial States. This practice is understood as going beyond mental discipline and actually refining the objects of concentration themselves. The purpose of this practice is to eliminate all visualizations and other sensations that may remain after the dhyanas.

In the four Immaterial States, one first refines infinite space, then infinite consciousness, then non-materiality, then neither perception-nor-not-perception. The work at this level is enormously subtle. So is this enlightenment? Not quite yet, some teachers say. In other schools, it is understood that enlightenment is already present, and Right Concentration is a means for realizing this.

MEDITATION STYLES

Religious and Spiritual

Some meditative traditions, such as yoga or tantra, are common to several religions.

Baha'í Faith

The Baha'í Faith teaches that meditation is necessary for spiritual growth, alongside obligatory prayer and fasting. 'Abdu'l-

Baha is quoted as saying: Meditation is the key for opening the doors of mysteries to your mind. In that state man abstracts himself: in that state man withdraws himself from all outside objects; in that subjective mood he is immersed in the ocean of spiritual life and can unfold the secrets of things-in-themselves.

Although the founder of the Faith, Baha'u'llah, never specified any particular forms of meditation, some Baha'í practices are meditative. One of these is the daily repetition of the Arabic phrase Allahu Abha (God is Most Glorious) 95 times preceded by ablutions. Abha has the same root as Baha' which Baha'ís consider to be the "Greatest Name of God".

Christianity

Christian meditation is a form of prayer in which a structured attempt is made to get in touch with and deliberately reflect upon the revelations of God. The word meditation comes from the Latin word *meditari* which means to concentrate. Christian meditation is the process of deliberately focusing on specific thoughts (e.g. a biblical scene involving Jesus and the Virgin Mary) and reflecting on their meaning in the context of the love of God.

Christian meditation contrasts with cosmic styles of eastern meditation as radically as the portrayal of God the Father in the Bible contrasts with discussions of Krishna or Brahman in Indian teachings. Unlike eastern meditations, most styles of Christian meditations do not rely on the repeated use of mantras, but are intended to stimulate thought and deepen meaning. Christian meditation aims to heighten the personal relationship based on the love of God that marks Christian communion.

In *Aspects of Christian meditation*, the Catholic Church warned of potential incompatibilities in mixing Christian and eastern styles of meditation. In 2003, in *A Christian reflection on the New Age* the Vatican announced that the "Church avoids any concept that is close to those of the New Age". Christian meditation is sometimes taken to mean the middle level in a broad three stage characterization of prayer: it then involves more reflection than first level vocal prayer, but is more structured than the multiple layers of contemplation in Christianity.

Hinduism

The earliest clear references to meditation in Hindu literature are in the middle Upanishads and the Mahabharata, which includes the Bhagavad Gita. According to Gavin Flood, the earlier Brihadaranyaka Upanishad refers to meditation when it states that "having becoming calm and concentrated, one perceives the self (*atman*) within oneself".

The practices of Yoga help one to control the mind and senses so the ego can be transcended and the true self (*atman*) experienced, leading to *moksha* or liberation. Yoga practice includes ethical discipline (Yamas), physical postures (Asanas), breath control (Pranayama), withdrawal from the senses (Pratyahara), one-pointedness of mind (Dharana), meditation (Dhyana), and eventually Samadhi, which is often described as the union of the Self (Atman) with the omnipresent, and is the ultimate goal of all Hindu Yogis.

Meditation in Hinduism is not confined to any school or sect and has expanded beyond Hinduism to the West. Today there is a new branch of Yoga which combines Christian practices with Yogic postures known popularly as Christian Yoga.

The influential modern proponent of Hinduism who first introduced Eastern philosophy to the West in the late 19th century, Swami Vivekananda, describes meditation as follows:

Meditation has been laid stress upon by all religions. The meditative state of mind is declared by the Yogis to be the highest state in which the mind exists. When the mind is studying the external object, it gets identified with it, loses itself. To use the simile of the old Indian philosopher: the soul of man is like a piece of crystal, but it takes the colour of whatever is near it. Whatever the soul touches... it has to take its colour. That is the difficulty. That constitutes the bondage.

Islam

A Muslim is obliged to pray at least five times a day: once before sunrise, at noon, in the afternoon, after sunset, and once at night. During prayer a Muslim focuses and meditates on God by reciting the Qur'an and engaging in dhikr to reaffirm and strengthen the bond between Creator and creation, with the purpose of guiding the soul to truth. Such meditation is intended to help maintain a feeling of spiritual peace, in the face of whatever challenges work, social or family life may present.

The five daily acts of peaceful prayer are to serve as a template and inspiration for conduct during the rest of the day, transforming it, ideally, into one single and sustained meditation: even sleep is to be regarded as but another phase of that sustained meditation. Meditative quiescence is said to have a quality of healing, and—in contemporary terminology—enhancing *creativity*. The Islamic prophet Muhammad spent sustained periods in contemplation and meditation. It was during one such period that Muhammad began to receive the revelations of the Qur'an.

Following are the styles, or schools, of meditation in the Muslim traditions:

- *Tafakkur* or *tadabbur*, literally means *reflection upon the universe*: this is considered to permit access to a form of cognitive and emotional development that can emanate only from the higher level, i.e. from God. The sensation of receiving divine inspiration awakens and liberates both heart and intellect, permitting such inner growth that the apparently mundane actually takes on the quality of the infinite. Muslim teachings embrace life as a test of one's submission to God.
- Meditation in the Sufi traditions is largely based on a spectrum of mystical exercises, varying from one lineage to another. Such techniques, particularly the more audacious, can be, and often have been down the ages, a source of controversy among scholars. One broad group of ulema, followers of the great Al-Ghazzali, for example,

have in general been open to such techniques and forms of devotion, while another such group, those who concur with the Ibn Taymiya, reject and generally condemn such procedures as species of bid'ah or mere innovation.

Numerous Sufi traditions place emphasis upon a meditative procedure similar in its cognitive aspect to one of the two principal approaches to be found in the Buddhist traditions: that of the concentration technique, involving high-intensity and sharply focused introspection. In the Oveyssi-Shahmaghsoudi Sufi order, for example, this is particularly evident, where muraqaba takes the form of tamarkoz, the latter being a Persian term that means *concentration.*

Jainism

Meditation has been one of the core spiritual practices undertaken by the Jains since the era of first Tirthankar Lord Rishabha. All the twenty four Tirthankars have practiced deep meditation and attained enlightenment. They are all shown in meditative postures in the images or idols. Lord Mahaveer practiced deep meditation for twelve years and attained enlightenment. The Acaranga Sutra dating to 500 BC, addresses the meditation system of Jainism in detail. Jain Acharya Bhadrabahu of 4th century BC practiced deep *Mahaprana* meditation for 12 years. Acharya Kundakunda of 1st century BCE, opened new dimensions of meditation in Jain tradition through his books Samayasara, Pravachansar, etc.

Jain meditation and spiritual practices system was referred to as salvation-path. It has three important parts, Right perception and faith, Right knowledge and Right conduct, which are also known as Three Jewels.

Meditation in Jainism aims at realizing the self, attaining salvation, take the soul to complete freedom. It aims to reach and to remain in the pure state of soul which is believed to be pure consciousness, beyond any attachment or aversion. The practitioner strives to be just a knower-seer (Gyata-Drashta). Jain meditation can be broadly categorized to *Dharmya Dhyana* and *Shukla Dhyana.*

There exists a number of meditation techniques such as *pindastha-dhyana, padastha-dhyana, rupastha-dhyana, rupatita-dhyana, savirya-dhyana*, etc. In *padastha dhyana* one focuses on Mantra. A Mantra could be either a combination of core letters or words on deity or themes. There is a rich tradition of Mantra in Jainism. All Jain followers irrespective of their sect, whether Digambara or Svetambara practice Mantra. Mantra chanting is an important part of daily lives of Jain monks and followers. Mantra chanting can be done either loudly or silently in mind. Yogasana and *Pranayama* has been an important practice undertaken since ages. Pranayama – breathing exercises – are performed to strengthen the ten *Pranas* or vital energy. Yogasana and *Pranayama* balances the functioning of neuro-endocrine system of body and helps in achieving good physical, mental and emotional health.

Contemplation is a very old and important meditation technique. The practitioner meditates deeply on subtle facts. In *agnya vichaya*, one contemplates on seven facts-life and non-life, the inflow, bondage, stoppage and removal of *karmas*, and the final accomplishment of liberation. In *apaya vichaya*, one contemplates on the incorrect insights one indulges into and that eventually develops right insight. In *vipaka vichaya*, one reflects on the eight causes or basic types of *karma*. In *sansathan vichaya*, when one thinks about the vastness of the universe and the loneliness of the soul.

Acharya Mahapragya formulated Preksha Meditation in 1970s and presented a well organised system of meditation. It is an important milestone in the history of Jain meditation system. Yogasana and *Pranayama*, meditation, contemplation, Mantra, therapy are its integral parts. Numerous Preksha meditation centres came into existence around the world and numerous meditations camps are being organized to impart training in it.

Judaism

There is evidence that Judaism has had meditative practices that go back thousands of years. For instance, in the Torah, the patriarch Isaac is described as going *lasuach* in the field—a term understood by all commentators as some type of meditative practice (Genesis 24:63), probably prayer.

Similarly, there are indications throughout the Tanach (the Hebrew Bible) that meditation was central to the prophets. In the Old Testament, there are two Hebrew words for meditation: *haga* (Hebrew), which means *to sigh* or *murmur*, but also *to meditate*, which means *to muse*, or *rehearse in one's mind.*

The Jewish mystical tradition, Kabbalah, is inherently a meditative field of study. The Talmud refers to the advantage of the scholar over the prophet, as his understanding takes on intellectual, conceptual form, that deepens mental grasp, and can be communicated to others. The advantage of the prophet over the scholar is in the transcendence of their intuitive vision.

The ideal illumination is achieved when the insights of mystical revelation are brought into conceptual structures. For example, Isaac Luria revealed new doctrines of Kabbalah in the 16th Century, that revolutionised and reordered its teachings into a new system. However, he did not write down his teachings, which were recounted and interpreted instead by his close circle of disciples. After a mystical encounter, called in Kabbalistic tradition an "elevation of the soul" into the spiritual realms, Isaac Luria said that it would take 70 years to explain all that he had experienced. As Kabbalah evolved its teachings took on successively greater conceptual form and philosophical system. Nonetheless, as is implied by the name of Kabbalah, which means "to receive", its exponents see that for the student to understand its teachings requires a spiritual intuitive reception that illuminates and personalises the intellectual structures.

Bibliography

Adikaram, E. W.: *Early History of Buddhism in Ceylon,* Buddhist Cultural Centre, Dehiwala, 1994.

Ahmad, Imtiaz: *State and Foreign Policy: India's Role in South Asia,* Vikas, New Delhi, 1993.

Auboyer, Jeannine: *Buddha: A Pictorial History of His Life and Legacy,* Crossroad, New York, 1983.

Aurobindo, Sri: *Vyasa and Valmiki,* Acharya Press, Pondicherry, 1956.

Avalon, Arthur and Ellen: *Hymns to the Goddess,* Ganesh and Co., Madras, 1964.

Awasthi, J.D. : *Agricultural Development of Himalayas with Special Reference to Bhutan,* India: University of North Bengal, 1984.

Bagchi, P. C.: *Studies in Dharmashastra,* University of Calcutta Press, Calcutta, 1939.

Banerjea, J. N.: *Pauranic and Vedanta Religion,* University of Calcutta, Calcutta, 1996.

Bankimchandra, C.: *Essentials of Dharma,* Sanskrit Book Depot, Calcutta 1979.

Basu, Manoranjan: *Dharmashastra: A General Study,* Shrimati Mira Basu, Calcutta, 1976.

Batchelor, Martine and Kerry Brown: *Buddhism and Ecology,* London, Cassell, 1992.

Bhattacharyya, B.: *Nispannayogavali of Mahapandita Abhyakara Gupta,* Oriental Institute, Baroda, 1949.

Blofeld, John: *The Tantric Mysticism of Tibet,* New York, Dutton, 1970.

Bose, D. N.: *Dharmashastra: Their Philosophy and Occult Secrets,* Kali Press, Calcutta, 1965.

Bromley, D.: *Krishna Consciousness in the West,* Bucknell University Press, Lewisburg, 1989.

Buddhadasa, Bhikkhu: *Teaching Dhamma by Pictures,* Social Science Association Press of Thailand, Bangkok, 1968.

Candragomin, F. : *Difficult Beginnings: Three Works on the Bodhisattva Path,* Boston, MA: Shambhala, 1985.

Chakravarti, Uma: *The Social Dimensions of Early Buddhism,* Oxford University Press, Delhi, 1987.

Collcutt, Martin : *Five Mountains: The Rinzai Zen Monastic Institution in Medieval Japan,* Cambridge, MA: Council on East Asian Studies, Harvard University, 1981.

Collins, Steven: *Nirvana and Other Buddhist Felicities: Utopias of the Pali Imaginaire,* Cambridge, Cambridge University Press, 1998.

Cook, Elizabeth: *Holy Places of the Buddha,* Berkeley, Dharma Publishing, 1994.

Coomeraswamy, Ananda K.: *Buddha and the Gospel of Buddhism,* MacMillan, London, 1928.

Cummings, Mary: *The Lives of the Buddha in the Art and Literature of Asia,* University of Michigan, Ann Arbor, 1982.

Davids, T. W. Rhys: *Buddhist India,* Delhi, Motilal Banaradass, 1980.

Dayal, Har: *The Bodhisattva Doctrine in Buddhist Sanskrit Literature,* London, Kegan Paul, 1932.

Dompnier, Robert : *Bhutan: Kingdom of the Dragon,* Boston, MA: Shambhala, 1999.

Gethin, R. M. L.: *The Buddhist Path to Awakening: A Study of the Bodhi-Pakkhiya Dhamma,* Leiden, E. J. Brill, 1992.

Gonda, Jan: *Vedic Literature: Samhitas and Brahmanas,* Wiesbaden, 1975.

Grant, Beata : *Mount Lu Revisited: Buddhism in the Life and Writings of Su Shih,* Honolulu, HI: University of Hawaii Press, 1994.

Grousset, Rene: *In the Footsteps of the Buddha,* Routledge and Kegan Paul, London, 1932.

Gupta, Vinay Kumar : *Buddhism in Mathura : A Detailed Study of Buddhist Tradition, Archaeology and Art*, Bharatiya Kala Prakashan, Delhi, 2009.

Hakeda, Yoshito S.: *Kukai, Major Works,* New York, Columbia University Press, 1972.

Haldar, J. R.: *Early Buddhist Mythology,* New Delhi, Manohar, 1977.

Hazra, Kanai Lal : *Buddhism and Buddhist Literature in Early Indian Epigraphy*, Munshiram Manoharlal, Delhi, 2002.

Holt, John Clifford: *Buddha in the Crown: Avalokitesvara in the Buddhist Traditions of Sri Lanka,* New York, Oxford University Press, 1991.

Horner, I. B.: *The Living Thoughts of Gautama the Buddha,* Cassell, London, 1948.

Jacobson, Nolan Pliny: *Buddhism, the Religion of Analysis,* London, Feffer & Simons, 1974.

Jayatilleke, K. N.: *Early Buddhist Theory of Knowledge,* London, George Allen & Unwin, 1963.

Johansson, Rune E. A.: *The Psychology of Nirvana,* New York, Doubleday, 1970.

Kabilsingh, Chatsumarn : *Thai Women in Buddhism,* Berkeley, CA: Parallax Press, 1991.

Ketelaar, James Edward : *Of Heretics and Martyrs in Meiji Japan: Buddhism and Its Persecution,* Princeton, NJ: Princeton University Press, 1990.

Lamotte, Etienne: *The Suramgamasamadhi Sutra,* London, Curzon, 1998.

Lamrimpa, Gen : *Calming the Mind: Tibetan Buddhist Teachings on Cultivating Meditative Quiescence,* Ithaca, NY: Snow Lion, 1995.

Lauf, Detlef Ingo : *Tibetan Sacred Art: The Heritage of Tantra,* Berkeley, CA: Shambhala, 1976.

Lopez, Donald S.: *The Religions of Tibet in Practice,* Princeton, NJ: Princeton University Press, 1997.

McDermott, James P.: *Karma and Rebirth in Classical Indian Traditions,* University of California Press, Berkeley, 1980.

Miksic, John: *Borobudur: Golden Tales of the Buddha,* Shambala, Boston, 1990.

Mills, Martin A. : *Identity, Ritual and State in Tibetan Buddhism,* London: RoutledgeCurzon, 2004.

Morrell, Robert: *Early Kamakura Buddhism: A Minority Report,* Berkeley, Asian Humanities Press, 1987.

Nagao, Gadjin: *Madhyamika and Yogacara: A Study of Mahayana Philosophies,* Albany, SUNY Press, 1991.

Nagar, K.S. : *India's Northern Security: Including China, Nepal, and Bhutan,* New Delhi: Reliance, 1986.

Nakamura, Hajime: *Gautama Buddha,* Buddhist Books International, Los Angeles, 1977.

Nyanaponika, Thera: *Abhidamma Studies,* Kandy, Buddhist Publication Society, 1965.

Ortner, Sherry B.: *Sherpas through Their Rituals,* Cambridge, Cambridge University Press, 1978.

Pal, Pratapaditya : *Art of the Himalayas: Treasures from Nepal and Tibet,* New York: Hudson Hills Press, 1991.

Pande, G. C.: *Studies in the Origins of Buddhism,* Allahabad, University of Allahabad, 1957.

Poppe, Nicholas: *The Twelve Deeds of Buddha,* Seattle, University of Washington Press, 1967.

Pruthi, R.K. : *Buddhism and Indian Civilization,* Discovery Publishing House, Delhi, 2004.

Ray, Reginald A. : *Indestructible Truth: The Living Spirituality of Tibetan Buddhism,* Boston, MA: Shambhala, 2000.

Rogers, Minor: *Rennyo: the Second Founder of Shin Buddhism,* Berkeley, Asian Humanities Press, 1991.

Snellgrove, David L.: *The Image of the Buddha,* Kodansha International, Tokyo, 1978.

Sprung, Mervyn: *The Problem of Two Truths in Buddhism and Vedanta,* Boston, Reidel, 1973.

Titmuss, Christopher: *The Green Buddha,* Devon, Insights, 1995.

Wagle, Narendra: *Society at the Time of Buddha,* Humanities Press, New York, 1967.

Wells, Kenneth E.: *Thai Buddhism, Its Rites and Activities,* Bangkok, Christian Bookstore, 1960.

Wray, Elizabeth: *The Ten Lives of the Buddha,* Weatherhill, New York, 1972.

Yang, C. K.: *Religion in Chinese Society,* University of California Press, Berkeley, 1961.

Yushin Yoo: *Books on Buddhism: An Annotated Subject Guide,* Scarecrow Press, Metuchen, 1976).

Zürcher, Erik: *Buddhism, Its Origin and Spread in Words, Maps, and Pictures,* E. J. Brill, Leiden, 1959.

Zwalf, W.: *Buddhism: Art and Faith,* British Museum Publications, London, 1985.

Index

❑❑❑